Educational Research, Policymaking and Practice

Educational Research, Policymaking and Practice

Martyn Hammersley

Paul Chapman
Publishing

Paul Chapman Publishing
A SAGE Publications Company
6 Bonhill Street
London EC2A 4PU

SAGE Publications Inc
2455 Teller Road
Thousand Oaks, California 91320

SAGE Publications India Pvt Ltd
32, M-Block Market
Greater Kailash - I
New Delhi 1 10 048

Library of Congress Control Number: 2001135448

A catalogue record for this book is available from the British Library

ISBN 0 7619 7419 9
ISBN 0 7619 7420 2 (pbk)

Typeset by Anneset, Weston-super-Mare, Somerset
Printed and bound in Great Britain by Athenaeum Press,
Gateshead

Contents

Acknowledgements

I am grateful to Roger Gomm for much discussion of the issues covered in this book; and to him and to Helena Foster for permission to include Chapters 3 and 7, respectively, in this volume. I am also indebted to Phil Hodkinson for comments on the Introduction and Chapter 5, to Paul Atkinson, Richard Edwards, and Donald Mackinnon for comments on an early version of Chapter 1; to Geoffrey Price for supplying many references to the work of Michael Polanyi which I used in writing Chapter 5, and to Rachel Hammersley for advice about the literature on republicanism.

Earlier versions of Chapter 1 appeared in the *British Educational Research Journal* (23, 1996: 41–61), and in L. Trinder and S. Reynolds (eds) *Evidence-Based Practice: a critical appraisal* (Oxford: Blackwell Science, 2000). Chapter 2 has not previously been published, but it is based on presentations given to seminars at the University of Warwick, the Open University, and the University of Oxford. Chapter 3, co-authored with Roger Gomm, was given at a conference on 'The transformation of knowledge: theorising, production and application' at the University of Surrey in January, 1999. Chapter 4 was presented at a conference on 'Current issues in qualitative research' held by the Centre for Applied Research in Education, University of East Anglia in July 2000. An initial version of Chapter 5 was given at a conference on 'Diversity or control in educational research?' organised by City University's Department of Continuing Education, in January 2000. I am grateful to all those who organised and participated in these seminars and conferences. Chapter 6 was published in the *International Journal for Social Research Methodology* (3, 3, 2000: 221–9). Chapter 7, co-written with Peter Foster, was published in the *British Educational Research Journal* (24, 5, 1998: 609–28).

Introduction

This book focuses on a perennial issue: the relationship between educational research and policymaking or practice. Announcements of the failure of research to perform its proper function for these activities have occurred frequently over the past century, often leading to attempts at improving the situation.[1] However, for the most part, responses to each new crisis have failed to draw on earlier ones. And, perhaps as a result, the discussions have not always distinguished clearly between the various types of question that must be addressed: factual questions about the roles that research *has actually played*, theoretical questions about the roles that it *can* play, and value questions about the roles that it *ought to* play. Against this background, my aim in this book is to contribute to a deeper analysis of the relationship between research and policymaking or practice, particularly as regards what it is possible for educational research to contribute, and what the implications of answers to this question are for its justification and organisation.

While the issue addressed here is a perennial one, and while I have drawn on a wide range of previous work, my thinking was stimulated in large part by what has been happening to educational research in England and Wales in the past decade. In particular, it has been subjected to increasing public criticism for failing to support evidence-based practice and policymaking. And there have been moves to subject it to greater external and central control, designed to remedy the problem. In the first part of this Introduction I will sketch these developments, since references to them occur in subsequent chapters, and because they embody views – about how research can be (and ought to be) useful to policymakers and practitioners – that are the focus for my discussion. In the final part of the Introduction I will outline the argument of each chapter.

The current crisis in educational research

Recent criticism of educational research in England and Wales probably needs to be understood against the background of longer-term changes in the nature of professional education for teachers (both pre- and in-service); of changing patterns in social research funding; and of the growth of demands for, and attempts to establish, 'transparent account-ability' in the public sector generally.

Teacher education

To a large extent, the expansion of educational research in Britain in the 1960s and 1970s was a result of the shift towards educating teachers in universities, rather than in training colleges. With this move, the academic component of teacher education was expanded, with some disciplines coming to be treated as foundational, notably the philosophy, psychology, sociology, and history of education. What informed this shift away from more practical forms of teacher preparation was a commitment to the goal of making teaching a full profession; in the sense of an occupation that could only be entered by university graduates who had been inducted into the ways of thinking and bodies of academic knowledge relevant to educational practice. However, for a variety of reasons, in the 1970s, 1980s and 1990s both teachers and teacher education came under increasing public criticism. This was closely related to the collapse of the previous broad political consensus about education, a collapse that had begun in the early 1970s. This was stimulated initially by the influence of 1960s leftist radicalism, but more strongly shaped by the subsequent resurgence of right-wing ideas (crowned by the political triumph of Thatcherism in the 1980s). As a result, there were moves to shift teacher education away from the academic model, regarded by many critics as too theoretical and political, back towards a more practical form of preparation, this time based primarily in schools.[2]

One component of these developments was that in the late 1960s and early 1970s educational research had come to be strongly infused by radical ideas: anarchism and Marxism initially, feminism and anti-racism later. To a large extent, this arose from a change within the sociology of education (announced as 'the new sociology of education'), and its spreading influence was facilitated by the success of that subdiscipline in challenging its main competitors – the philosophy and the psychology of education. These radical ideas had a considerable effect on the pro-fessional education of teachers in the 1970s, though this was not as great as right-wing critics later claimed. Subsequently, the shift to the Right in the external political climate led to a waning in influence of the sociology of education, and to growth in other areas of educational research – notably curriculum studies, educational administration and management, school effectiveness, and policy studies. However, in this process the influence of the methodological and theoretical legacy of the new sociology – which was mainly qualitative in methodological terms and social constructionist in theoretical commitment – continued to spread across the field of educational research (see Hammersley 1996).

The funding of social and educational research

The election of a Conservative government also brought moves to reduce the public funding for social research, and even led to questions being raised about whether it had any justification at all. In 1981 a review of the work of the Social Science Research Council, the main funding body for social science research in England and Wales, was ordered. It was widely believed at the time that the motive behind this review was to provide a justification for closing the organisation down. In the event, the review was broadly favourable (Rothschild 1982), and what happened instead was that there was a change of name, to the Economic and Social Research Council (ESRC), and continued reduction in funding. Subsequently, there have been recurrent changes within the ESRC which have moved it more and more towards an emphasis on funding research directly relevant to current policy priorities. Early on, there was a shift to allocating a substantial proportion of funds via specific initiatives, rather than through the responsive funding mode that had previously been the norm. Furthermore, there have been increasing requirements that those bidding for funds involve potential 'users' and develop dissemination strategies designed to encourage 'implementation' of the findings.[3]

Closely related to these changes in the mode of operation of the ESRC has been the growing influence of ideas about the 'knowledge economy', the 'socially distributed' character of knowledge production and the need for 'interactive' social science (see Caswill and Shove 2000). An influential contribution to this line of argument was provided by an ex-chair of the ESRC, Douglas Hague. He argued that current economic development depends more and more on knowledge and information, and that this has very important implications for universities and for the researchers based in them. In particular, he suggests, they will find themselves in an increasingly competitive market for producing and distributing knowledge; and he argues that, to survive, they will have to reform themselves so that they can operate in ways that are closer to those of commercial knowledge businesses, and/or to form alliances with these businesses (see Hague 1991). More recently, along similar lines, Gibbons et al. have argued that an important change is taking place in the organisation of research across a whole range of fields, away from more traditional, disciplinary forms towards ones that involve interdisciplinary teams tackling practical problems, and working at the sites where those problems arise rather than in universities (Gibbons et al. 1994).

Moves towards 'transparent' accountability in the public sector

The third important background factor has been attempts to apply 'transparent accountability' to many parts of the public sector in Britain in recent years. This form of accountability is central to the 'new public management' that has become so influential within government circles across many Western societies (see Ferlie et al. 1996). It requires that publicly funded activities be accountable through the monitoring of performance, in the same way that private enterprises are believed to be accountable to investors in terms of sales, profits and dividends. The assumption is that private enterprise is naturally more efficient and effective than state organisation, an idea made more influential by the collapse of East European economies in the 1980s. So, the goal of the new public management is to introduce forms of organisation within the public sector that approximate to the 'discipline of the market'.

One element of this is the establishment of quasi-markets, but equally important is the provision of information about institutional per-formance. In neo-classical economic theory, on which the new manageri-alism partly relies, markets are seen as generating information – about relative costs, about the relative quality of goods and services etc. – on the basis of which consumers act in ways that reward efficient producers and penalise inefficient ones. Investors, in turn, respond according to the market performance of different firms, investing in successful ones, dis-investing from unsuccessful ones. Analogously, from the point of view of the new public management, the publication of league tables and of the results of audits and inspections provides information about the performance of particular units or policies which can be used by those who fund the public sector, both government and citizens generally, to judge its effectiveness and efficiency.[4]

In relation to research there has been a gradual move towards trying to implement this kind of 'transparent' accountability. The introduction of the Research Assessment Exercise can be seen as an early step, plus the already mentioned shift within the ESRC towards greater emphasis on the role of users, the introduction of procedures designed to test whether projects have met their objectives, and attempts to measure the 'impact' of funded research.

However, it is important to stress that social research has a dual rela-tionship to this new form of accountability. Not only are there demands for research itself to be made more 'accountable', like other activities, but it is seen by governments as able to generate information about the effec-tiveness and efficiency of policies and institutions. In other words, it is regarded as a major tool in promoting 'accountability' and 'modernisa-tion' across the public sector and beyond. And, of course, this view of its function has significant implications for the *kind* of research that is believed to be of value. Above all, this is research which tells us 'what works', 'what works best' or 'what works most efficiently'.[5]

Mounting criticism of educational research and government intervention

These broad developments over the last few decades of the twentieth century – in policies towards teacher education, in the funding of social research, and in public sector accountability – are the background against which recent attempts to reform educational research can be understood. It is difficult to identify precisely when these attempts began. As early as 1991, a working party was set up by the ESRC to review research in education and to set priorities for it (see Rudduck and McIntyre 1998:8–9 and *passim*). However, the main trigger seems to have been the Teacher Training Agency (TTA) annual lecture given by David Hargreaves in 1996. Hargreaves was well known as an educational researcher, but had also been Chief Inspector of Schools for the Inner London Education Authority. Moreover, he had been in the forefront of criticism of university-based initial teacher education. When he gave the TTA lecture he was professor of education at the University of Cambridge. In this lecture, he repeated some of the criticisms he had made of the sociology of education many years earlier (see, for example, Hargreaves 1981), generalising these to educational research as a whole, and focusing in particular on what he saw as its failure to serve the education system. In this he drew an analogy with the situation in the health service, where a movement towards 'evidence-based medicine' had recently emerged. This movement had been primarily concerned with facilitating and encouraging medical practitioners to draw more on the findings of relevant research. By contrast, Hargreaves argued that while teachers did not make much use of educational research, the blame did not lie with them but with researchers. He argued that, for the most part, the latter had not been doing the kind of research which was necessary to serve evidence-based practice. Furthermore, he proposed that some of the money currently allocated to universities for educational research should be transferred to the Office for Standards in Education (OFSTED), to facilitate analysis of the reports of school inspectors.

Hargreaves' lecture reinforced the commitment of the TTA to the concept of teaching as a research-based profession. And this organisation began a funding programme to enable more teachers to carry out small research projects and to disseminate their findings to colleagues. The idea was that such research would be more practically focused than most academic educational research, and would thereby have a much more direct and beneficial impact on practice.[6]

Hargreaves' critique generated a great deal of attention, both within the educational research community and outside. Most significantly, it led to the setting up of two investigations into educational research, one sponsored by OFSTED and the other by the Department for Education and Employment (DfEE). Furthermore, while these investigations were under way, the controversy was kept on the boil by media commentary, such as criticism of papers given at the British Educational Research Association annual conference in the *Spectator* (McKinstry 1997). This announced that the research reported at the conference simply 'indulged the ideological whims of academics' rather than 'studying possible improvements in teaching', 'which is what educational researchers are paid for' (ibid.:24–5). There was also a book review in the *New Statesman* by Chris Woodhead, Chief Inspector of Schools and head of OFSTED, in which he dismissed the value of much recent sociology of education. The headline of this read: 'Academia gone to seed: once upon a time, educational research helped teachers and illuminated how children learn. Today's academics produce little more than badly written dross.' In the course of this review, Woodhead referred back to Hargreaves' TTA lecture and also quoted from the report of the OFSTED-sponsored investigation, which was at that time still unpublished (Woodhead 1998).

The Tooley report eventually appeared just before the DfEE-funded Hillage report (Tooley 1998; Hillage et al. 1998). James Tooley was research fellow in the School of Education, University of Manchester, and later professor of education at the University of Newcastle; but he was also Director of Education at a right-wing think tank, the Institute of Economic Affairs. In his report, Tooley examined a sample of recent articles in four education journals, and came to the conclusion that a substantial proportion of them suffered from serious methodological defects, though he also concluded that most of them could be judged educationally relevant in a broad sense, and he warned against generalising from his sample. As head of OFSTED, the sponsoring agency, Woodhead wrote a brief introduction to this report, in which he declared that much educational research 'is, on this analysis, at best no more than an irrelevance and a distraction', and in the press release for the report (which was headed 'Majority of academic educational research is second-rate') he suggested that 'considerable sums of public money are being pumped into research of dubious quality and little value'.[7]

The DfEE report, produced by researchers in the Institute for Employment Studies at the University of Sussex, also raised questions about the quality and, especially, the usefulness of educational research. It suggested (following Hargreaves) that an independent forum should be set up – on which researchers, representatives of government agencies, members of funding bodies, and teachers should be represented – to determine 'national strategy' in educational research. Building on this, in the accompanying press release the DfEE declared that 'public money is wasted on poor educational research, which is too often irrelevant to teaching practice or inaccessible to teachers'; and the Department promised a 'fundamental shake-up of the educational research establishment'

(*Times Higher Educational Supplement* [hereafter *THES*] 28 August 1998).[8]

These two critical reports on educational research were followed by a government initiative designed to remedy the problems identified. In the words of Charles Clarke, then Parliamentary Under-Secretary of State at the DfEE, the aim was to 'resurrect educational research in order to raise standards' (Clarke 1998:2), a comment which implies a rather negative view about the health of this field of enquiry, to say the least. In the course of outlining the Government's proposed remedies, Clarke makes clear the conception of educational research which lies behind the proposed reforms. He declares that educational research is important because 'it can identify the most effective approaches which will contribute to raising standards at all levels [of the education system]' (Clarke 1998:2). This was to be achieved by: the promotion of 'centres of excellence', in other words funding particular institutions for specific areas of research; the encouragement of 'longitudinal studies, literature reviews, replications and, where appropriate, randomly controlled trials'; the development of an information centre collating and reviewing the findings of educational research in a way that is accessible to users; and increased user involvement in setting priorities for educational research, and indeed in the 'entire process'.

As part of this government intervention, an Evidence for Policy and Practice: Information and Co-ordinating Centre (EPPI-Centre) was set up at the Institute of Education, University of London. This was charged with the task of coordinating the development of systematic reviews that would make research findings accessible to policymakers and practitioners. In addition, a National Educational Research Forum was established, designed to set priorities for the funding of educational research in a way that is more responsive to the needs of its 'users'. The intention was that these priorities would coordinate the decisions of all the relevant funding agencies, both public and private. In addition, an ESRC programme was established on 'teaching and learning' – funded in large part, it seems, from finance that would otherwise have gone directly to university education departments, this money now to be competed for on the basis of specific research proposals. Moreover, the framework of this programme laid great emphasis on research that has immediate practical payoff, being designed to support projects 'which will lead to significant improvements in the achievements of learners' (ESRC 2000).

In early 2000, in a speech to an ESRC gathering, the then Secretary of State for Education and Employment made clear that he saw these developments as a model for what was needed across social research generally. The title of his lecture – 'Influence or irrelevance?'- makes clear the options from his perspective. He asks: 'can the social science community have a major influence in improving government, or is it destined to be ever more detached and irrelevant to the real debates which affect people's life chances?' The Secretary of State then goes on to list what he calls 'our frustrations': that social research either 'addresses issues other than those which are central and directly relevant to the political and policy debates' or addresses those issues in ways that do not take into account 'the reality of many people's lives' and/or are 'driven by ideology' (Blunkett 2000:12).[9]

There is a strong hint here about whom David Blunkett believes should be setting the research agenda. Clearly, it is not researchers. As he comments later in his speech: 'there is a widespread perception both within and beyond government that too much social science research is ... too "supplier-driven" ' (ibid.:15). Furthermore, it is evident from this speech that external control is taken to be desirable not just in relation to *what* is studied, but also as regards *how* it is studied. In particular, emphasis is to be placed on large-scale, interdisciplinary, quantitative studies.

Early in 2001, the National Educational Research Forum (NERF) produced a consultation paper. The aim of this was to generate a national strategy designed to coordinate educational research, so that it serves evidence-informed policymaking and practice more effectively. This strategy has several elements. One is to establish effective systems for summarising the results of research and making them available to users, along the lines of the Cochrane Collaboration in the field of health. The work of the EPPI Centre at the London Institute of Education and the international Campbell Collaboration are seen as tackling this. Another element is to set priorities for research and development in education, and to establish a mechanism to 'implement this priority-setting process on an ongoing basis' (NERF 2000:8). A further aim is to coordinate assessments of research proposals and research products by funders – and by other key gatekeepers in the field, such as journal editors – in terms of an agreed set of quality criteria. Furthermore, as an adjunct to this, the impact of particular research projects is to be assessed and lessons from this built into the quality criteria.[10]

These recent events in England and Wales raise, in the sharpest possible way, the issue of what relationship is feasible and desirable between research and policymaking or practice. Underlying most of the criticism of educational research, and even some of the responses to it, has been what I refer to in Chapter 3 as a one-worldist view: the idea that the two activities can and must be brought into a close relationship, so that the requirements of educational policymakers and practitioners determine the kind of research that is done, and the results of that research directly shape future policies and practice. The belief is that this will generate a progressive spiral of increasing standards, on both sides. However, the arguments in this book raises fundamental questions about such an assumption: about what research can offer, about what policymaking and practice require, about whether there can be frictionless relationships among these three activities, and about what conditions are required for educational research to flourish.

Outline of the chapters

In the first chapter I look in detail at what, in England at least, has been the most influential recent critique of educational research: David Hargreaves' 1996 lecture to the TTA. I outline and assess the two key criticisms that Hargreaves makes of educational research: that it has failed to produce a cumulative body of knowledge; and that what it has generated is often of little use to teachers. While I accept that both these issues are important, and that some elements of Hargreaves' case are sound, I argue that much of his argument is based on fallacies. His criticism of the failure of educational research to be cumulative neglects the difficult methodological problems that such research faces. And his claim that educational research does not offer a valuable contribution to educational practice presupposes a narrowly instrumental conception of that relationship, one that seems unlikely to be generally applicable in the field of education. Indeed, there are respects in which it may not apply even to medicine, the major source for ideas about the role of research in evidence-based practice on which Hargreaves relies. I argue that his proposals for the radical reform of educational research, proposals which have shaped subsequent policy developments, are likely to be counterproductive. Far from improving the quality of educational research, they are more likely to damage it.[11]

One influential way of thinking about the contribution that research can make to policymaking or practice is in terms of the contrast between what have come to be referred to as the engineering and enlightenment models. While current attempts to reform educational research seem to be based on the former, most researchers adopt the latter. Chapter 2 looks closely at the enlightenment model, suggesting that it can be interpreted in two quite different ways, and that the most convincing interpretation is a 'moderate', rather than a 'strong', form of it. The central part of the chapter examines the various limits on what research can offer policy-making and practice; and outlines the indeterminate relationship between research findings, evaluations and recommendations based on these, and desirable practical outcomes. One element of this is a challenge to the idea that well-executed research always has desirable, and never undesirable, consequences. My argument amounts to a deflationary account of the contribution that research can make to practice, compared with what is generally assumed; though I also outline the sorts of con-tribution that it *can* make. I conclude by considering the likely conse-quences of researchers adopting this moderate enlightenment model in defending their position. My argument is that researchers, funders, and users need to recognise and value the modest practical contribution that research offers, rather than assigning it a master role and then complaining that it has failed to live up to this.

Chapter 3, written with Roger Gomm, examines the idea that research, policymaking and practice represent different 'worlds', involving distinctive orientations that differ from one another in unavoidable respects. The history of this idea is outlined, as well as some problems with it. These are addressed, and an attempt is made to develop the idea by drawing on the literature of phenomenological philosophy. Against this background, the various metaphors that have been employed to conceptualise the relationship between research and practice are examined: such as 'application', 'implementation', 'dissemination', and 'translation'. We conclude that the last of these is the most fruitful, because it takes account of the differences in orientation between research and other forms of practice. In the final section it is argued that educational policy making and practice also differ from one another in important respects, and that current attempts to reform educational research are part of a wider process in which the occupational world of teaching is being managerialised; and that the proposed reforms must be viewed in this wider context.

Chapter 4 focuses on the way in which qualitative enquiry has sometimes been singled out for particular attention in recent criticisms of educational research. This stems from the fact that, in Britain over the past two decades, it has become very popular among researchers; and it is indeed of uneven quality. However, the source of the criticism may be more fundamental. I argue that there is a conflict between the engineering model of the relationship between research and practice, which underpins current attempts to reform educational research, and the picture of social life generated by qualitative research, a picture that has much to commend it. The key elements of that picture are outlined, and they are contrasted with the functionalist conception of society which underlies the engineering and medical analogies. It is pointed out that such functionalism has long been subjected to cogent criticism within the sociological literature. At the same time, it is argued that some of the opposition to the engineering model, especially that influenced by critical theory and postmodernism, shares a similarly functionalist conception of society. Links are identified between qualitative researchers' ideas about the nature of society and the moderate enlightenment model.

Chapter 5 starts from a contrast between the idea that educational research needs to be subjected to external and central control if it is to serve policymaking and practice more effectively, and the proposal that diversity of approach within educational research should be tolerated or even celebrated. The latter position is sometimes justified on the grounds that 'difference' must be respected, and/or that educational research should represent marginalised voices. By contrast, here I question current attempts to increase central control over research by appealing to Michael Polanyi's conception of 'the republic of science'. His understanding of the nature of research communities is spelled out, along with the historical context in which it developed. I then examine the question of whether Polanyi's arguments against external and central control are applicable to educational research, given that it is a social, and applied, form of enquiry, whereas he was concerned with natural science; and given widespread recognition that educational research is not currently in a good state. I propose that his arguments *are* applicable, especially to scientific (rather than practical) research on education, but that they do not justify celebration, or even toleration, of all diversity in approach. Instead, they point to the need for the local exercise of control, on the basis of internal scientific considerations. In conclusion, I argue that while the critics of educational research may be right to claim that its current state is not healthy, central control is no remedy.

One problem with many discussions of social and educational research is a failure to recognise the different forms it can legitimately take, and/or inadequate conceptualisation of these differences. In Chapter 6, the distinction between basic and applied research is the focus. Problems with this distinction are identified, and an alternative typology is presented. This distinguishes, first of all, between scientific and practical research, in terms of their audience and mode of validation. Further distinctions are then made within each of these categories. This chapter underlines the importance of recognising the heterogeneity of social and educational research, if we are to clarify its relationship to various forms of practice. I try to provide a better way of conceptualising this heterogeneity, one which recognises both what is generic and what is distinctive to different approaches.

Chapter 7, written with Peter Foster, focuses on reviews of research, as the most important means by which the findings of scientific educational research can be communicated to audiences outside the researcher community. We look at some aspects of the production of reviews in the light of this function. Attention is given to issues surrounding the initiation of reviews, their intended audience, the definition of the field, the coverage and treatment of relevant studies, and the drawing of conclusions. The discussion is illustrated by reference to some recent examples of reviews of educational research. As noted earlier, one of the elements of current attempts to reform educational research in England and Wales is attempts to increase the number and quality of research reviews. While recognising the value of this, we show that there are some difficult choices, and easily overlooked problems, involved in producing reviews.[12]

Conclusion

There is nothing in this book which denies that there is room for considerable improvement in the quality of educational research. Indeed, elsewhere, some colleagues and I have pointed to serious problems with much of the work in one field: that concerned with educational inequalities (see Foster et al. 1996). Moreover, there is little doubt that there is scope for improvement in the relationship between educational research and policymaking or professional practice. However, it seems to me that much recent conceptualisation of this relationship is misguided, including that on which current attempts to reform educational research are based. False assumptions are made about both sides of the divide, and, as a result, excessive expectations are generated about the contribution that research can make to improving educational policymaking and practice, analogous to the false expectations which currently hold sway about the contribution that education can make to national economic success.[13] I hope that this book will contribute to a more realistic understanding of what is possible and desirable; one that will facilitate the flourishing of educational research, and perhaps thereby aid the improvement of education.

Notes

1. Nisbet and Broadfoot (1980) outline the history of recurrent crisis in the relationship between research and policymaking in education. As they make clear, concern over what educational research contributes to policymaking and practice has by no means been restricted to Britain. For a useful collection of articles about the issue, most of them from the United States, see Anderson and Biddle (1991).
2. In fact, there had already been changes in some pre-service teacher education courses towards closer and more extended links with schools, in order to encourage the integration of theory and practice: see Lacey and Lamont (1976) and McIntyre et al. (1993).
3. For an illuminating account of the rationale behind the early stages of this shift in the orientation of the ESRC, see Hague (1990). On the prominence of 'users' in ESRC thinking, see Shove and Rip (2000). They suggest that what is involved here is a form of 'strategic mythologising' (ibid.:181).
4. It is important to emphasise that 'transparency' is not the only form of accountability there is, even though this is sometimes implied or claimed by its advocates. What has happened is that earlier forms of accountability, involving occupational self-regulation and relying on lay trust, came to be seen as inadequate. For useful discussions of these developments, see Pollitt (1990), Clarke and Newman (1997), and Power (1997).
5. See, for example, Oakley (2000); for a review of her arguments, see Hammersley (2000d).
6. For a methodological assessment of the first wave of TTA funded studies, see Foster (1999).
7. For responses from educational researchers to the Tooley report, see *Research Intelligence*, the newsletter of the British Educational Research Association (65, August 1998).
8. In fact, the prospect of such a shake-up had been announced when the Hillage enquiry was initially established. At that time, under a headline 'Shake-up on the way as research is scrutinised', Michael Barber, then head of the Standards and Effectiveness Unit at the DfEE, was quoted in the *Times Educational Supplement (TES)* as saying: 'It is extremely unlikely that the status quo will survive this review' (*TES* 20 February 1998). For responses to the Hillage report, see *Research Intelligence* (66, October 1998) and the *Times Educational Supplement* (9 October, 1998:25).
9. For assessments of this speech, see Hodgkinson (2000) and Hammersley (2000a). Even before this, Blunkett had criticised some educational research on homework (see Farrow 1999), and research findings about 'antisocial'

council tenants (BBC News web page, 20 November 1999), because they ran counter to his own views. Both these criticisms were repeated in his ESRC lecture.

10. For responses to this consultation paper, see Hodkinson (2001) and Ball (2001).
11. A version of this chapter was previously published in the *British Educational Research Journal*, and Hargreaves wrote a response to it: see Hargreaves 1997. A reply to his response is available from the author.
12. This chapter was previously published in the *British Educational Research Journal*, and a critical response appeared in the same issue relating to one of the reviews we discuss: see Gillborn and Gipps (1998). For a complementary paper on 'systematic' reviews, see Hammersley (2001b).
13. On the relationship between education and national economic success, see Robinson (1997).

Chapter 1

Research and Evidence-Based Practice in Education: An Assessment of David Hargreaves' Critique

There is some variation across different fields in what a shift to evidence-based practice is believed to require. In medicine, most of the emphasis has been on the need for practitioners to make more use of research evidence in their work. In education, by contrast, the stress has been on the inadequacy of the research evidence that is available, as regards both its rigour and its applicability. In short, while the focus in medicine has generally been on the quality of practice, in education it has been on the quality of research.

It is only very recently that the term 'evidence-based practice' has appeared in the field of education. In England, the Teacher Training Agency (TTA) has played a crucial role in this development, announcing its commitment to the promotion of teaching as a research-based profession (see, for example, TTA 1996). And a central theme in its literature is that there is insufficient educational research that is focused on the classroom and that supplies practical knowledge which can be used to improve the quality of teaching. In an attempt to correct this, the TTA mounted a research programme designed to encourage such research on the part of teachers.[1]

It should be noted that, while use of terms like 'evidence-based' or 'research-based' practice is relatively new, the idea that teaching ought to be based on research evidence has a long history (see, for instance, Dunkin and Biddle 1974). One of the preoccupations of much American educational research in the first half of the century, and of later research in Britain, was the relative effectiveness of different pedagogical techniques and styles. And probably the most common view among educational researchers today is that this project failed; and not just for contingent reasons but because it was mistaken in principle (Chambers 1991 and 1992; Glass 1994; though see also Gage 1985 and 1994). As a result, over the past few decades, the role of research has come to be seen by many educational researchers more in terms of the 'enlightenment' than the 'engineering' model (Janowitz 1972; Bulmer 1982; Finch 1986).

Rather than supplying or validating effective techniques or policies, the payoff of research is now widely believed to lie more in terms of raising questions about current assumptions, and of supplying alternative perspectives on the work of teachers, education managers and policymakers, and on the contexts in which they operate.

The promotion of teacher research, another component of the TTA project, is also far from new. There was an influential classroom action research movement in the United States during the 1950s (see Corey 1953), and in Britain and elsewhere from the 1970s onwards (Stenhouse 1975; Nixon 1981; Hustler et al. 1986; Elliott 1991). Moreover, these developments have also been subjected to critical assessment. There have been questions raised, from within and outside, about whether such work is an adequate substitute for more conventional kinds of research, and about the contribution of some versions of it to classroom practice and to educational change (see, for example, Wiles 1953; Hodgkinson 1957; Carr and Kemmis 1986; Hammersley 1993).

Recent advocacy of evidence-based teaching in Britain has not drawn much on this past experience, the proposal being presented instead as a radically new venture. Furthermore, it has occurred in a context where, as in the public sector generally, there has been growing emphasis on 'transparent' public accountability, framed in terms of attempts to measure the 'value added' by institutional practices. From this point of view, research is often seen as playing a crucial role in providing the means by which to monitor the inputs, processes, and outputs of institutions; and in offering guidance about how best to render services more 'effective', 'efficient' and, sometimes, 'equitable'. It is against this background that educational research has recently been criticised as inadequate.

By far the most considered and effective presentation of the case for the failure of educational research to facilitate evidence-based teaching is to be found in David Hargreaves' TTA lecture *Teaching as a Research-Based Profession* (Hargreaves 1996). This attracted a great deal of attention and drew much comment.[2] Hargreaves claims that the effectiveness of teaching in schools would be substantially improved if it were a research-based profession. And he lays the blame for the fact that it is not on researchers rather than on teachers. He argues that current educational research is neither sufficiently cumulative nor sufficiently relevant to practical concerns for it to make the contribution required of it. To support his argument, Hargreaves draws a contrast between the role of research in relation to education and its contribution to the practice of medicine. He uses as a model the recent development of evidence-based medicine, in which clinical decision-making is to be founded on, and justified in terms of, research findings about the relative effectiveness of different medical treatments. On the basis of his critique of educational research, Hargreaves argues that radical changes are required in the way that it is organised and carried out. In particular, 'practitioners and policy makers must take an active role in shaping the direction of educational research' (ibid.:6). He proposes the establishment of a National Educational Research Forum to facilitate dialogue amongst the various stakeholders. This would sponsor research foresight exercises to provide the basis for a national strategy, specifying short- and long-term priorities. And he recommends the reallocation to the TTA and to OFSTED (the Office for Standards in Education) of some of the money currently given to universities for educational research. Above all, he argues that more educational research should be carried out by practising teachers, since this would enhance its practical relevance.

In this chapter I will assess Hargreaves' criticisms of educational research and the remedies he proposes. First, though, I need to spell out his critique in a little more detail.

Hargreaves' diagnosis of the ills of educational research

Towards the end of his lecture, Hargreaves summarises his criticisms as follows: 'what [should] come to an end is the frankly second-rate educational research which does not make a serious contribution to fundamental theory or knowledge; which is irrelevant to practice; which is uncoordinated with any preceding or follow-up research; and which clutters up academic journals that virtually nobody reads' (ibid.:7). Two main charges seem to be involved here.

The first is that much educational research is non-cumulative, in the sense that it does not explicitly 'build on earlier research – by confirming or falsifying it, by extending or refining it, by replacing it with better evidence or theory, and so on'. The problem is that 'a few small-scale investigations of an issue which are never followed up inevitably produce inconclusive and contestable findings of little practical relevance'. Moreover, replications, 'which are more necessary in the social than the natural sciences because of the importance of contextual and cultural variations, are astonishingly rare'. This situation is worsened by the fact that 'educational researchers, like other social scientists, are often engaged in bitter disputes among themselves about the philosophy and methodology of the social sciences'. This means that lines of research are abandoned when there is a change in fashion, rather than because problems have been solved. As a result, despite considerable work, 'there are few areas which have yielded a corpus of research evidence regarded as scientifically sound and as a worthwhile resource to guide professional action' (ibid.:2).

As can be seen, this first argument leads straight into the second: that research is not found useful by teachers. Hargreaves claims that 'few successful practising teachers' use the knowledge provided by the foundation disciplines (psychology, sociology, philosophy, and history) or think it important for their practice. Indeed, 'teachers are able to be effective in their work in almost total ignorance of this infrastructure'. As a result: 'the disciplines of education are seen to consist of "theory" which is strongly separated from practice. Trainee teachers soon spot the yawning gap between theory and practice and the low value of research as a guide to the solution of practical problems' (ibid.:2). The fundamental defect is that there is no substantial body of research 'which, if only it were disseminated and acted on by teachers, would yield huge benefits in the quality of teaching and learning'. Thus, Hargreaves asks:

> just how much research is there which (i) demonstrates conclusively that if teachers change their practice from x to y there will be a significant and enduring improvement in teaching and learning and (ii) has developed an effective method of convincing teachers of the benefits of, and means to, changing from x to y? (Ibid.:5)

On this basis, Hargreaves argues that the money allocated to educational research is not well spent: 'Something has indeed gone badly wrong. Research is having little impact on the improvement of practice, and teachers I talk to do not think they get value for money from the £50–60 millions we spend annually on educational research' (ibid.:5).

Assessing Hargreaves' argument: educational research as non-cumulative

Criticism of the non-cumulative character of research on education has been a persistent theme in Hargreaves' writings. As long ago as 1981 he took the sociology of education to task for its failure to develop a cumulative body of knowledge:

> As time goes by, theories do not become better, by which I mean broader in scope and more economical in content, either as a result of careful testing or as a result of subsuming earlier theories. Theories simply 'lie around' in the field, relatively vague and relatively untested. Empirical research fares no better. Very few studies actively seek to build on the work of earlier researchers, confirming or disconfirming earlier findings to put our knowledge on a sounder basis. Too often research evidence is inconsistent or incompatible. It is thus that many of the introductory text books to the sociology of education inevitably end up as *catalogues* of theory and research, for there is no way that a reviewer can integrate the field into a coherent whole. There are very few areas in our discipline where we can confidently say that either theory or research is much better established than it was several years ago. (Ibid.:10)

I agree with Hargreaves' argument here. Commitment to one-off studies is an important defect of much educational research, and indeed of social research generally. It reduces the extent to which findings from particular investigations are tested across different situations and minimises the division of labour, thereby undermining the cumulation of knowledge. There is little doubt that we need to move to a situation where new research builds more effectively on earlier work, and where greater attention is given to testing competing interpretations of data, whether descriptive or explanatory. And this may require replications; though the form these take cannot be the same in naturalistic as in experimental research, since here the researcher has less control over the course of the research process. In addition, as might be inferred from the above, I believe that Hargreaves is right to assume the appropriateness of a scientific approach to the study of education, despite the strong trend towards the opposite conclusion on the part of many educational researchers in recent times.

Nevertheless, I think that there are also some serious problems with this aspect of Hargreaves' critique: about the criteria of evaluation he uses, concerning the causes of the problems facing educational research, and about the pressure on educational enquiry to serve policymaking and practice.

Criteria of evaluation

A first problem is that he is not as clear as he might be about what criteria he is using to assess educational research. In the early parts of his lecture he stresses its failure to accumulate knowledge by building on earlier work, but the concept of cumulation is not a simple one: there are different forms it can take (see Freese 1980:40–9). Moreover, many educational researchers *do* claim that their work has produced theoretical development (see, for example, Woods 1985 and 1987). Hargreaves does not make clear why he would deny these claims. Moreover, later in his lecture, this first criticism turns into the charge that educational research is not, or that not enough of it is, 'evidence-based'. Again, clarification is required. What is and is not being accepted as evidence here, and what counts as basing claims on evidence? Some of the language that Hargreaves uses implies commitment to a methodological perspective that many educational researchers would dismiss as positivist. That dismissal would be a mistake, in my view; but some specification and justification of the model of research he is employing is necessary. Reference to *examples* of evidence-based and non-evidence-based educational research might also have been illuminating.[4]

The sources of the problems facing educational research

A second problem is that Hargreaves seems to present the failings of current educational research as if they stemmed solely from a lack of proper commitment on the part of researchers to rigorous and cumulative inquiry, and/or from a lack of effort. There is no doubt that this commitment has become attenuated. But, to some extent, this is a response to genuine problems. It should be pointed out that the move away from the scientific model is relatively recent. Much educational research in the first two-thirds of the twentieth century was devoted to scientific investigation of educational institutions and techniques. As Hargreaves knows, since he was a leading figure in it, the shift to qualitative method in the 1970s was prompted by powerful criticisms identifying unresolved problems in this 'positivist' research. Some of these related to the difficulties of measuring what is of educational significance (Barrow 1984:ch. 6; Delamont and Hamilton 1984). Others concerned the peculiar complexities of 'social causation', including interaction effects (Cronbach 1975). The most radical versions of these arguments drew on philosophical writings to the effect that human social life is quite different in character from the physical world studied by natural scientists (and, we might add, from that investigated by most medical researchers) (see, for example, Winch 1958 and Schütz 1967). From this it was often concluded that the kind of knowledge produced by natural scientists is not available to social and educational researchers.

In my judgement, the arguments for the distinctiveness of the social world have been overplayed, and are associated with too homogeneous a view of the phenomena studied, and of the methods used, by natural scientists. Nevertheless, there can be no denying the serious problems involved in producing conclusive knowledge about causal patterns in social phenomena. This is one reason why educational researchers, like social scientists generally, have become embroiled in philosophical and methodological disputes. Hargreaves treats these disputes as if they were merely a matter of fashion. It may be true that some of the discussion is self-indulgent, but the underlying problems are real enough. At the core of them is precisely the question of the extent to which one can have a science of human behaviour of a kind that models itself, even remotely, on the natural sciences. By failing to mention these problems, Hargreaves implies that the sort of cumulative, well-founded knowledge he wants can be created simply by researchers pulling themselves together and getting back to work (under the direction of teachers). The situation is not so simple; and not so easily remedied.

I can only sketch the problems briefly here.[5] As already noted, they centre on two areas: the measurement of social phenomena, and the validation of causal relationships amongst those phenomena. As regards the former, there are problems involved in identifying distinct and standardised 'treatments' in education, witness the difficulties faced by researchers seeking to distinguish teaching styles (see Bennett 1976 and 1985; Wragg 1976; Galton et al. 1980). Indeed, there are unresolved measurement problems in relation to even the most specific and concrete aspects of teaching, for example types of questions asked (Scarth and Hammersley 1986a and 1986b). The problems are also formidable at the other end of the causal chain, in operationalising the concept of learning. There is room for substantial disagreement about what students *should* learn, but also about what they *actually* learn, in any particular situation: in terms of different knowledge, skills, and/or values; different areas of content; depth versus surface learning; degrees of transferability etc. More than this, very often what are regarded as the most important kinds of learning – relating to high-level, transferable cognitive skills or to personal understanding – are extraordinarily difficult to measure with any degree of validity and reliability. And there are reasonable doubts about whether replicable measurement of them is possible, even in principle. In short, in both areas, there are questions about whether it is possible to move beyond sensitising concepts to the definitive concepts that seem to be required for scientific analysis of the kind proposed by Hargreaves.[6]

The problems relating to the establishment of causal patterns are equally severe. Since we are interested in what goes on in actually operating educational institutions, and because strict experimentation is often ruled out for practical or ethical reasons, this task becomes extremely difficult. How are we to control competing factors in such a way as to assess the relative contribution of each one in what is usually a complex web of relationships? More than this, can we assume that causation in this field involves fixed, universal relationships, rather than local context-sensitive patterns in which interpretation and decision on the part of teachers and students play an important role? Unlike in many areas of medicine, in education the 'treatments' consist of symbolic interaction, with all the scope for multiple interpretations and responses which follows from that. What kind of causal relations are involved here, if they are causal at all? And what kind of knowledge can we have of them?

These, then, are some of the fundamental problems facing educational researchers attempting to produce the kind of knowledge that Hargreaves demands. I do not want to suggest that such knowledge is impossible. Indeed, I have claimed elsewhere that Hargreaves' earliest work forms part of one of the few cumulative programmes of research that develops and tests theory to be found in sociology and education. Nevertheless, problems remain with that programme, and there are questions about whether it can provide a model for work in other areas (Hammersley 1985).

Effects of the pressure on educational research to serve policymaking and practice

In my view, one important cause of the unsatisfactory nature of much educational research is that it is too preoccupied with producing information that will shape *current* policy or practice. This seems likely to be one source of the lack of testing and cumulation of knowledge that Hargreaves complains about. He touches on this when he notes that educational researchers have fallen between two stools: 'achieving neither prestige from the social scientists ... nor gratitude from classroom teachers' (Hargreaves 1996:3). The problem, in part, is that while working under the auspices of academic disciplines concerned with contributing to theory, researchers have also sought to address the changing political agendas that define pressing educational problems. This is partly a product of sharp competition for funds. But it has also been encouraged by conceptions of research which imply that it is possible simultaneously to contribute to scientific theory and to provide solutions to practical or political problems. This view is characteristic of some forms of positivism and also of Marxism, both of which have been influential in the field; and there are signs that Hargreaves is committed to a version of it, though these are more obvious in his 1981 article than in his 1996 lecture. However, it seems to me that this view is fallacious, since the production of information of high practical relevance usually depends on a great deal of knowledge that does not have such relevance. In other words, for science to be able to contribute knowledge that is relevant to practice a division of labour is required: a great deal of coordinated work is necessary which tackles smaller, more manageable problems that do not have immediate practical payoff. Moreover, this requires sustained work over a long period, not short bursts of activity geared to political and practical priorities. In other words, in recent years, the wrong time schedule has been in control: that of educational policymaking and practice rather than that appropriate to scientific research.

In my judgement, then, the commitment of educational researchers to addressing the 'big questions' and to producing answers to them in the short rather than the long term, along with parallel expectations on the part of funders, has been a major contributing factor to the weaknesses that Hargreaves identifies. And his call for educational research to be more practically effective will only worsen this problem. He insists that 'curiosity-driven, long-term "basic" and "blue skies" research is as vital in education as in any other scientific field' (ibid.:7). But he neglects the extent to which the funding for this has already been eroded. For example, the main source which he mentions, the ESRC (the Economic and Social Research Council), has increasingly moved towards non-responsive funding of research, much of which is of a strategic or even applied character. This is despite the fact that its predecessor, the SSRC (the Social Science Research Council), was specifically established to fund basic research – government departments and other sources were expected to finance applied work. Moreover, Hargreaves applauds 'the pressure the ESRC now puts on researchers to demonstrate consultation with, and involvement of, users as a condition of getting a research grant' (ibid.:6). Yet it is a feature of basic research that who the users will be and what use they might make of it are largely unknown.

Assessing Hargreaves' argument: the contribution of research to educational practice

Let me turn now to the other main complaint in Hargreaves' lecture, to what is indeed its central theme: that educational research has not produced sufficient practically relevant knowledge.[7] I certainly agree that an important ultimate aim (but, for reasons already explained, not an immediate one) of all research should be to produce knowledge which is practically relevant. But there is room for much disagreement about what such relevance amounts to, and about what kinds of knowledge are possible and of value. In his lecture, Hargreaves adopts a narrowly instrumental view of practical relevance: that research should be able to tell practitioners which is the best technique for dealing with a particular kind of problem. In this respect, though his analogy is with medicine, he seems to be committed to the 'engineering model' of the relationship between research and practice. This portrays research as directed towards finding or evaluating solutions to technical problems.[8]

The question of whether educational research can supply the sort of knowledge assumed by the engineering model has already been dealt with in the previous section, but there is also the issue of whether the problems that teachers face are of a kind that is open to solution by research; in other words, whether they are technical in character. Early on in his lecture, Hargreaves seems to recognise that they may not be. He comments: 'both education and medicine are profoundly people-centred professions. Neither believes that helping people is merely a matter of a simple and technical application but rather a highly skilled process in which a sophisticated judgement matches a professional decision to the unique needs of each client' (ibid.:1). Yet his subsequent discussion of the contribution which he would like to see research making to educational practice seems to contradict this; for example, his reference to research needing to 'demonstrate conclusively' that a particular pedagogical approach will produce 'a significant and enduring improvement' (ibid.:5).

Teaching as a practical rather than a technical activity

At one time it was widely assumed that educational practice could, and should, be based on scientific theory, with teachers using techniques whose appropriateness had been determined by the results of scientific investigation (O'Connor 1957; Dunkin and Biddle 1974). However, much recent work on the nature of teaching by philosophers, psychologists, and sociologists has emphasised the extent to which it is practical rather than technical in character; in short, that it is a matter of making judgements rather than following rules (Schwab 1969; Hammersley 1979; Hirst 1983; Carr 1987; Olson 1992; Woods 1996). In an earlier article, Hargreaves himself contributed to this line of thinking, referring to the 'enormous complex whole which we call the teacher's common sense knowledge of life in classrooms'. He emphasised its largely tacit nature, and the fact that it must have this nature if it is to enable the teacher to do his work: 'Decisions are made partly on the basis of social skills and partly on the basis of certain value commitments: both are encapsulated and rapidly processed in every routine classroom decision' (Hargreaves 1979:79). This line of argument throws doubt on the idea that teaching can be *based* on research knowledge. It implies that it necessarily depends on experience, wisdom, local knowledge and judgement. And, I suggest, it is precisely the practical character of teaching, as much as any failing on the part of researchers, which is the main source of the 'yawning gap' between theory and practice; indeed, complaints about such gaps are a commonplace of professional education in all fields.[9]

One of the features of much practical activity, and particularly of teaching, is that goals are multiple, and their meaning is open to debate and difficult to operationalise. In this context, Hargreaves' focus on the 'effectiveness' of pedagogy obscures some of the most important issues. Put into practice, an exclusive focus on effectiveness leads to an overemphasis on those outcomes which can be measured (at the expense of other educational goals), or results in a displacement of goals on to the maximisation of measured output. We see this problem in some currently influential research on 'school effectiveness'. While researchers in this field are usually careful to note that the outcome measures they use do not exhaust or measure all the goals of schooling, their work is sometimes presented and often interpreted as measuring school effectiveness *as such*.[10]

Now, of course, we need to take care not to adopt too sharp a distinction between technical and practical activities.[11] What is involved is more of a continuum, and it seems likely that educational practice is not homogeneous in this respect: there may be some educational problems that are open to technical solution, even though many are not. Nevertheless, all teaching beyond that concerned with very elementary skills seems likely, in general terms, to come closer to the practical end of the dimension. And the practical character of most teachers' work is increased by the fact that they deal with *batches* of pupils, rather than with single clients, one by one, in the way that doctors do.[12] It is this which makes the classroom situation a particularly demanding one in terms of the need for reliance on contextual judgement (Jackson 1968; Doyle 1977).

The contribution that research can make to practice

All this is not to suggest that research can make no contribution to teaching. But it may mean that the contribution cannot take the form of indicating what is the appropriate technique to use in a particular situation, or even what are the chances of success of a technique in a particular *type* of situation. One reason for this is that, even less than doctors, teachers are not faced with exemplars of standard forms of problem, but rather with much more complex clusters of problematic factors. Given this, the nature of the contribution that research can make may be closer to the enlightenment model, involving the provision of information that corrects assumptions or alters the context in which teachers view some aspect of their situation, for example by highlighting possible causal relations to which they may not routinely give attention. Equally important is the capacity that research has for illuminating aspects of teachers' practices that are below their normal level of consciousness. A good example of this is research on teachers' typifications of children. Documentation of how these are built up, how they affect the ways in which teachers deal with pupils, and the consequences of this, is surely of considerable value (see, for example, Hargreaves et al. 1975). For the most part, such contributions are not dramatic in their consequences. But it is just as much a mistake to try to judge the value of research in terms of its immediate and identifiable practical impact as it is to judge the quality of a school solely by its examination results.

In earlier publications Hargreaves seems to adopt a position closer to the enlightenment than the engineering model. In the preface to his book *Interpersonal Relations and Education* he argued that the most important task in applying the human sciences to education is to 'shed light on the old problems as well as throwing up new problems, or at least problems that are not adequately acknowledged, formulated or discussed' (Hargreaves 1972:2).[13] This seems to me to be a more realistic expectation than the instrumental function he assumes in his TTA lecture. And it parallels conclusions that have been reached in studies of the relationship between research and policymaking (Weiss 1980). In his lecture, Hargreaves quotes Nisbet and Broadfoot's (1980) and Taylor's (1973) arguments for the enlightenment view, but he does not show that their conclusions are false. Instead, he simply asserts that this view is a self-fulfilling prophecy.

Hargreaves' evaluation of the contribution of educational research

All this raises questions about Hargreaves' conclusion that educational research does not offer value for money. This phrase has become a popular one, but it involves a judgement that is a good deal more complex and uncertain than its use generally suggests. Thus, Hargreaves gives no indication of how he thinks the cost-benefit analysis involved could be carried out. Even measuring the real cost of a particular piece of research would be a formidable task, and measuring the value of its 'impact' would be virtually impossible and the conclusion reached always open to debate. Nor does he acknowledge the problems with the whole cost-benefit approach. These have long been recognised within economics, if not always given the weight they deserve (see Little 1950 and Graaff 1957). Because of their reliance on values, all judgements about cost-effectiveness are likely to be subject to considerable instability across time, circumstances, and judges. So the question arises of who is to judge, when and how. Aside from his own assessment, Hargreaves seems to rely primarily on the judgements of teachers he has talked to (Hargreaves 1996:5). Yet, even ignoring the sampling and reactivity problems involved here, we can ask whether teachers are the best judges, given that according to him they have little knowledge of the findings of educational research. Furthermore, teachers are not the only proper audience for such research. Its main function, it seems to me, is to inform public debates about educational issues: to provide information for use by anyone concerned with those issues, not only teachers but also parents, governors, administrators, pressure groups, politicians, and citizens generally. How well it does this is an important question, and some assessment of its cost-effectiveness in this respect may be unavoidable; but this can be no more than a speculative and contestable estimate.

Hargreaves' lecture is effectively an evaluation of educational research, and as with all evaluations the conclusions reached are very sensitive to the standard of assessment employed. One's attitude to the practical value of current educational research will depend a great deal on one's expectations about the contribution to practice that it *could* make. In my view, researchers have promised – and funders, policymakers and prac- titioners have expected – too much, assuming that, in itself, research can provide solutions to practical problems (Hammersley 1995:ch. 7; see also Chapter 2 in this volume). Disappointment, recriminations and a negative attitude towards research have been the result. Hargreaves' lecture is more of the same in this respect, and as a result it is not likely to improve the situation. By reinforcing the idea that research can provide a scientific foundation for practice he exaggerates the contribution that it can make, *even in principle*. And the risk is that when it fails in this task, as it almost certainly will, it will be dismissed by even more potential users – and by funders – as worthless.

The parallel with medicine

In his critique of the practical failure of educational research, Hargreaves leans heavily on an analogy with medicine. I have no doubt at all that this comparison can be illuminating, but it ought to be pointed out that implicit in its use is a conception of professionalism which emphasises reliance on an established body of scientific knowledge. And this conception ought not to be taken for granted. We should remember that this has never been a feature of the other occupation whose status as a profession has generally been accepted as beyond question: the law.

Furthermore, as with all analogies, it is important to recognise that there may be significant differences, as well as similarities, between what is being compared. Also, analogies are sometimes based on misconceptions about that which is being used as a comparative standard. We must be very cautious, then, about using medicine as a basis for evaluating educational research and practice. Its appropriateness has to be argued for, not assumed.

Differences and similarities between education and medicine

Earlier, I discussed aspects of education which mark it off from medicine, in ways that challenge Hargreaves' negative judgements about the relative success of educational research. Certainly, it seems likely that much medical research avoids some of the problems that face educational researchers, in particular those deriving from the peculiarities of the social world. Where it does not, I suggest, we find the same lack of cumulative evidence that Hargreaves bemoans in education (Edwards 1996:9). Similarly, medical practice may generally be closer to the technical rather than to the practical end of the spectrum, so that research is able to play a role there which is much nearer to that envisaged by the engineering model than is possible in education.

However, it is easy to exaggerate the differences between the two cases. Thus, I think it is misleading to claim that in the case of medicine 'there is little difference between researchers and users; all are practitioners', whereas in educational contexts, 'by contrast, researchers are rarely users' (Hargreaves 1996:3). As Hargreaves recognises, much medical research is laboratory-based rather than clinic-based; and is not carried out by practising clinicians.[14] Equally, most educational researchers are also educational practitioners (though they may not be practitioners in the same type of context as that in which they do research). Moreover, in their role as academics, they use their own and others' research for teaching purposes, much in the manner that secondary school teachers use subject knowledge in theirs.[15] It is also worth noting that many educational researchers are ex-schoolteachers whose research relates to schools of the same general type to that in which they previously taught. (Hargreaves is himself an example of this.) I do not want to deny that there are important differences in the organisation of research and practice in the fields of education and medicine, but the differences are less sharp and more complex than Hargreaves implies.

Doubtful assumptions about medical research

There are also respects in which the assumptions Hargreaves makes about medical research, and about the way it contributes to medical practice, are open to doubt. One concerns the contrast in quality that he draws between medical and educational research. It is important to note that rather similar criticisms to those made by him of educational research have been directed at medical research carried out by doctors. In an article entitled 'The scandal of poor medical research', Altman comments:

> When I tell friends outside medicine that many papers published in medical journals are misleading because of methodological weaknesses they are rightly shocked. Huge sums of money are spent annually on research that is seriously flawed through use of inappropriate designs, unrepresentative samples, small samples, incorrect methods of analysis, and faulty interpretation. (Altman 1994:283)[16]

And it is worth emphasising the reasons that Altman puts forward for the poor quality of much medical research, since these relate directly to what Hargreaves claims to be its great strength: the fact that it is carried out by practising doctors. Altman lays the blame on the fact that doctors are expected to engage in research, but are often inadequately prepared for or committed to it. What we may conclude from this is that while there is undoubtedly a great deal more cumulation of well-founded knowledge in medicine than in education, it is not at all clear that this results primarily from the participation of clinicians. And we might therefore reasonably fear that increasing the proportion of educational research that is carried out by practising teachers would not provide a remedy for the methodological ills that Hargreaves has identified.

Doubtful assumptions about medical practice

There are also questions about the assumptions which Hargreaves makes about medical *practice*. Sociological research investigating this has highlighted the role of clinical judgement, and pointed to the emphasis that clinicians themselves place on this component of their work (Becker et al. 1961:231–8; Freidson 1970:ch. 8). Thus, Becker et al. argue that clinical experience 'can be used to legitimate a choice of procedures for a patient's treatment and can even be used to rule out use of some procedures that have been scientifically established' (Becker et al. 1961:231). Similarly, Atkinson describes the clinician as 'essentially a pragmatist, relying on results rather than theory, and trusting in personal, firsthand knowledge rather than on abstract principles or "book knowledge"' (Atkinson 1981:5). Furthermore, in a more recent study of haematologists, he shows how personal, traditional, and scientific knowledge interpenetrate in clinical discourse away from the bedside (Atkinson 1995:48 and *passim*).

There are two closely related aspects of the picture of clinical practice presented by this research that are relevant here. First, clinical decision-making is not based solely, or even primarily, on knowledge drawn directly from research publications. Secondly, it often does not conform to what we might call the rational model of medical procedure. According to this (rather economistic) model, practice takes the following form: the relevant problem is clearly identified at the start; the full range of possible strategies for dealing with it are assessed in terms of their costs and benefits, on the basis of the best available evidence; and, finally, that strategy is selected and implemented which promises to be the most effective. As has been pointed out in many fields, including economics, for a variety of reasons practical activity deviates substantially from this rationalistic model: goals are not always clearly formulated and undergo change over the course of the activity; only a limited range of strategies may be considered, with little search for information about alternative strategies, stock assumptions being relied on; and the aim may not be to maximise payoff but only to achieve a satisfactory solution, with scope for disagreement about what this amounts to.[17]

In one way, Hargreaves recognises these features of medical practice. Referring to some comments by Caroline Cox about teachers, he points out how medical practitioners also often rely on 'tradition, prejudice, dogma, and ideology' (Hargreaves 1996:7–8). In adopting this loaded characterisation, he aligns himself with the proponents of evidence-based medicine, who propose that research must play an increased role in clinical practice if the latter's effectiveness is to reach acceptable levels. It is argued that there are reasons to doubt the effectiveness of a substantial proportion of medical treatments currently used by clinicians. Advocates of evidence-based medicine put forward two main explanations for this. First, they claim that the quality of clinical practice deteriorates over the course of the careers of medical practitioners. This is because they are dependent on the state of research knowledge when they were trained, which becomes progressively outdated. The second argument is that the huge number of medical research reports now produced is too great for clinicians to access directly. What is required, therefore, is the use of bibliographical strategies and information technology for summarising and making available the information produced by research, and the training of clinicians in using these.

Problems with evidence-based medicine

What does not come through in Hargreaves' lecture is that evidence-based medicine is by no means an uncontroversial matter.[18] Critics have argued that it places too much emphasis on the role of research findings in clinical decision-making; in fact, that it is a misnomer, since all medicine is evidence-based, even when it does not make the kind of systematic use of the research literature that advocates of evidence-based medicine recommend. One critic points out that the latter would be better referred to as 'literature-based medicine' (Horwitz, cited in Shuchman 1996:1396). Another suggests that the presumption built into the term is that the practice of medicine 'was previously based on a direct communication with God or the tossing of a coin' (Fowler 1995:838). What is at issue is not the use of evidence as against reliance on something else ('tradition, prejudice, dogma, and ideology'), but the relative importance of different kinds of evidence. And we should perhaps also note that the appropriate balance amongst these will not just vary across medical specialities but also at different stages of treatment. In diagnosis, for example, particular emphasis is likely to be given to evidence from medical histories, physical examinations and/or test results.

Critics also point out some problems in the use of research evidence to inform clinical decision-making. One is that the literature is very variable in quality, and that there is much more research in some areas than others. A consequence of this is that there are significant gaps in knowledge which render the practice of evidence-based medicine problematic in many fields. More significantly, the fact that there may be evidence about some treatments and not others, or better evidence about them, could result in misleading conclusions being drawn about their relative efficacy. A second point is that there may be biases in the research literature, for example resulting from the tendency of journals to be less interested in publishing negative than positive findings.[19] A third problem is that the process of summarising the findings and methods of re-search may itself introduce distortions. Certainly, it may make the critical appraisal of evidence, which advocates of evidence-based medicine emphasise, more difficult and subject to increased threats to validity.

There are also problems surrounding the application of information about aggregates to particular patients. The authors of a key text in clinical epidemiology, one of the foundations of evidence-based medicine, report a senior doctor as opining that it is immoral to combine epidemiology with clinical practice (Sackett et al. 1985:ix). It is not clear from the context what the reasoning was behind this criticism, but two problems seem relevant. One is that there may be circumstances where the requirements of research conflict with those of treating a particular patient. An illustration is provided by Jadad (1996), in an article entitled 'Are you playing evidence-based medicine games with our daughter?'. He seems to have fed his three and a half year old daughter shrimp in order to test a consultant's diagnosis of allergy, which he believed was not based on sound research evidence. Whatever the rights and wrongs of this particular case, it is not difficult to see that conflicting motivations can be involved where clinicians (or parents!) are also engaged in research (see also Dearlove et al. 1995:258). Another issue relates to the problem of treating a patient as an instance of a category for which one has research data. Clinicians are directly responsible for the treatment of individual patients, not primarily concerned with what works in general. Patients always have multiple characteristics, some of which may be such as to render the treatment indicated by the research literature inappropriate; and these characteristics can include patients' preferences (see Thornton 1992; Charlton 1995:257; Jones and Sagar 1995:258; Entwistle et al. 1998).[20]

Even putting aside the problem of applying aggregate data to individual cases, it is not necessarily in a patient's best interests for a clinician to use what is reported in the literature as the most effective treatment. Treatments can demand distinctive skills, which a particular practitioner may not have, most obviously (but not exclusively) in the case of surgery. Thus, a formally less effective treatment of which the doctor already has experience may be more advantageous than a less than fully successful attempt at something more ambitious (see Burkett and Knafl 1974:94–5). Literature-based knowledge can only provide a guide, it is no substitute for first-hand experience or for that of immediate colleagues, who can be questioned further in the event of unforeseen complications that need to be corrected. Thus, a particular technique may be used because it seems to have been effective in the past, and also because much is known about what to expect from it: one knows what normally happens as well as the routine deviance associated with it. Using new drugs or surgical techniques can increase the level of uncertainty, and the danger of running into situations that one does not know how to deal with.

It seems unlikely that any clinician would deny the value of research evidence. What is at issue is the degree and nature of its use. The advocates of evidence-based medicine vary in what they recommend. Sometimes, they simply point to the capacity for searching the research literature that is now provided by information management technology, emphasising that this cannot substitute for experience and clinical judgement. On other occasions, however, more radical proposals seem to be implied, where systematic literature searches are treated as obligatory and as providing benefit/risk ratios which can form the basis not just for clinical decision-making but also for accountability regimes designed to regulate medical practitioners. In this latter version, advocates of evidence-based medicine follow Cochrane's dismissal of clinical *opinion*, and his argument that there is little or no evidence about the effectiveness of many routinely used techniques, where 'evidence' is interpreted as the outcome of randomised controlled trials or as 'immediate and obvious' effects (Cochrane 1972:30). What is at issue here, then, is not just what is, and is not, to count as adequate evidence, but also the approach to be adopted in clinical decision-making, how it is to be assessed, and by whom.

Evidence-based practice and accountability

Sociologists have often noted the role that an emphasis on clinical judgement and uncertainty has played in the power that the medical profession exercises. Evidence-based medicine threatens this, in that there is a close association between it and demands for greater accountability on the part of doctors, in terms not just of efficacy but also of cost-effectiveness. It is this that has led to much of the reaction against evidence-based medicine; and perhaps also some of the support for it among lay people, including health service managers.[21] However, only if there were good reasons to be confident that research evidence could replace clinical judgement, and that the rational model could be applied, would it be justifiable to dismiss the resistance of doctors as ingrained conservatism or self-interested concern with preserving professional power. And it seems to me that there are no grounds for such confidence, even though moves towards clearer guidelines for clinicians and increased use of the medical literature may well be desirable.

As in the NHS (National Health Service), so also in the education system there has been growing emphasis on professional accountability, and attempts to set up quasi-markets which are held to maximise efficiency. Moreover, Hargreaves clearly has accountability very much in mind when he argues that: 'expertise *means* not just having relevant experience and knowledge but having *demonstrable* competence and clear *evidence* to justify doing things in one way rather than another' (Hargreaves 1996:7). From this point of view, a research-based teaching profession is one that accounts for itself in terms of the details of its practice to those outside by appeal to the following of explicitly formulated procedures backed by research evidence. As Hargreaves comments, though with questionable predictive validity: 'when educational leaders have evidence for their practices, they may even command the respect of politicians' (ibid.:8).

In practice, however, this move towards evidence-based accountability seems unlikely to enhance the professionalism of teachers; quite the reverse. Just as evidence-based medicine threatens to assist attacks on the professionalism of doctors and nurses by managers in the NHS, so Hargreaves' arguments may be used by those who seek to render teachers more 'transparently' accountable. In both areas there are grave doubts about whether this will improve the quality of service. This is because the kind of accountability involved undermines trust in professional judgement. As a result, it seems more likely further to demoralise and undermine the professional judgement of practitioners; in occupations that have already been seriously damaged in these respects.[22]

Conclusion

Hargreaves' lecture raises very important issues, and in my view some of his criticisms of educational research are sound. It does seem to me that researchers need to be more focused about what their goals are, about the degree of success they have had in achieving them and about the problems they face. Furthermore, we need to try to make our research both build more effectively on earlier work and provide a better foundation for subsequent investigations. We also ought to take more care in disseminating the results of research, and to think more clearly about how it is used. Hargreaves' arguments could play a productive role in stimulating developments in these areas. Moreover, the parallel with medicine is surely worth exploring. Indeed, I think we could learn much from examining the role of research in relation to a range of occupations and organisations.

Problems with Hargreaves' diagnosis

At the same time, I have argued that there are some fundamental problems at the core of Hargreaves' analysis. One is that he is not very explicit about the form he believes educational research *should* take, in terms of which he evaluates current work negatively. Another is his neglect of the severe methodological problems that educational researchers face. His failure to address these problems is exemplified by his comment that *'without question* OFSTED has the most comprehensive data-base on what teachers do and how it relates to their effectiveness' (ibid.:8, my emphasis). While he refers only to comprehensiveness not to validity, the fact that he recommends the transfer of money to OFSTED from universities in order to fund analysis of these data implies that he thinks they could provide a sound basis for reaching scientific conclusions about the relative effectiveness of different pedagogical techniques. What evidence is there to support this assumption? Hargreaves does not provide or refer to any; nor is the claim plausible. This is partly because of the problems I discussed earlier relating to measurement and causal analysis. On top of this, though, the quality of the data collected by OFSTED is likely to be poor, given the pressures under which the inspectors work, the range of different aspects of schools they have to cover, and the nature of the framework within which they operate.[23] Hargreaves seems to see the task of developing cumulative knowledge about the effectiveness of different pedagogical techniques as much more straightforward than it is.

Here, as elsewhere, his reliance on the medical analogy is potentially misleading. Much medical research, while by no means easy or unproblematic, does not involve the distinctive problems associated with studying social phenomena. We might also note that while he stresses the amount of money spent on educational research, this is only a tiny fraction of that allocated to medical research (for which he provides no estimate). Like is not being compared with like here, in either respect.

Another problem concerns the nature of the relationship that is possible between research and practice in the field of education. In my view, Hargreaves uses a standard to judge current educational research which assumes too direct and instrumental a form of that relationship. Even in the field of medicine it is not clear that this model can be closely approximated. And the thoroughly practical character of most teaching – the diverse and difficult-to-operationalise goals, the multiple variables and complex relationships involved – may mean that research can rarely provide 'actionable knowledge' about the relative effectiveness of different techniques. The history of research on 'effective teaching' points strongly in this direction. Furthermore, in my view there is a tension between seeking to improve the rigour of educational enquiry so as to contribute to the cumulation of knowledge, on the one hand, and trying to make its findings of more direct practical relevance, on the other. There are, of course, those who see no tension here at all; but Hargreaves does not make a case for this, and I do not believe that a convincing one is possible. In the past, he has quoted Lewin's dictum that 'there is nothing so practical as a good theory' (Hargreaves et al. 1975:ix). Yet, the history of action research, in education and elsewhere, suggests that there is considerable tension between these two orientations.[24]

Evaluating Hargreaves' proposed remedies

While I disagree with Hargreaves' diagnosis, I do not reject his prescriptions entirely. I have no doubt that practical research carried out by teachers and educational managers in order to further their work can be useful, so long as it is recognised that not every problem needs research to find a solution and that not every question can be answered by research. However, there are dangers, I think, in this kind of work being required to be scientific. It is designed to serve a different purpose, so that, while there will be some overlap in techniques and relevant considerations, the orientation should be different.[25] Such inquiries are no substitute for academic research; just as the latter is no substitute for *them*.

I also accept that the establishment of a forum for discussing educational research and its relationship to educational policymaking and practice could be worthwhile. However, I do not believe that giving such a forum a role in planning educational research would be at all helpful. In my view, the currently fashionable view that research can be centrally planned is based on fallacious assumptions about the nature of research and how it can best be coordinated and pursued. The arguments against this were well put by Michael Polanyi in the context of natural science many years ago (Polanyi 1962; see Chapter 5). The problems and dangers involved in previous attempts to plan educational research are also instructive (Nisbet and Broadfoot 1980:14–17). Moreover, down the road that Hargreaves recommends, and not very far down it at all, lies the extension to the whole of educational research of the contract model recommended by Rothschild for applied research funded by government departments (Rothschild 1971). That is a destination from which there is probably no return, and it is not one that is likely to lead to the flourishing of educational research; instead, the latter may become little more than one more public relations tool.

I recognise, then, that the current state of educational research is not healthy, but I do not believe that what Hargreaves proposes will remedy it. The diagnosis is mistaken and, taken as a whole, the prescription is likely to be lethal. He emphasises several times the radical nature of what he is proposing, chiding educational researchers for shying at such radicalism. Personally, I have no problem in refusing to jump high fences: radical change is not *necessarily* a good thing; it will often be for the worse rather than for the better. It ought to be adopted only as a last resort, when there is little to be lost; at best, it is much more likely to result in unforeseen consequences or unacceptable side effects than less radical change. And I do not accept Hargreaves' judgement that educational research suffers from a *'fatal* flaw' (Hargreaves 1996:3, my emphasis) or that *'there is . . . little to lose* in moving as soon as possible to an evidence-based teaching profession' (ibid.:8, my emphasis). What could be lost is the substantial researcher and teacher expertise that we currently have, which Hargreaves apparently discounts.[26]

It is also of significance, though Hargreaves does not emphasise it, that the evidence-based education which he recommends involves a trans-formation of teaching as well as of research.[27] In particular, it involves extending the accountability of teachers beyond examination league tables and national tests to justifying the details of classroom practice in terms of research evidence. In my view the consequences of this aspect of his proposals are likely to be as disastrous for the quality of teaching as for educational research. I do not deny that there is much wrong with the quality of teaching in some schools, nor do I believe that research is incapable of providing knowledge that is of practical relevance to improving it. But educational research can only play a fairly limited role in resolving the problems. It can highlight and analyse them, and thereby attempt to provide some understanding. However, remedying the failings of schools is a practical business that necessarily depends on professional expertise of a kind that is not reducible to publicly available evidence, even that provided by research. Moreover, in large part, the problems in schools stem from external factors, including the repeated imposition of radical, and often ill-conceived, policy initiatives.

The rhetorical form of Hargreaves' critique and anti-professionalism

There is one further aspect of Hargreaves' lecture that deserves attention. This is to do with its rhetorical form rather than its content. It is not simply a contribution to debate among researchers about how their work should be organised and carried out. The audience for his lecture was wider. Of course, there is nothing wrong with this, in principle; but what is unfortunate is that Hargreaves engages in pre-emptive dismissal of the arguments of fellow researchers who disagree with him, implying that these are rationalisations. Thus, he writes: 'The research community has yet to face up to the problem. It protects itself and the status quo by a series of defences' (ibid.:5) and 'Rationalising failure to improve practice through research became a self-fulfilling prophecy' (ibid.:5). Along with this, Hargreaves dismisses those who are committed to a more conven-tional approach as simply unwilling to put their house in order: 'Left to ourselves, we educational researchers will not choose the necessary radical reforms' (ibid.:1) and 'Researchers continue their work on their own self-validating terms; they are accountable to themselves; so there is absolutely no reason why they should change' (ibid.:6). In effect, he directs what he has to say over the heads of researchers to those who have the power to intervene: he is inviting in the state troopers! In this sense, his lecture is a political intervention not just a contribution to scholarly debate; and it has been responded to as such. It has made a substantial contribution to the increasing attempts to exert central and external control over educational research, discussed in the Introduction.

For me research, like teaching, is a profession. This does not mean that researchers should have total control over their own affairs, but it does mean that they must have considerable independence. And Hargreaves is quite open that what he is proposing would involve 'some loss of autonomy' (ibid.:8). He argues that this is justified because educational research is not in a healthy state. But where is the evidence to show that his proposed treatment is the most effective means of curing the illness, and that its side effects will fall within acceptable limits? If we are to have evidence-based practice, surely we should have evidence-based policymaking about educational research?[28]

Advocates of evidence-based medicine have often been challenged because they are not able to support their proposals with the kind of evidence that they demand of medical practitioners (see, for example, Norman 1995). Hargreaves is particularly vulnerable to this challenge, given the admittedly radical character of the surgery proposed. He certainly does not provide evidence that 'demonstrates conclusively that if [researchers] change their practice from x to y there will be a significant and enduring improvement in teaching and learning'. Even less has he 'developed an effective method of convincing [researchers] of the benefits of, and means to, changing from x to y'. Indeed, instead of seeking to meet this latter requirement, he puts it aside, calling for external intervention. Moreover, his view of researchers is in danger of being self-fulfilling. The rhetorical strategy he employs – which is not dissimilar to the anti-professional mode of speech found in many government communications directed at teachers, for example in the report of the 'three wise men' (see Hammersley and Scarth 1993) – is likely to lead to political opposition and counter-argument, rather than to reflection and considered discussion. Researchers are not a powerful constituency, of course. However, to the extent that the aim is to improve educational research rather than to save money by eliminating it (and the motives of those who listen to Hargreaves may well differ from his own), little progress can be made without their support. In these terms, too, his lecture seems unlikely to help the situation.

Notes

1. For a review of the first fruits of this research, see Foster (1999).
2. See the *Times Educational Supplement* (28 June 1996), plus letters in subsequent issues, and *Research Intelligence* (57 and 58).
3. Though I think he is right to deny them, see Hammersley (1987a and 1987b).
4. Hargreaves did provide some examples in a response to this chapter when it was first published as a journal article: see Hargreaves (1997).
5. For a fuller treatment, see Chapter 4.
6. On the contrast between sensitising and definitive concepts, see Blumer (1969). For a review of the distinction, see Hammersley (1989).
7. Hargreaves begins his lecture by stressing the need for cumulative and well-founded research knowledge, as well as for greater applicability. By the end, the emphasis is largely on the latter. In the final paragraph he claims that the changes he is recommending would produce 'far more research that is closely related to policy and practice, that is carried out by and with users, and that leads to results which are more likely to be applied in practice' (Hargreaves 1996:8). By this point, the issue of the quality of the research seems, at best, to have become absorbed into applicability.
8. Hirst (1990) has pointed out that this model may not be an accurate picture of the relationship between theory and practice even in science and technology.
9. See Schön (1983 and 1987) for an influential response to this problem.
10. For a highly critical assessment of school effectiveness research along these lines, see Elliott (1996); see, also, the response from Sammons and Reynolds (1997).
11. In an influential article, Jamous and Pelloile seek to operationalise the distinction between professional and non-professional occupations in terms of a ratio between 'technicality' and 'indetermination', see Jamous and Peloille (1970:112–13).
12. For an underused account of 'the structure of formally organized socialization settings' that highlights this dimension, see Wheeler (1966, especially pp. 60–6).
13. Also relevant here is his identification of appreciative, designatory, reflective, immunological, and corrective capacities of symbolic interactionist research (Hargreaves 1978:19–21). For a discussion, see Hammersley (2001).
14. Indeed, there is evidence to suggest that in some areas at least it is non-clinical research that has led to the major advances, see Strong (1984:342–3).
15. It is my view that one of the problems with social science research generally is that this use of research has come to dominate all others.
16. For a substantial discussion of methodological failings in medical research, see Anderson (1990); see also Feussner (1996).
17. On deviation from the rational model see, for example, Simon (1955) and March (1988). In a recent book explicating the assumptions involved in his research in the health field, and elsewhere, Anselm Strauss argues that these empirical features of action, at odds with the so-called rational model, are central to the model of action adopted by symbolic interactionists. See Strauss (1993:ch. 1).
18. See Tanenbaum (1993); *Lancet* (1995); Grahame-Smith (1995); Court (1996); Smith and Taylor (1996); *Journal of Evaluation in Clinical Practice* (3, 2, 1997); and the letters in *Lancet* (346, 1995:837–40 and 1171–2); and in the *British Medical Journal* (311, 1995:257–9, and 313, 1996:114–15 and 169–71). It is worth noting that evidence-based medicine could be seen as part of what Strong

has referred to as statistical imperialism, as also could the critiques of medical research quoted earlier. See Strong (1984:344–5 and 350–1).

19. Pharmaceutical companies may also suppress negative findings about their products.

20 As a common saying has it: 'no patient is ever like a textbook' (cited in Burkett and Knafl 1974:89). For an illuminating discussion of this issue which provides grounds for caution about reliance on clinical judgement, see Meehl (1957). It is worth noting that, in part, what is involved in the evidence-based medicine movement and the responses to it is a clash between epidemiological and other ways of thinking about medicine: see Tanenbaum (1993).

21. For some evidence that what is feared is no mirage, see Culyer (1986), Jenett (1988), Brahams (1991), Deighan and Hitch (1995), Clancy (1996), and Watson (1996). The person who is widely cited as laying the basis for evidence-based medicine, A. L. Cochrane, had no doubt that efficiency as well as effectiveness is important. His aim was the application of cost-benefit analysis throughout the NHS, see Cochrane (1972). For a recent discussion of some of the dilemmas and how they should be resolved, which involves medical practitioners being free to override guidelines in particular cases, see Sackett (1996).

22. For arguments for and against evidence-based practice across a range of fields, see Trinder (2000).

23. Hargreaves' recommendation of better training is unlikely to resolve these problems. On the relationship between inspection data and research, in the context of OFSTED, see Smith (2000).

24 For a discussion of the dilemma, see Marris and Rein (1967:ch. 8) and Rapoport (1970:505–7). It is puzzling that Hargreaves gives no attention to the history of educational action research, in the United States and in Britain. Its advocates anticipated some of the criticisms he makes of academic research on education, and in some respects it is close to the kind of development he wants to see. Moreover, there is much to be learned from it, not all positive; see Hammersley (1993).

25 Indeed, at one point, Hargreaves seems to recognise that what may be most useful in developing the professional culture of teachers is not so much scientific research as 'accumulated wisdom' in the form of case records, with commentaries and critiques (Hargreaves 1996:4 and 8). See Chapter 6 for discussion of the contrast between practical and scientific research.

26 My own views about what is wrong with social and educational research and the direction it should move in can be found elsewhere: Hammersley (1992 and 1995), and Foster et al. (1996).

27 This comes out more clearly in Hargreaves (1994). See also Hargreaves (1999a).

28 On the latter, see Ham et al. (1995) and the letters in *British Medical Journal* (30 1995:1141).

Chapter 2

Why Research into Practice Does Not Go: Some Questions about the Enlightenment Function of Educational and Social Enquiry

It has come to be accepted by many social and educational researchers that the usual, and perhaps also the most appropriate, way in which research shapes practice is through 'enlightenment': through providing knowledge or ideas that influence the ways in which policymakers and practitioners think about their work. This 'enlightenment' model is usually contrasted with the 'engineering' model, which views research as providing specific and immediately applicable technical solutions to problems, in the manner that natural science or engineering research is assumed to do (Janowitz 1972; Weiss 1977 and 1980; Nisbet and Broadfoot 1980; Bulmer 1982; Finch 1986).[1]

There are several reasons why the enlightenment model is generally regarded as most appropriate for the social sciences. Some of these relate to the nature of the knowledge that those disciplines can produce. It is often argued that this hardly ever consists of scientific laws, which is what would seem to be required by the engineering model. Commitment to the goal of discovering laws is now widely regarded as an error deriving from a discredited positivist philosophy. What research provides instead, it is suggested, is a deeper understanding of the contexts in which action takes place, and of the action itself; or, at the very least, some specific concepts or items of information that illuminate important features of those contexts and actions.

Equally important, often, are arguments about the forms of practice that social and educational research serves. In particular, it is claimed that the problems which these practical activities face are not of a kind that can be solved technically; that is, by the *application* of scientific theories or research findings, or by the *specification* of rules or procedures based on them. It has been suggested that medicine, education, social work, public policymaking, organisational management, etc, are necessarily judgement-based and reflective activities; so that the adoption of a technical approach to them is detrimental (see, for example, Schön 1983 and 1987). Thus, attempts to specify in abstract terms the relative effectiveness of different strategies for dealing with a problem overlook important variations in the contexts where the problem arises, and in how the strategies can be used. They also threaten to lose sight of the multiple goals often involved or to reduce these to spurious performance indicators whose application undermines good practice as well as the autonomy and morale of practitioners. Indeed, it is sometimes claimed that the engineering model represents an ideology of technique – an overextension of natural science thinking into the social world – that dominates contemporary life in modern societies and that must be resisted (Habermas 1971; Fay 1975).

There is much to be said for many of these arguments supporting the enlightenment model. At the same time, that model is by no means unproblematic. In what follows I will examine some of the issues it raises, and consider their implications. The first problem relates to the meaning of the term 'enlightenment'. Two very different interpretations can be identified, and one of these seems to suffer from many of the same problems as the engineering model.

The weaknesses of 'strong' enlightenment

A literal reading of the word 'enlightenment' implies that policymakers and practitioners are normally in the dark, and that research is needed to provide the light necessary for them to see what they are doing, and/or what they ought to be doing. This literal, or strong, interpretation of 'enlightenment' can be traced back to some of the Enlightenment ideas of the eighteenth century. The *philosophes* generally took over from Renaissance thinkers the notion that Europe had been in intellectual darkness from the collapse of the Roman Empire, but had begun to emerge from this in the fifteenth century. However, whereas the Renaissance was based largely on rediscovery and reinterpretation of ancient texts, many Enlightenment thinkers no longer saw the ancients as offering superior knowledge to what could be produced by moderns: they were greatly impressed by the new knowledge generated by natural scientists (or 'natural philosophers', as they were then called).[2] Moreover, the exercise of reason was regarded as offering not just knowledge but also the prospect of social betterment. The fog of myth and tradition which had enveloped the past was to be dispelled by the light of reason, clearing the way for a reorganisation of society to make it more rational, prosperous, and just.[3]

This strong Enlightenment conception of the social role of reason was inherited to one degree or another by influential nineteenth-century thinkers, especially by Saint-Simon, Comte, Hegel, and Marx. What distinguished their views from most earlier ideas was that they saw rationalisation as a process of historical development not as an act of intellect or will; and, for some of them, the ideas of the past were not simply erroneous but contained seeds of an emerging truth. Nevertheless, to one degree or another, they shared a strong interpretation of 'enlightenment', whereby science – albeit conceived in different ways – can provide a comprehensive worldview that should govern practice; thereby realising, or at least facilitating movement towards, the ideal society. The watchword for all these thinkers was, therefore, the unity of theory and practice; and through them the strong interpretation of enlightenment has had considerable influence in twentieth-century social research, in the form of both positivist and Marxist or 'critical' traditions.

It is important to note that the engineering and the strong enlightenment models share some of the same historical sources. The engineering model arose in large part from the seventeenth-century scientific revolution, its main features being anticipated by Bacon's view of science as providing the technological base for 'the relief of man's estate' (see Quinton 1980). And, as already noted, the growth in natural science was a major influence on the *philosophes* (Berlin 1979). Given this, it is perhaps not surprising that, despite their differences, these two models also have some important features in common. First, both treat the knowledge provided by science as having a very high level of validity, and as properly replacing existing commonsense 'knowledge'; indeed, some versions of strong enlightenment even depend on the idea that science can produce laws which enable human behaviour to be understood and changed (see Fay 1987). As a result, like the engineering model, it seems to set aside (or at least to downplay) the role of wisdom and accumulated experience in practical affairs (as part of its rejection of tradition), in favour of a governing role for scientific knowledge (though with the latter sometimes interpreted in a very different way from that characteristic of the engineering model).[4] Indeed, commonsense or practical knowledge may be treated as necessarily false, as reflecting mere appearances and/or as serving a conservative social function. For both these models, science plays an emancipatory role; though what emancipation is from, and to what it leads, are usually different. Crudely speaking, in one case it is from folk ideas and unproven practices to effective and efficient alternatives that will generate a happy and prosperous society; in the other it is from ideology to a new form of society, and perhaps even a new kind of humanity, that is characterised by genuine freedom.[5]

Given this overlap in assumptions between the engineering and strong enlightenment views, to the extent that the arguments against the former are sound many of them also count against the latter. Furthermore, the strong interpretation of enlightenment involves some additional assumptions that are questionable. One is the idea that science or philosophy (and the distinction between the two is less clear in this context than it is in others) can produce a comprehensive perspective on the world; rather than just specific items of knowledge, or perspectives useful for particular purposes. A second questionable feature is the assumption that practical conclusions can be derived from factual evidence, either directly or by reliance on a naturally produced value consensus.[6]

Neither of these two additional assumptions is very plausible. The first is at odds with the tendency towards specialisation and fragmentation that has been characteristic of the development of research in most fields.[7] While it is true that the development of scientific knowledge carries implications for areas outside its focus – so that, for example, Western religious beliefs have had to be modified as a result of the rise of science – the latter does not seem to be able to supply us with a single, comprehensive alternative worldview; at least, not without highly speculative inferences. Its implications are often negative rather than positive, in the sense that in many areas (such as those covered by morality and theology) it simply indicates what *cannot* any longer be believed rather than what *should* be believed, and even this is often open to reasonable disagreement. As regards the second assumption, it seems to me that the arguments against deriving 'ought' from 'is' are sufficiently strong to throw doubt on the claim that research can tell us what is to be done. The traditional Humean argument is that any value conclusion depends on at least one value assumption besides factual knowledge. And the idea that there is a *natural* value consensus is undermined by arguments about value pluralism: that, within Western culture at least, we frame our evaluations and prescriptions in terms of multiple values, and indeed different meta-ethical perspectives, that will often be in conflict.[8]

Of course, this strong, one might even say intoxicating, version of the enlightenment model can be diluted, and we find this occurring in the twentieth century. Both positivism and Marxism were affected by internal problems, and other philosophical tendencies became influential which offered more moderate versions of the enlightenment model. One of these was pre-modern philosophy. Thus, in recent times there has been a resurgence in the influence of Aristotle and of medieval philosophical ideas (Wallach 1992), and an important aspect of this relates to the nature of practice. This is now interpreted by many as goal-directed or even goal-embodied action that is founded on experience, judgement and wisdom more than on theory; above all, it does not consist of the simple application of rules, even though these may be used as guidelines (see Beiner 1983; Larmore 1987).[9] Another source of more moderate versions of the enlightenment model is hermeneutic philosophy. While internally diverse, the core of this position is the idea that human action is different in character from the behaviour of physical phenomena, so that our knowledge of it must be obtained in a different way from that which is characteristic of the natural sciences. Here, while the classical notion of the teleology of praxis is retained, albeit now in contrast to a non-teleological view of nature, it is injected with historicism. This means that diversity in ways of life is treated not as a product of deviation from natural law (as was the tendency in pre-modern philosophy) but as reflecting legitimate cultural differences, in the form of discrepant understandings of the world and conflicting ideals. Necessarily, this implies the local and culturally variable character of praxis.[10]

So, the strong enlightenment view of the relationship between research and practice shares many of the same problems as the engineering model, and has some additional ones of its own. Given this, a more moderate version of the enlightenment model seems preferable.[11] However, as we shall see, this carries some implications that (at face value, at least) may be difficult for researchers (and others) to live with, especially at the present time.

The implications of the moderate enlightenment model

According to the engineering and strong enlightenment models, research can supply much, perhaps everything, that practitioners need. It can tell them what action is required, in principle, and perhaps even in specific terms. The knowledge it provides is taken to be true, and to be capable of replacing practical commonsense. By contrast, according to the moderate view, the role that research plays in relation to practice is more limited. This model involves revised judgements about what research can supply, about what practice needs, and about the consequences of research for practice. Here, research is one among several sources of knowledge on which practice can draw. Morever, the use made of it properly depends on practical judgements about what is appropriate and useful.

Limits to what research can supply

One limitation on what research is able to provide concerns the fallibility of research-based knowledge.[12] While this knowledge may be more likely to be valid than information from other sources, its truth cannot be guaranteed. The fallibility of even natural scientific knowledge is now widely accepted. For example, Popper's philosophy of science argues that the only epistemological distinctions of any significance are those between falsifiable and unfalsifiable claims, and between falsifiable claims that have already been disproved and those that have *not yet* been disproved. On this view, the knowledge produced by natural science can only be accepted as valid *until further notice*: it may be revised or even transformed by subsequent investigations.[13] And how much more true is this of the knowledge produced by the social sciences? Moreover, once it is recognised that falsification is no more absolutely conclusive than verification, the difference in validity between what research produces and the information coming from other sources lessens still further, and the role of research-based knowledge in society is correspondingly reduced.[14] Where before there was a contrast between knowledge and opinion – with research supplying the former, everyday experience the latter – according to the moderate enlightenment view there is only a *dimension* along which are ranged judgements of varying degrees of probable validity; with research having some authority, because providing knowledge with a higher level of likely validity, but no guaranteed access to and no monopoly on truth.

A second feature of research-based knowledge which limits its contribution to practice concerns the standards in terms of which knowledge claims are accepted or rejected. On some cogent accounts, educational and social research modelled on science involves 'organised scepticism' (Merton 1973b): the requirement that, in determining what is and is not valid, researchers operate in such a way as to err on the side of rejecting what is true rather than of accepting as true what is in fact false. By contrast, practitioners' assessments do not usually have this consistent emphasis: what we might call the 'acceptability threshold' by which they judge the validity of information typically varies according to circumstances. In particular, they are likely to be concerned with the relative costs in practical terms of different types of error, and also with the extent to which actions leading to error are reversible (or are remediable in some other way). Where the cost of some type of error threatens to be high, or where it is irremediable, standards of assessment will usually be such as to minimise this danger. Where the likely cost of an error is judged to be low, standards of assessment will not usually be designed to minimise it, and other possible errors will be given a higher priority. Moreover, the potential costs that are addressed by practitioners will often not be solely to do with the intrinsic requirements of tasks, but will also relate to what we might call the politics of the situations in which they operate. And the priority they give to different kinds of cost will reflect their particular responsibilities and value orientations.

What this means is that while both researchers and practitioners take much for granted (neither can afford to question everything, nor is there any reason for them to do so), *what* they take for granted will vary, reflecting the different activities in which they are engaged and the different accountability regimes associated with these. The result of this contrast in orientation between researchers and practitioners is that (despite considerable overlap) there will often be a mismatch between what the two groups treat as valid knowledge, *and with good reason*. Thus, practitioners may be ill-advised simply to accept the conclusions of research at face value or to assess them solely in research terms.[15]

It is also worth pointing out that an enterprise set consistently to err on the side of rejecting as false what is in fact true, rather than vice versa, will produce knowledge at a comparatively slow rate, and this is another reason why research often cannot supply practitioners with the knowledge that they require. For the same reason, even when knowledge relevant to practice *is* produced, it may not be sufficiently up to date to meet the needs of practitioners. It is widely recognised that there is a difference in the time scales on which research and other kinds of practice typically operate; it is therefore very difficult to coordinate them in the way that both the engineering and strong enlightenment models assume is possible and desirable.

A third feature of research which limits its practical contribution is that particular studies tend to be narrowly focused on single issues, whereas practitioners have to take a range of considerations into account in making decisions. For example, it is not uncommon for researchers to be concerned with documenting the extent to which institutions or practices are equitable on some particular value interpretation, for example in the treatment of males and females, different ethnic groups, 'able' and 'disabled', etc. This narrowness of focus is desirable, since otherwise it will not usually be possible to complete an investigation satisfactorily from a research point of view. However, in doing *their* work, practitioners are properly concerned with multiple considerations, not just with one. For example, schoolteachers will not only be concerned with equity issues, these relating to various categorisations of student, but also with how best to educate those in their care, how to cover everything in the National Curriculum or examination board syllabus, how to survive an upcoming OFSTED inspection, etc. So, the perspectives of practitioners typically cover a broader range of considerations than the researcher focuses on, many of which will have to be taken into account in deciding how best to act on particular occasions. For this reason, as well as others, researchers are not able to supply practitioners with a replacement perspective, nor able to recommend a readymade solution to their problems solely on the basis of research. Instead, they will only be able to provide partial information relevant to particular practitioner concerns.

A fourth point is that the knowledge produced by research is usually general in character, and inference from it to conclusions about the particular situations in which practitioners operate is problematic. Research conclusions typically take the form of empirical generalisations about a whole population of cases, or theories about a particular type of phenomenon. From a practitioner point of view, the problem with empirical generalisations is that their relationship to the particular cases that are of concern is, at most, only probabilistic. If these cases are atypical, the knowledge produced by the research will not be applicable, and treating it as if it were will be misleading. With theories, even if the cases faced by practitioners match the conditions where the theory holds, the factors it refers to may be counterbalanced or overdetermined in these cases by others not dealt with by that theory. For this reason, a single theory cannot provide the sole basis for satisfactory practice. Nor is it possible, usually, to infer the consequences of interactions among factors dealt with by different theories from the theories themselves. A substantial element of contingency therefore surrounds the value for practice of both empirical generalisations and theoretical knowledge.[16]

A fifth point is that, as we saw earlier, research can only validate factual claims, it cannot in itself justify practical evaluations and recommendations. This follows from the argument that practical value judgements cannot be logically derived from facts. Indeed, while we are often inclined to forget it, there is always the possibility of deriving quite different practical conclusions from any set of factual findings. To take a controversial example, it is frequently assumed that the idea that intelligence is largely genetically controlled implies that social class differences in educational performance ought simply to be accepted as natural; that the allocation of more resources to middle-class than to working-class children would be justified by the 'fact' that they are better able to benefit from them, etc. Yet such value conclusions would not follow automatically even if the factual assumptions about the genetic determination of intelligence on which they rely were sound. Thus, we might argue that schooling ought to be directly concerned with remedying such natural inequalities, and this would be possible (in principle at least) so long as the environment played at least *some* role in generating differences in intelligence and achievement. Conversely, if we believe that differences in intelligence are entirely the result of environmental factors, the conclusion does not *necessarily* follow that efforts should be made to eradicate these. It might be argued that this is undesirable, given the fundamental changes to social structure and massive policy interventions into local community and family life that would probably be necessary to achieve it.[17]

This relative autonomy of value conclusions from the factual knowledge that research provides has important implications for the relationship between research and practice. Since practitioners are primarily concerned with what is good or bad, acceptable or unacceptable, etc., and with 'what is to be done', the fact that research can only produce factual conclusions limits considerably the contribution it can make to their work. Certainly, it cannot solve their practical problems on its own.[18] In these terms, notions of 'applying' research to practice are misconceived. And research conclusions formulated as practical (rather than conditional) evaluations or prescriptions are ideological, in one important sense of that much abused term.[19]

This misconception about the contribution of research derives from a central strand of much Enlightenment thinking: the idea that there is an intimate relationship or affinity between scientific enquiry and pursuit of the good society. It is assumed, in effect, that once people employ reason they will come to recognise the truth about what is in everyone's interests, and how those interests can best be served. This is an assumption that has been subjected to recurrent criticism; from the time of David Hume onwards; and most recently by some of those writers identified as postmodernists. What we can conclude from this criticism, I think, is that research-based knowledge is a resource which can be used to improve people's lives, but that it can also be used to serve sectional interests, and indeed purposes that most of us would judge to be evil.[20] On top of this, we cannot assume that in any particular situation there is always some single correct line of action which reason dictates. Even if we do not accept one or another kind of value pluralism, we ought to recognise that there is often room for reasonable disagreement about what is and is not desirable, who has a right to what, etc. (Larmore 1996).

The final point about the capabilities of research from the moderate enlightenment point of view is that even in factual terms every research report is open to multiple, more or less reasonable, interpretations; and usually *is* interpreted in different ways by different people. It is not necessary to go to Derridean extremes about the 'dissemination' of meaning to recognise that there is a sense in which readers construct the meaning of any research report, and may do so in diverse ways.[21] This arises in part because every report makes both central and more marginal claims, and differential emphasis can be given to these, but also because readers come to research reports with different preoccupations and assumptions, from which they may generate conclusions about the significance of research findings that are remote from those of the researcher. Furthermore, the researcher's presentation of her or his findings may be reinterpreted by readers on the basis of their own methodological assessments of the research – these necessarily relying on substantive assumptions about the state of the world.[22] While some possible interpretations will be unreasonable, often there will be more than one reasonable interpretation of any set of findings; and, as a result, there may be disagreements even among researchers about what factual conclusions can be properly drawn. Furthermore, as a result of this, different studies focusing on the same problem will often come to contradictory conclusions, so that practitioners are faced with no clear research consensus on the matters about which they want information.[23]

What practice needs

The moderate enlightenment model also raises questions concerning the assumptions about the nature of practice, and about the needs of practitioners, that are built into both the engineering and strong enlightenment models. There are several aspects to this. The first point to be made, one that follows from what was said earlier about the nature of research-based knowledge, is that research cannot even supply all of the *knowledge* required by practitioners. Some of what is needed will consist of up-to-date and local information. Moreover, it must take account of what can and cannot reasonably be relied on for practical purposes, given the costs and remediability of different sorts of error. Yet, as we saw, research (especially, scientific research) is not well designed to meet these needs.

A second point is that the engineering and strong enlightenment models tend to imply that knowledge is *all* that practitioners need. And it is fairly obvious, I think, that this reflects an exaggerated estimate of the role of propositional knowledge and of cognition in practical activities. Indeed, it is an exaggeration that is characteristic of Enlightenment thinking, perhaps reflecting the fact that, in an important sense, it was an ideology of intellectuals. Against this, we should note the influential distinction between knowing that and knowing how, and the fallacy of reducing the latter to the former; what Ryle calls 'the intellectualist legend' (Ryle 1949). Also relevant is Polanyi's emphasis on the role of tacit knowledge. Indeed, he argues that this plays an essential role even in the activity of doing scientific research (Polanyi 1959).

Equally significant in this context is the growing recognition, throughout the nineteenth and twentieth centuries, of the important role of affective and unconscious factors in human behaviour (see Hughes 1959). This was emphasised by some of the positivists, notably by Saint-Simon and Comte, who saw that if reason was to take on the role that had previously been played by religion it would have to acquire some of the latter's characteristics; in order, for example, to motivate action and to sustain social solidarity. Thus, at one point, Saint-Simon proposed a religion centred on Newton, and later he advocated a 'new Christianity'; while Comte and his successors set up the church of positivism (Charlton 1959; Manuel 1962; Simon 1963; Taylor 1975). Later still, Sorel took this argument further, claiming that it is the motivating power of ideas, not their truth, which is most important in practical affairs (Horowitz 1961), while pragmatists like William James and John Dewey defined 'truth' in instrumental terms (see Bird 1986 and Tiles 1989). Here we find some of the resources on which contemporary forms of relativism and postmodernism rely.

At the very least, one implication of this for the relationship between research and practice is that action is a product of attitudes, defined as propensities to act; not just of factual beliefs. Thus, any knowledge produced may have little impact, however well-founded or relevant in principle, if it does not find its place in a motivational context that encourages practitioners to use it. Here, much may depend on what this knowledge is taken to imply for practice, and on whether it chimes with currently influential practitioner ideas; not least on whether it opens practitioners up to potential criticism or gives them a valued identity or a new role. Information which questions the rationale for an activity or occupation can be demotivating, and may well be ignored for that reason alone. While the fact that many practitioners reject research on these grounds does not make the response legitimate, researchers who criticise them ought to remember that this orientation is analogous in some ways to the attitude of natural scientists towards anomalous results which do not provide a promising alternative to the current paradigm (Kuhn 1970). Nor does it follow automatically from the fact that practitioners resist acceptance of research findings that it is desirable (in practical terms) that the sources of resistance be removed. Such resistance may have beneficial consequences. For instance, a degree of conservatism may protect practice from damaging effects caused by the adoption of new research findings that later turn out to be spurious and/or misleading.

The consequences of research for practice

The point I want to make under this heading is perhaps the most difficult of all for researchers to accept. This is that the production and dissemination of knowledge deriving from research can have negative as well as positive consequences for practical decisions and outcomes. This tends to be obscured by the Enlightenment idea that the true and the good are two sides of the same coin. That notion underlies currently influential demands for researchers to maximise the impact of their work on practice (see, for example, Hillage et al. 1998). Yet, not only is it false to assume that doing so will always be of practical advantage, we need to recognise that on occasions it may even be undesirable.

This is not a new idea. As noted earlier, it was discussed by some of those involved in the Enlightenment, notably by Rousseau in his 'Discourse on the sciences and the arts' (Gourevitch 1997). He claims that progress in the sciences and arts has been accompanied by a decline in morality, and that these two trends are closely linked. A different version of the argument is to be found in Nietzsche's 'untimely meditation' on 'the uses and disadvantages of history for life' (Nietzsche 1874). He argues that historical knowledge, unless artistically shaped and thereby mythologised, is unlikely to stimulate bold and noble actions, but encourages torpor and weakness instead. Later, we find Pareto echoing Plato in arguing that society is held together by indispensable illusions, and suggesting that sociological analysis is only justifiable because no one will take much notice of it. If they were to do so, he implies, the result would be catastrophic (Bryant 1976:26)!

There are two immediately obvious ways in which research can have negative consequences. One is that the 'knowledge' produced is false and may thereby lead us astray (Degenhardt 1984). And, given the fallibility of all research findings, this is an ever-present danger. The other problem is that sound knowledge can be used for bad purposes. However, the point I am making here is a more fundamental one: that even sound knowledge used in a good cause can have bad effects.

There are several reasons for this. One is that research may generate too much information, or information that is too detailed, for the practical purpose concerned. A consequence may be information overload, and this can damage decision-making. More generally, assimilating the information produced by research always takes time, and practitioners often work under great pressure, so that giving attention to research involves cost; and in some circumstances this may outweigh the practical payoff to be derived from using it. In this respect, then, research can have damaging effects on the practical activities it was supposed to serve.

A second problem is that research tends to complexify rather than to simplify (Lindblom and Cohen 1979; Finch 1986). Thus, it often shows that the world is more complicated than practitioners think it is, that widely held stereotypes are false or only true in a very approximate way, that assumed causal relationships are more contingent than often supposed, etc. Under some circumstances, showing practitioners the complexity and uncertainty of the situations they face, or defects in their knowledge, can be beneficial, but in others it will not be. It may demotivate or even paralyse them, and this is especially likely where no viable alternative seems to be available. Or it may lead them to conclude that their task is impossible and that any action is as good as any other; or that they should make decisions solely on the basis of what serves their own interests, for example protecting themselves against future criticism by sticking rigidly to guidelines.

This second problem reflects a fundamental difference between what is rational in the context of research and what is rational in other kinds of practical activity (Schütz 1962; Garfinkel 1967b:ch. 8). Research cannot provide the knowledge base for practice because what it produces is not attuned to the contexts in which practice operates, for all the reasons outlined earlier. What follows as a corollary of this is that if research findings are given too much weight by practitioners, as against their own background assumptions or information from other sources, the outcome may be undesirable.

A related problem is that the effects of practitioners relying on some set of research findings depend on the local circumstances in which action takes place – and even on the manner in which it is carried out – as much as on the validity of the research findings or the intentions of the actor. In other words, the consequences of 'applying' the products of research will vary according to context. Not only may the same findings be interpreted in different ways in different situations, but the same type of action informed by the same research results may well have different consequences in different circumstances. By contrast, much discussion of the impact of research seems to assume that its effects will be (or ought to be) standard or determinate, as if these were logically built into it and could be read off without knowledge of the context in which it is to be used.

A fourth reason why sound research may have bad effects is that any line of action produces multiple consequences, in both the long and the short term. And these may be mixed as regards benefits and costs. One of the problems with the Enlightenment assumption of an affinity between pursuit of the true and pursuit of the good is that it ignores the fact that it is rare to gain benefits without incurring *some* costs. And, given value pluralism, there is room for disagreement in judgements about overall gain and loss, especially since the specific gains and losses may well be differentially distributed across those parties making the judgements. Furthermore, very often, in the case of already institutionalised patterns of action, the mix of consequences produced is known and more or less accepted by those involved. By contrast, a new approach, shaped by research findings, might produce better results in some respects but generate other novel consequences that are neither desirable nor regarded as acceptable by key audiences. Much discussion of the impact of research, and indeed of policy, seems to assume that consequences form a single set that is *intrinsically* good or bad, better or worse, so that a consensus can be assumed. However, this essentialism is misconceived, and the chances of consensus are correspondingly less than is often believed.

What all this implies, then, is that research findings can be true but misleading. And the obverse also holds. The fact that some of the information on which practitioners rely is false does not necessarily mean that their practical orientation ought to be changed. While in various respects the perspectives of practitioners will need to conform to the nature of the situations in which they operate, error in these perspectives does not necessarily result in practical failure. The factual assumptions of practitioners are tested all together, rather than one at a time, and any package of assumptions is judged as better or worse against specific alternatives. Moreover, unlike researchers, practitioners may not be able to afford simply to acknowledge ignorance or uncertainty about some matter until further notice. In the absence of anything better, they are likely to stick with what has previously worked satisfactorily (in their terms); and perhaps rightly so. Furthermore, the factual assumptions on which practice is based are tested in association with or through the practical inferences that are drawn from them; yet, as we saw earlier, different implications can be drawn from any set of factual conclusions. They are also tested under particular sorts of conditions and according to what is necessary for specific practical purposes. For all these reasons, some kinds of error identified by research may simply not matter in a practical context, and researchers challenging them may do more harm than good.[24]

There is another, and perhaps more obvious, way in which research can have negative consequences for practitioners. This stems from the fact that it is often used to justify activities or decisions, or to argue for policy changes that would facilitate future work. In this context, any research findings which appear to run counter to the case being made are not simply of no use but may be employed by others to undermine that case. In a context where balanced consideration is given to research evidence and to all other relevant matters, this might not be a problem. However, the contexts in which many practitioners operate today are not usually like this; they are much more politically charged situations in which the 'implications' of research findings are used in battles among those advocating different policies. Furthermore, given value pluralism, even in less contested areas there are likely to be conflicting views even about what 'balanced consideration' of relevant considerations would amount to.

It is not just the substantive content of research findings which may be a problem in this respect. If they are presented in a manner that properly respects their fallibilistic and qualified nature, they will be of limited value in public debate, at least where soundbites are the currency. Practitioners may find knowledge claims that are presented as indubitably true more useful than those put forward with greater circumspection. Indeed, for this purpose, invalid 'knowledge' which has appealing features in other respects will be found more useful by practitioners than sound knowledge. *And it may be used to good effect.*

Conclusion

There is widespread agreement that, currently, social and educational research does not have the substantial impact on policymaking and practice that the engineering and strong enlightenment models promise. The usual responses to this failure have been either to blame practitioners for not using research (for example, for not making their practice evidence-based), or to blame researchers for failing to disseminate their findings, for not collaborating effectively with practitioners, and/or for not producing findings that are practically useful. What is distinctive about the moderate enlightenment model is that it challenges the master role that the other two models assume research can and should play in relation to policy or practice. In doing so, it suggests that while there may be some scope for improving the relationship between research and practice, this is more limited than is often supposed. In other words, it suggests that expectations about the practical contribution of research need to be revised downward.

The fallibilistic character of research, its reliance on organised scepticism, its narrow focus, the *general* character of its findings, and the fact that these are open to contestable interpretations and cannot be translated into practical evaluations or prescriptions, all serve to limit the contribution of research to practice. From the other side, the fact that practice does not depend on knowledge alone, that research cannot meet even all of the *knowledge* requirements of practitioners, and that research-based knowledge can have *negative* as well as positive consequences, all reinforce the point. Thus, the moderate enlightenment model presents practice as more independent and proactive than is implied by the other two views. Where before the task of practitioners was to take knowledge and apply it, or to be persuaded to see the world in a different light and thereby transform it, this model portrays them as *selecting* what is relevant and useful to their purposes, according to the situation, and *interpreting* and *employing* this in the context of other knowledge and of a motivational framework that is adapted to circumstance. The implication is that judgement is necessarily involved in practical affairs, and that this must be based on other considerations besides the research validity of the knowledge available. Moreover, practical rationality is portrayed by the moderate enlightenment model as significantly different from that of the researcher. This challenges the tendency of many researchers to operate with a deficit model of practitioners, especially of policymakers and administrators, which treats them as falling short of research ideals in terms of their open-mindedness, etc.[25]

What the moderate enlightenment model implies, then, is that much of the dissatisfaction with the practical role that social and educational research currently plays stems from false expectations set up by the engineering and strong enlightenment models. And what is required is not just a reduction in the *scale* of the contribution expected of research, but also recognition that the practical implications and effects of research are not determinate; they are not built into it in the way that these models assume. Thus, practice cannot be *founded on* what research produces, and the contribution that research makes to practice is not measurable and cannot even be assumed to be predictably beneficial in specific terms. As we have seen, contingency is involved in interpretations of the factual findings of research, and in the derivation of practical implications from these. Different contexts of interpretation may produce different conclusions. And we can add to this that in making their decisions practitioners will properly take account of other considerations than research findings, that the consequences of the course of action selected will vary according to the manner and circumstances in which it is pursued, and that it will generate (in association with other factors) a *range* of consequences in the short term and over the longer term. Finally, these consequences will be open to a variety of interpretations as good or bad on the basis of different value frameworks.

In the present climate it is perhaps necessary to emphasise that the moderate enlightenment model does not imply that research has no value for practice. The tendency to draw that conclusion is a function of commitment to the other two models, which tend to treat the contribution of research to practice as all or nothing. For my argument here it is essential to be clear about the different demands that can be involved in the requirement that research be useful or effective. This can mean:

1 that it produces and disseminates knowledge that is policy- and/or practice-relevant;
2 that it provides information that practitioners currently need;
3 that what it produces has specifiable practical implications for action, and perhaps also that:
   (a) these are taken up by practitioners;
   (b) these are taken up by practitioners and the resulting action achieves their goals; and/or
   (c) these are taken up by practitioners and the resulting action has desirable consequences overall, in terms of some external standard of evaluation.

In the present situation, where the inclination is to apply value-for-money assessments to research, as to everything else, outcomes of Type 3 are used as the standard in assessing the effectiveness and efficiency of research. And strong versions of the enlightenment model adopt much the same interpretation of relevance. However, for all the reasons presented in this chapter, this is not defensible. Instead, the moderate enlightenment model treats research as being designed to contribute to practice through outcomes of Type 1 or 2 (these representing the goals, respectively, of scientific and practical research). This is not to deny that research can sometimes make a decisive contribution to practice, but the moderate enlightenment model underlines the fact that this will always occur in the context of other factors over which researchers (and often policymakers and practitioners) do not have control. Moreover, it is important to recognise that such decisive contributions are not the only valuable ones, and may not be the most important ones, even in the short term.

The implications of the moderate enlightenment model are deflation-ary, then; but not to the point of denying any practical contribution at all from research. It can and should attempt to provide policy- and practice-relevant information. But, in terms of the list of possible contributions given above, it should attempt no more than this. And this means some reduction is required in the claims about its contribution to practice that many researchers currently make for their work, and in the demands that funding agencies and external audiences place upon it. Equally important, where the other two models assume a fundamental harmony between research and practice, the moderate enlightenment model treats mutual frustration with one another on the part of researchers and prac-titioners as normal, and sees conflict between them as ineradicable; though, of course, greater tolerance could and should be developed on both sides.[26]

Coda

As I noted earlier, even those researchers who regard the arguments for the moderate enlightenment model as convincing may find its implica-tions difficult to accept and live with. After all, several disadvantages could result from embracing this position, especially at the present time. One danger is complacency. Acceptance of this view may lead researchers to reduce their efforts at making research accessible to policymakers and practitioners. And this would be unfortunate given that there are undoubtedly still respects in which researchers do not do enough to make their work available to lay audiences.[27] Of course, complacency does not follow logically from the moderate enlightenment model, but this could nevertheless be its practical result.

Another possible consequence is a dramatic reduction in motivation on the part of researchers. It would seem that many people are involved in research because they believe that it can make a big difference in practical terms, perhaps even that it can fundamentally change the world. (I readily admit that this was one of my reasons for becoming a researcher.) Yet, if the moderate enlightenment view is correct, this is a mistake. And recognising this fact may sap much of the energy that many researchers put into doing research. But such practical or political ambitions are not the sole source of motivation for doing research. Nor is careerism the only alternative to them, as is sometimes implied. An essential element of the moderate enlightenment model, it seems to me, is a defence of the pursuit of value-relevant knowledge for its own sake, against the instrumentalist view of enquiry which now seems to dominate on all sides.[28]

Finally, and perhaps most worrying of all, there is the question of the external effects of adopting the moderate enlightenment view. Clearly, it may lead funders to conclude that research can make no significant contribution to practice. This is especially likely at the present time because of the instrumentalism just mentioned. Currently influential views of accountability assume that there should be a strong and measurable relationship between the quality of work done and the benefit that it has for those who are in some sense its users or beneficiaries. Against this background, if it were to become widely accepted that social and educational research cannot routinely make such a contribution, funding for it might be removed or severely reduced.

Given these dangers, what should our response be to the moderate enlightenment model? One answer is that the proper orientation of researchers, indeed of professionals or intellectuals of any kind, is to accept and proclaim the truth; no matter what the costs are to themselves or to others. In the words of Alvin Gouldner, we must be prepared to acknowledge 'hostile information' (Gouldner 1973:59). But, whatever the general appeal of this principled response, it runs into paradox in the present context. There is a reflexive dilemma involved in the moderate enlightenment model, since the argument for it can be folded back on itself. This arises because the relationship between methodological conclusions of the kind presented in this chapter and the necessarily practical orientation of researchers is not very different from that between the products of social and educational research and the orientations of other kinds of practitioner. And, to the extent that this is true, the moderate enlightenment model suggests that rather than simply accepting such methodological conclusions as valid in abstract terms, and embracing them, researchers ought also to judge them in the context of their own practical experience; not least in terms of the likely consequences of acting on them. So, given that there are certainly undesirable consequences that *could* follow from accepting and acting on the moderate enlightenment model, it might be argued that *on the basis of that model itself* commitment to one of the other models ought to be retained because, even though it is false, this would nevertheless best serve the interests of research. The analogy is with sound research-based knowledge not being adopted because in the relevant practical context it carries undesirable consequences.

I do not believe that this is a sensible conclusion. It is certainly true that, to be consistent, an advocate of the moderate enlightenment model must accept that researchers ought to judge it not only in terms of the cogency of its supporting arguments but also according to its practical implications. It is also true, as we have seen, that there are negative consequences that could result from adopting it. So, even if researchers were convinced by the arguments for the validity of the model, pragmatic considerations *might* override acceptance of it as the basis for our actions as researchers (at least in public). However, this does not follow automatically. The moderate enlightenment model does not imply that practitioners – in this context, researchers – should adopt whatever views serve their own immediate interests. While researchers (like others) cannot afford to act as if they lived in a world that is perfectly suited to their work, they must nevertheless give weight to the main goal that guides it: in this case, the production of knowledge. Relaxation of their commitment to that goal should be contemplated only *in extremis*.[29] Furthermore, the cogency of methodological arguments is implicated in any assessment of the consequences of accepting them. Espousal by researchers of ideas that they knew to be false would probably damage their work in the long run, both internally and externally – whatever its other advantages. To operate in 'bad faith' has a corrosive effect on commitment, generating cynicism for which there would be no antidote available. Moreover, were researchers discovered to be living a lie in this way, the effect on their status and influence would be to reduce these even further. In this respect and others, the practical assessment of methodological arguments must encompass their likely contribution to the effective pursuit of research in the long as well as in the short term.

Furthermore, as I pointed out earlier, the negative consequences of adopting the moderate enlightenment model do not necessarily follow. The first two consequences that were mentioned relate to researchers themselves; and it should be possible to counter any complacency or reduced motivation in that quarter. Researchers have less control over the third possible negative consequence: the likely reaction of funders. But it seems to me that sticking to the engineering or strong enlightenment models is unlikely to save research from criticism for recurrent failure to deliver what was promised or expected, or from punitive action based on this. At most, it would only delay the final judgement. And promotion of the moderate enlightenment model might even minimise the damage, at least over the longer term.

It is also important to take account of negative consequences flowing from continued commitment to the engineering and strong enlightenment models. One of these, I suggest, is a tendency to exaggerate the validity and significance of the research findings we produce (see Foster et al. 1996:ch. 7). And this cannot be avoided without abandoning those models, or admitting our failure in terms of them. This inflation of the claimed payoff of our work not only represents a betrayal of its central ideal, but is also likely to serve practice badly.

In my judgement, then, the moderate enlightenment model is sound, and using it to guide our research, even in our dealings with those who fund or use it, is on balance the best available option. This does not mean, however, that it promises a harmonious relationship between the world of research and that of practice or politics; nor does it offer researchers the prospect of an easy life.

Notes

1. Under the engineering model, what is produced must be decisive in enabling something to be done that was impossible before, or in enabling what was previously do-able to be done much more effectively or efficiently. Hirst (1990) raises questions about the extent to which the engineering model actually applies even to engineering. This is an important issue, but not one I can address here. Of course, views along the lines of the engineering model have by no means completely disappeared among social and educational researchers. And, recently, there have been signs of a resurgence: see, for example, Hargreaves (1996) and Reynolds (1998). Hargreaves' position is discussed in Chapter 1.
2. This is not to suggest that the ideas of the ancient world had no influence on the *philosophes*. On this influence, see Gay (1966) and Venturi (1971:introduction).
3. This is close to a caricature of Enlightenment ideas, but it is an image that has been influential. A more accurate account is provided by Hampson (1968), who characterises the Enlightenment in terms of an initial commitment to the notion of a beneficent providence, a notion which subsequently disintegrated into deterministic materialism, on the one hand, and deep scepticism, on the other. Furthermore, early on, some philosophers, notably Rousseau, raised fundamental questions about the superiority of the modern world. And, in the German discussions of 'What is enlightenment?', there was much play on the literal meaning of the term, for example as to whether allowing freedom of the press would provide illumination or start fires (in the form of political revolution). There was also considerable discussion of the difference between 'true' and 'false' enlightenment, and even suggestions that reason could itself lead to tyranny (see Beiser 1987 and Schmidt 1996), an idea which resurfaced in critical theory and postmodernism in the second half of the twentieth century.
4. An example is Habermas' use of psychoanalysis as a paradigm, see Habermas (1968).
5. As a result of what they share, both the engineering and strong enlightenment models fall under the heading of what Oakeshott calls modern rationalism. And his criticisms of this relate precisely to the abandonment of tradition, see Oakeshott (1962).
6. For a discussion of this issue in the case of Marx, see Wood (1991). These assumptions highlight an important difference between the strong enlightenment and engineering models. The former implies a greater role for research (broadly conceived) in relation to practice than does the engineering model. Where the latter focuses on means alone, strong enlightenment is also concerned with the goals of practice – in other words, with the perspective within which both goals and means are conceptualised.
7. This fragmentation was the basis for the critique of modern science by Goethe, Hegel and others in the nineteenth century, a critique whose influence has

persisted into the twentieth century. It was central, for example, to discussions of Max Weber's conception of science as a vocation (Lassman and Velody 1989) and also to Heidegger's doomed attempt to transform Freiburg University under the National Socialists, see Heidegger (1977). In the late nineteenth and early twentieth centuries, this critique was part of a response to what was believed to be a general cultural crisis: see Ringer (1969:ch. 5).

8. The arguments for and against the derivation of ought from is can be found in Hudson (1969). On value pluralism, see Larmore (1987), Berlin (1990) and Gray (1996). For further discussion of this point in the context of educational research, see Foster et al. (2000).

9. Denial that action can be governed by rules is also central to some versions of postmodernism, notably that of Lyotard, on which see Drolet (1994).

10. It also opens the way for another sort of attempt to derive ought from is: from factual information about local norms and values. However, this suffers from much the same problems as other attempts to do this.

11. For accounts which suggest a moderate enlightenment view, see Weiss (1977 and 1980), Lindblom and Cohen (1979), and Nisbet and Broadfoot (1980). Shotland and Mark (1985:14) suggest that an embryonic version of this model is the most common view among social scientists, in the form of the belief that 'the social sciences can contribute to policymaking processes, but these contributions are likely to be modest in many if not most cases'.

12. It is worth remembering that the fallibility of reason was often recognised by eighteenth-century writers, see Hampson (1968:192). For a similar account to that presented here of the limitations on what academic research can supply to policymakers, see Scott and Shore (1979:appendix).

13. See Shahar's application of a Popperian perspective to clinical trials and the implications he draws for 'evidence-based medicine' (Shahar 1997).

14. Indeed, if one adopts some of the more epistemologically radical views currently to be found in the philosophy and sociology of science, the distinctiveness of research as a source of 'knowledge' may disappear (see, for example, Woolgar 1988). My point here is that even the fallibilist position denies some of the characteristics that the engineering and strong enlightenment models assume research-based knowledge to have. In fact, some commentaries on Popper's work imply that it undermines these models completely. Thus, Putnam (1993:356) concludes: 'the distinction between *knowledge* and *conjecture* does real work in our lives; Popper can maintain his extreme scepticism only because of his extreme tendency to regard theory as an end for itself'.

15. I am not suggesting that they will, or should, judge them in an *entirely* different manner. I see the organised scepticism of academic research as simply a modification of what is integral to everyday practical enquiry, a modification that is necessary for the specialised pursuit of knowledge. Note too that some social and educational research is practical rather than academic in character and probably does not operate on the basis of *this* kind of scepticism. For a typology of forms of research in these terms, see Foster et al. (1996:32–4). See also Chapter 6. However, most of the arguments about the limited contribution that research can make to practice apply as much to practical as to academic research.

16. There are some who argue that educational and social researchers do not need to aim at general conclusions; that instead they should provide case studies of particular situations, whose findings may then be 'transferred' to other cases by practitioners and put to use (see, for example, Lincoln and Guba 1985). However, this does not make research findings any more directly

applicable than in more traditional approaches. Here, too, unless there is a very high degree of homogeneity in relevant respects in the population of cases with which both researchers and practitioners deal, the validity of 'transferability' is uncertain. And a high level of homogeneity is unusual, if we are to judge by everyday experience of the social world. Moreover, this problem is worsened by the concern of practitioners with a wide range of considerations. For a discussion of problems associated with the notion of 'transferability', see Gomm et al. (2000:ch. 5).

17. Another example of variation in interpretations of the same research is provided by responses to Bernstein's theory of sociolinguistic codes. See Bernstein (1971:introduction).

18. Of course, on some occasions, the knowledge it produces, as interpreted by practitioners within the context of their own experience, may be the decisive factor leading to one course of action rather than another.

19. Problems of this kind arise with much research on educational inequalities, which conflates equality with equity, and research on effective schooling or teaching, which often confuses the latter with good education. On the first of these cases, see Foster et al. (1996 and 2000). Discussion of the distinction between practical and conditional evaluations or prescriptions can also be found in these sources.

20. That is one of the features of the holocaust which gives it its peculiarly appalling character.

21. See Shahar's discussion of the scope for differential presentation and interpretation of the results of clinical trials in medicine: Shahar (1997:112–13).

22 That there is inevitable reliance on substantive assumptions is an implication of the use of the criterion of plausibility in assessing claims to knowledge. On this criterion, see Hammersley (1998a:ch. 3).

23. This is not a problem that is restricted to social and educational research, but it is probably worse in that field than elsewhere.

24. This is obscured by the close relationship between arguments for maximising the impact of research findings, on the one hand, and a conception of practice that is perfectionist, on the other. Perfectionism is one of the features that Oakeshott identifies as central to modern rationalism, see Oakeshott (1962).

25. This is not to suggest that practitioners of any kind should be regarded as beyond criticism. The argument is simply that they should not be criticised for being bad researchers, any more than researchers should be criticised for being bad politicians. For an example of the latter, see the previous Secretary of State for Education and Employment's complaint that some social researchers are insufficiently 'street-wise in their approach and in the conclusions they draw': Blunkett (2000:13).

26. It is perhaps worth underlining that in one of the main senses of the term, 'tolerance' means allowing things to pass of which one disapproves: see Mendus (1988).

27. In my view, the main way in which this should be done for academic research is through providing reviews of work concerned with particular practically relevant issues. However, even this task is not unproblematic: see Chapter 7.

28. I have elaborated on this defence elsewhere Hammersley (1995a:140–3).

29. I have spelt out this argument elsewhere, in relation to the ethics of research. See Hammersley and Atkinson (1995:ch. 10).

Chapter 3

Research and Practice, Two Worlds for Ever at Odds?
(written with Roger Gomm)

The failure of social and educational research to serve practice – or at least to do so in the ways or to the extent desired – has been a recurrent theme of discussion both within the research community and outside. Typically, the explanations put forward for the failure of research properly to serve policymaking and practice fall into two main categories. First, there are explanations which identify the problem as lying with researchers. Here research is seen as:

- insufficiently geared to the concerns of practitioners;
- failing to produce findings at the time they are needed;
- generating conflicting evidence;
- producing evidence that does not point to clear policy actions;
- offering evidence that simply confirms what is already known or that is at odds with what is well-known to practitioners so that its validity seems to be weak; and/or
- producing conclusions that are inaccessible to practitioners (because too elaborate and qualified, jargon-ridden, and/or published in journals that practitioners do not read).

Researchers may also be criticised for putting insufficient effort into *disseminating* findings, leading to demands that they must collaborate with practitioners (or 'users') in 'implementing' the results of their research. Thus, on the basis of this explanation, a more 'interactive' relationship between researchers and various kinds of practitioner may be recommended; or even one which eliminates the distinction between the two.[1]

The second type of explanation, by contrast, puts the blame on policymakers and practitioners. They may be portrayed as

- closed-minded, set in their ways, and therefore resistant to new perspectives;
- committed to the dominant ideology and therefore unwilling to accept research findings which fall outside that;

- untrained in the capacity to understand and make use of research; and/or
- lacking in the commitment required to seek out research evidence and to reflect on their decisions in light of it.

In the current jargon, they may be criticised for failing to make their practice evidence-based. Indeed, it may be suggested that their very mode of practice is incompatible with what is required; for example because it involves explicit or implicit reliance on experience, judgement and values (or, to use the more loaded terms of one critique, on 'tradition, prejudice, dogma, and ideology': Cox, quoted in Hargreaves 1996:7–8). And, very often, the implication is that practice should be reformed so as to approximate to the model of research. This is the implicit message, for example, of some versions of action research (see Hammersley 1993).

Despite appearances, these two explanations are by no means incompatible. Implicitly, if not explicitly, there is often criticism of – and a demand for change on – both sides. Thus, while the most recent report on problems with educational research in England and Wales is not entirely even-handed in this respect – most of the blame seems to fall on researchers – the failure of policymakers to base their decisions on research evidence is also criticised (Hillage et al. 1998). And, while the initial criticisms of educational research which triggered the current crisis focused on its alleged failure to serve teachers (Hargreaves 1996), they also carried substantial implications for teachers' work. Hargreaves began by contrasting the failure of educational enquiry with the success of medical research in contributing practically relevant knowledge. To remedy this failure, he recommended that practising teachers should play a greater role in educational enquiry, not only in shaping its agenda but also in doing research themselves; on the model of clinical research in medicine. And it is here that the radical implications of his critique for pedagogical practice become clear. These implications are made explicit in a more recent article, where he proposes that schools become 'knowledge creating' organisations. An immediate requirement for this is that they carry out a knowledge audit, and restructure their activities to pursue their research-and-development role more effectively (Hargreaves 1999b).

These two sorts of explanation – apparently contrasting, but in some ways complementary – dominate the literature on the relationship between research and practice, and have done so for many years. However, there is another, very different, perspective which is occasionally to be found in that literature; one which questions the underlying assumptions of the dominant accounts. This model accepts, to a large extent, the picture that they start from; in which research currently plays only a limited and apparently weak role in the work of policymakers and practitioners. However, it removes the negative evaluation attached to this. Also abandoned is the associated implication that the situation can be dramatically changed, and a close and harmonious relationship introduced between the two sides. This view argues that researchers and practitioners are engaged in two fundamentally different activities, and that this gives rise to divergent orientations on their part. The implication is that the lack of coordination that prevails is only to be expected. More than this, it implies that this difference in orientation is essential if these different activities are to be pursued effectively. To underline this, it is often said that researchers and policymakers or practitioners live in *different worlds*. We will therefore call this the 'two-worlds theory'. It is worth emphasising that, from this perspective, it is not just that research and practice *are* two worlds but also that they are *inevitably so*; and that they are necessarily in conflict to some degree.

In this chapter we begin by examining this two-world argument, and address some of the problems associated with it. Later, we will consider what might be learned from it about how the relationship between research and practice in education should be conceptualised, and about how current efforts to transform it ought to be evaluated.

Two-worlds theory

All ideas are said to be footnotes to ancient philosophy, and two-worlds theory is no exception. The idea that research and practice are different worlds derives in large part from the longstanding contrast between theory and practice. The Greek concepts of *theoria* and *praxis* were originally used to refer to two different ways of life. The first was focused on contemplation of what is eternal and unchanging, of things that cannot be otherwise than they are (Lobkowicz 1967:36). This way of life was, of course, that of the philosopher; with 'philosophy' interpreted in a broad sense to include mathematics and what we would today call natural science (though not engineering or the study of human society). Within Greek thought this way of life was usually given high status, being treated as participation in the divine, on the grounds that 'he who concerns himself with the divine imitates it'. The theorist is a 'spectator of the sacred' who enjoys the highest and most rewarding form of life (Lobkowicz 1977). *Praxis*, by contrast, deals with the changeable and the local, in other words with human action and its orientation to the good; above all, with politics (in the sense of government). So, practical knowledge is concerned with the products of deliberate human choice, and with relationships that are contingent in character. Moreover, it is directly linked to the task of making decisions in the mundane world. As such it is human rather than divine in status, though this is not to say that it is unimportant – moreover, it was seen as superior in status to *techne*, to the making of things.[2]

Lobkowicz shows how ideas about theory and practice were transformed across the centuries. However, the ancient Greek conception has retained considerable influence. And it seems to have shaped some twentieth-century ideas about the distinction between scientific and common-sense ways of thinking. This is represented in a particularly clear form in the work of Alfred Schütz (Schütz 1962). Embree summarises Schütz's account of scientific rationality as follows:

1 All terms are to be as clear and distinct as possible;
2 Propositions are to be consistent and compatible not only within the particular discipline but also with all other scientific propositions and those of common-sense judgements accepted within the scientific subuniverse; and
3 All scientific thought is to be derived directly or indirectly from 'tested observation, that is from the originary immediate experiences of facts within the world' . . .; more specifically, each step in the construction and use of scientific models is open to verification by empirical observation. (Embree 1988:269).

Schütz contrasts these features with those characteristic of the 'natural attitude' which dominates everyday life. Similarly, in an article that builds on Schütz's work, Garfinkel argues that the above features 'occur as stable properties of actions and as sanctionable ideals only in the case of actions governed by the attitude of scientific theorizing. By contrast, actions governed by the attitude of daily life are marked by the specific absence of these rationalities either as stable properties or as sanctionable ideals' (Garfinkel 1967a:270). Like Schütz, then, Garfinkel draws a sharp distinction between what is rational in scientific and in practical terms, science being a theoretical not a pragmatic activity.[3] What is especially important for our purposes here is that, in distinguishing between two forms of rationality, these authors do not simply treat practical common sense as a defective form of scientific rationality.

One of the implications of this analysis of different forms of rationality is that where researchers and practitioners are both concerned with the same area of social life there will be a tendency for each to see the other's approach as irrational. Beiner suggests that this is true not just of natural and social science but also of political philosophy; even though he believes that the distinctive features of the latter are very different from those of science. He claims that 'radically different existential demands are made by civic life on the one hand and by the life of theory on the other' (Beiner 1997:ix). From this he concludes that:

> the purpose of the theorist . . . is not to offer sensible guidance on the conduct of social life, but rather to probe the normative adequacy of a given vision of social order by pushing that particular vision as far as it will go: hence the 'intellectual extremism' that is, as it were, built into the whole enterprise of theory (as exemplified by its most ambitious practitioners). The exemplary theorists are what J. S. Mill referred to (and celebrated) as 'one-eyed men' whose 'one eye is a penetrating one' precisely because it does not see the whole truth: 'if they saw more, they

probably would not see so keenly, nor so eagerly pursue one course of enquiry'. The practice of citizenship should be sober, sensible, prudential, moderate, and (in the best sense of the word) 'liberal', whereas theory should be radical, extravagant, probing, biting and immoderate. (Ibid.:ix–x)

Indeed, he argues that:

> To be sure, one has little reason to doubt that our political world of the last two centuries would have been a decidedly safer place if Rousseau, Marx, and Nietzsche had practised theory in more or less the way that John Stuart Mill practised theory. Yet the point of theory isn't to think safe thoughts; rather, the point is to open intellectual horizons which one is hardly likely to do with much effectiveness unless one hazards dangerous thoughts. Without Rousseau, Marx, and Nietzsche, our political world might well be a safer world; but unquestionably, our *intellectual* world would be radically impoverished if the great critics within the tradition had been merely Swiss and German clones of John Stuart Mill. (Ibid.:xi)

Two-world theory in the field of education

A milder version of the contrast between theory and practice is to be found in some examples of two-world theory in the field of education. For example, in their review of literature on the relationship between educational research and practice, Nisbet and Broadfoot argue that 'the worlds of research and decision-making are distinct: etymologically, a decision is "that which is cut off", and while decision makers must cut off enquiry in favour of action, the researcher's concern is to pursue enquiry'. As a result:

> the different sectors of the educational system have different 'ways of knowing', different ways of formulating problems and different interpretations of what are acceptable answers. These differences help to explain the often cynical and occasionally hostile perceptions which exist between 'sides' in the research enterprise, and why policy makers and researchers so frequently caricature each other. (Nisbet and Broadfoot 1980:51–2)

In much the same way, Levin refers to 'natural' or 'intrinsic' differences between educational research and the policy process, and sees these as leading to inevitable conflict (Levin 1991:77).[4]

Others, rather than seeing the difference between theory/research and practice as a universal feature of human life, have treated it as arising from the institutional differentiation that is characteristic of modern, large-scale societies. Thus, Taylor argues that 'the roots' of the problem of the relationship between research and practice 'lie in the fact that the knowledge about education that is possessed by all the people who are labelled teachers, administrators, inspectors, researchers and so forth, is to a large and increasing extent role-specific knowledge' (Taylor

1973:194). He claims that, given this, 'clearing the channels of communication' would not ensure 'some miraculous flowering of research and its
effective application to work in classroom and lecture hall, and a conse-
quential improvement in educational outcomes' (Taylor 1973:193). As this
indicates, Taylor does not believe the problem lies in an uneven distribution of knowledge that could be easily remedied. He sees the situation
in much more dynamic terms. He argues that: 'As part of the process of
exerting identity, each of the education professions and sub-professions
tends to develop its own language and style of expression, to legitimize
certain sources of knowledge and to devalue others' (ibid.:195). And these

> distinctive languages ... make it more difficult for individuals from
> different groups to 'take on the role of the other', and inhibit understand-
> ing and the development of shared meanings between such groups. Not
> only this, but the tendency to perceive the world in the terms of a particular
> specialism has the effect of shaping the very nature of the reality with
> which the individual sees himself as having to contend. (Ibid.:204–5)

Closely related to two-worlds theory is what was referred to in
Chapter 2 as the 'moderate enlightenment' model of the relationship
between research and practice. Taylor notes that only a very small
proportion of education professionals will read journals and books in
which research findings are reported. Thus,

> only a very limited part of the knowledge about education that all these
> people possess and employ in the performance of their everyday tasks can
> strictly be regarded as research-based. Only exceptionally will the daily
> discussion of a problem or difficulty include the citation of a particular
> piece of research that contributed significantly to resolution or decision.
> Yet even when there is no explicit reference to particular studies, it is
> unlikely that such discussions will be unaffected by research. It exerts its
> influence by helping to determine the agenda of problems and difficulties,
> and in providing some of the elements that shape individual and group
> orientations towards particular issues. ... The fact that material on research
> forms only a very small part of the literature on education, and that most
> discussions about education, except among researchers themselves and
> some of the education professionals in universities and colleges, contain
> few explicit references to research, is no real guide to its influence and
> certainly no basis on which to calculate its usefulness in cost/benefit terms.
> (Ibid.:199–201)

Moreover, in having an effect,

> research-based knowledge interacts with other kinds of knowledge that
> derive from experience, hunch, prejudice, commitment to principles and
> self-interest. An element in determining the extent to which research
> findings will be 'used' in decision-making, or in contributing to the
> definition of agendas, or the formulation of attitudes, is the extent to which

these findings are consonant with the knowledge that we derive from these other sources. Such knowledge also helps to define the kinds of research that we consider relevant and worthy of support, and thus serves to complete what is, to a certain extent, but never completely, a closed knowledge system. Never completely closed, because the variety of convictions and interests in a pluralistic society ensures a continuous process of change in what Schön has called 'ideas in good currency'. (Ibid.:201–2)

Of course, none of these authors denies that there is scope for improving the relationship between researchers and educational policy-makers/practitioners, but their analyses suggest that there are substantial limitations on this; and that these rule out the more optimistic proposals for reform, designed to create a single world in which the findings of research directly shape policy and practice.[5]

Some questions about two-worlds theory

Two-worlds theory is not without problems, of course. A first point to be made is that, however useful any metaphor is, there is always a danger that its metaphorical character will be forgotten. In other words, the respects in which it is *not* true may be neglected. One danger with the idea of two worlds is that it will obscure the sense in which research and practice operate in the *same* world, and may therefore be subject to common trends. It is important to notice, for instance, that recently increased demands for the accountability of research are very similar to those which have already been applied to practitioners in other parts of the public sector, and especially in the fields of health and education. Indeed, we will have something to say about these parallels later.

A second point that needs underlining is that research is itself a form of practice. This is something which Schütz recognised, but did not pay much attention to: the fact that, as an activity, research must gear into the world in various respects. His neglect of this is not surprising given the way in which he relies on his own intellectual activity as a basis for reflection, and the philosophical character of that activity: the picture that emerges from his writings is of the researcher, pen in hand in front of a sheet of paper, gazing thoughtfully out into his garden (see Schütz 1970:1). This is a kind of research that requires very limited resources. But, of course, research varies considerably in what resources it needs, and in how easily available these are to those who would engage in it.[6] The consequences of resource needs for the dependence of 'big science' on governments and large commercial enterprises have been noted (Price 1963; Rescher 1984); but even smaller scale work can be heavily resource-dependent.

Furthermore, resources are usually provided on the basis of an at least implicit contract; in other words, in return for some kind of product.[7]

Thus, to some degree at least, researchers must try to ensure that the expectations of those who provide the resources will be met. And, in recent times, both the expectations and the means employed for monitoring achievement have become increasingly demanding. Funding agencies now often require a specification of the intended product and an outline of plans for dissemination; and, afterwards, they usually carry out an assessment of whether the research has met its goals. Moreover, in the future, it seems likely that some evaluation will also be required of its 'impact' in practical terms (see National Educational Research Forum 2000).

Equally significant for the dependent character of social research is the problem of gaining access to research sites. Those carrying out social surveys have to secure the compliance of respondents, and deal with the potential error introduced by non-response. This is an increasing problem, perhaps because of the intensification of both work and leisure, and the spread of the expectation that nothing should be done without financial return. Similarly, ethnographers have to gain entrance to the natural settings that they want to study; and in some areas, including education, access is becoming more difficult (see Troman 1996). This seems to have resulted from greater fear of the effects of research, for example of bad publicity for the school or college being studied, along with less willingness to tolerate the presence of researchers, given that educational practitioners now work under even greater pressure than before.

Research is a practical activity in another sense too. Like many activities it is a highly uncertain business: success cannot be predicted. There is a parallel here with the work of the traditional professions. One way of conceptualising this is to say that research follows a trajectory that is not under the control of the researcher, much as illnesses often follow trajectories that are by no means completely under the control of medical staff.[8] Deviation from what is expected frequently occurs, and has to be made sense of. Initial understandings of the problem may need to be changed quite dramatically. At the very least, complicating factors will have to be recognised, and along with this a considerable degree of contingency acknowledged. Indeed, in this distinctive sense (where the contrast is with the *technical*), it might be argued that research is *more* practical than many other kinds of work: the prospects for success, and perhaps even an understanding of *what would count* as success, are matters for discovery. While Nisbet and Broadfoot may be wrong to suggest that there is *no* cut-off to the activity of research, in the way that there is for other activities, it is certainly true that research is often much more long-term in perspective than other activities. A doctor can face great uncertainty in trying to diagnose and treat a patient's illness, but the problem in most cases will be self-limiting: the patient is cured, improves or dies; or a point is reached where the doctor has grounds for declaring that nothing further can be done. We can contrast this with research investigating the physiological processes involved in cancer, where there is also uncertainty (for instance, about which line of investigation it is best to pursue and even about what it will be possible eventually to achieve) but no foreseeable cut-off point. There is no clear limit to what may usefully be discovered about the physical processes associated with various types of cancer; or, for that matter, about the psychological and social processes surrounding them. There are virtually endless roads ahead here, and no-one can be sure where they will lead. Even were a cure to be found, there is always scope for discovering new and better cures.

A third point of qualification is that to refer to the 'worlds' of research and practice is to ignore the diversity that is to be found under each of these headings. This is probably most obvious in the area of 'practice'. It is clearly wrong to assume that everything that is not research conforms to more or less the same pattern, or that those involved in diverse forms of practice all display the same orientation. Furthermore, it is false to assume that there is a sharp break between research and all other kinds of practice. There are sometimes close resemblances, in particular respects. This is illustrated by the fact that other occupations have sometimes been used as models for research method; for instance, the investigative journalist (Douglas 1976) and the detective (Sanders 1974; Alasuutari 1998). On the other side, the differences *within* research are also important: for example, between theoretical and applied, strategic and tactical, non-interventionist and interventionist, academic and contract or commercial research (see Chapter 6). Indeed, at the present time, it seems as if what goes under the label of research is becoming increasingly diverse.

In these various respects, then, the idea that research and practice are two quite different worlds carries dangers. It neglects the sense in which researchers and practitioners operate in a common arena, that research is itself a form of practice, and the heterogeneity within (and occasional overlaps between) what falls under the two categories. Nevertheless, two-worlds theory points to something important about the relationship between most forms of research and the kinds of practice to which their findings relate. It points to differences in purpose, and to the consequences of these; including the potential for conflict or at least friction. As we hinted earlier, the remedies usually recommended for this difference and conflict involve an attempt either to reconstruct research in the image of the practical activity it is supposed to serve, or to reconstruct practice in the image of research. Indeed, the history of action research nicely captures the equivocation frequently involved: about who is changing whom (Hammersley 1993). What two-world theory suggests, though, is that such remedies are unlikely to be successful, and that they may have unintended consequences which can be judged undesirable.

In the next section we want to try to develop the notion of multiple 'worlds' in a way that avoids the dangers we have mentioned and capitalises on the insights that this idea can provide.

Practical activities and their different horizons

In his discussion of the difference between the natural attitude (the orientation that we all adopt in everyday life) and the scientific attitude, Alfred Schütz emphasises the pragmatic character of the former. How we see and interpret the world in the natural attitude is strongly influenced by currently prevailing purposes. While, for reasons already explained, Schütz's contrast between the natural and the scientific attitudes needs to be handled carefully, much that he says is useful and can be employed to illuminate the differences between research and other forms of practice; and, equally important, the differences among those other forms of practice.

The concept of horizon

In effect, Schütz's argument is that activities set up frameworks of relevances which determine what, drawing on Husserl, he refers to as the 'horizons' in which actors operate. The basis for this metaphor is of course that our distinctive perceptual capacities as humans, and the fact that we are usually located at some particular point on earth's surface, determine what we see.[9] In her commentary on Husserl, Ströker (1987, 1993:88) characterises a horizon as follows: 'In the natural experience of the world something like a horizon is apprehended as the more or less diffuse boundary of hazy and eventually disappearing contours of what is intuitively given in the distance.' This Husserlian idea is used by Schütz to make sense of the fact that where we are socially located affects what we can see and also what we will notice. Not only do particular roles lead us along particular routes through the social world, but also the core concerns of our role and the perspective that has built up around them shape our experience, along with how we interpret that experience (the boundaries between experience and interpretation being by no means fixed or clear). Husserl comments at one point:

> The tradesman on the market has his truth – the truth of the market. Is that not, taken in its relations, a good truth and the best of which he may avail himself? Is it the mere semblance of a truth, because the scientist, forming his judgements with respect to other relations, other goals and other ideas, seeks a different sort of truth and because these truths, though instrumental within a far broader range of application, happen to be unfit just for the purposes of the market? (Husserl, quoted in Kuhn 1940:106–7).[10]

What this points to is the way in which what is true is judged somewhat differently in the context of different activities. We suggest that one reason for this is that in many activities such judgements are shaped by estimates of the likely practical costs of different types of error, and perhaps also of how these will be distributed. By contrast, academic researchers assess knowledge claims, generally speaking, in terms of whether they are likely to be, or ought to be, convincing to the relevant research community (see Chapter 2). So, as Taylor argued, it is not just a matter of differences in actual levels of *knowledge* between researchers and practitioners but of differences in *orientation* or *perspective*.

Now, it is an essential feature of a horizon that we know that there are things beyond it; though we may not know with much clarity or detail what those things are like. Ströker comments that: 'the horizon is apprehended in such a way that the experience of it at the same time anticipates a "beyond" of possibilities and "presumabilities" of new experiences' (Ströker 1987, 1993:88). Moreover, to some degree at least, we can modify the horizons of our experience. By shifting our position on the earth's surface, or acquiring some binoculars, we can bring new landscape into view. Similarly, we can modify our social horizons: for instance by putting ourselves in a position to see what goes on in settings that we would not normally experience, or by looking more carefully at the scenes we *are* familiar with.[11] Equally important, sometimes change in our horizons is forced upon us by problems which erupt into our normal patterns of activity: these may stem from reconceptualisations of the task we are engaged in, new external demands, alterations in the circumstances in which we are operating, etc.[12]

According to Husserl and Schütz, there are two sorts of horizon: outer and inner. If we extend our outer horizon we bring into view new phenomena that were previously left out, not attended to because they lie in the background around the edges of our focal concerns. By contrast, if we extend our inner horizon we bring into view aspects of the phenomena with which we are already concerned that were not previously given attention because they formed part of what was judged unnecessary to know: we see the internal structure of those phenomena in more detail. In physical terms, a pair of binoculars or a telescope extends our outer horizon, while a microscope extends our inner horizon.

It is important to underline that, while we can change our horizons, any change will involve loss as well as gain; in the sense that we will lose sight of some things as we gain sight of others. Moreover, while outer and inner horizons can always be extended, this cannot be done in such a way as to incorporate all that could, in principle, be incorporated; since the world is inexhaustible (in both directions). In extending our horizons we quickly reach psychological limits, or at least a point of diminishing returns, whereby it becomes difficult to pursue the activity we are engaged in.[13] In this sense, perspectival variation is built into life generally; it is not simply a product of modernity, though the latter has increased role differentiation. Pursuing an activity necessarily involves making certain things thematic and leaving others as background; even if, as we have suggested, the boundary between theme and background may vary over time as a result of changes in relevances.

Implications of the fact that different activities have different horizons

So, practices operate within perspectives which provide different pictures of the world; shaped by contours that reflect what is of central and what of marginal concern in terms of that activity, and that leave much out of account altogether. Some of what is treated as marginal or irrelevant will be largely unknown; other things will be known, and even recognised as important from other points of view, but specifically ruled out of consideration for this activity. This kind of differentiation in perspective is increased by the development of large-scale modern societies, and reinforced by notions like the separation of powers in politics and other arguments in favour of institutional autonomy or professionalism.

The contours of relevance will be determined not just by how practitioners define their occupational goals but also by assumptions about how these are currently interpreted by influential and powerful others; what is given and unchangeable in the situation, so that it can be relied on or (if it is an obstacle) must be worked round; what can normally be expected of others involved in the situation who play various roles; what are the normal procedures, deviation from which may result in negative sanctions; what must be avoided at all costs; what can be overlooked, etc. The implication of this is that practices of all kinds, including research, are socio-historically situated in ways that are locally variegated. And what is rational or reasonable will be judged from within that location and may look quite irrational from other points of view.[14] The effect of moving from one perspective to another is something like that of viewing a scene through a fish-eye lens, where small changes in orientation produce large changes in the picture produced.

Of course, we are not suggesting that every person is locked into a single perspective. We all engage in multiple activities in the course of our lives. Indeed, every occupation involves a cluster of tasks rather than a single one, and component tasks may entail rather different points of view. So, we are accustomed to coping with multiple perspectives, to one degree or another. To take an example, one's view of universities may vary as one moves from thinking about them as an academic to viewing them as the parent of a student. Nevertheless, one perspective, for example an occupational one, may come to dominate how a person views things even when he or she is engaged in other activities. This is the insight behind much literature, fictional and scholarly. Of the latter we might mention the notion of the 'bureaucratic personality' (Merton 1957) and Bensman and Lilienfeld's analysis of the perspectives associated with various different occupations (Bensman and Lilienfeld 1973).

The concept of horizon enables us to gain some understanding of the way in which research and other forms of practice can belong to the same world in the most fundamental sense, yet also be different worlds in another sense. Thus, activities operate within different horizonal perspectives even where they deal with the same objects: a teacher and the parents of the children in her or his class both relate to the same children, but they do so from different perspectives, perspectives that reflect their different roles. Yet, at a more basic level, using a common illustration and playing the argument the other way, while organisms with different types of eye see a different world, this does not imply that what generates their perceptions (in combination with their optical capabilities) is different in each case. It is the same world which produces different 'worlds' for those with different biological (and, in parallel terms, social) characteristics. What *is* true, though, is that there is no single picture that is all-encompassing; which can capture the world as a whole; that is, without horizons. This has very important implications for research, as we shall see.

Metaphors for 'research into practice': application, implementation, dissemination, enlightenment, and translation

At the centre of one-worldist views, of the kind outlined at the beginning of this chapter, is what has been called the 'engineering model', in which a direct and smooth relationship is assumed between scientific research and the forms of practice which it serves. From this point of view, the two mesh together, or ought to. Indeed, on some accounts, they merge into a single process of research and development. One-worldism is also built into some of the terms most frequently used in conceptualising the relationship between research and practice. An example is the notion that research findings can be *applied* in action. Here, the discretion of the practitioner consists, at most, in deciding *what* to apply at any given moment; that which is to be applied is assumed to be already compatible with the relevant practical world. The same holds in the case of the term 'implementation'. Another frequently used term, 'dissemination', involves a very different metaphor; but its implications are similar. Here, research produces the seeds that are to be sown by practitioners. Again, what research supplies is assumed to be ready made for use, and to carry particular practical results within it.[15]

Now, of course, the engineering model, and the terms associated with it, have not escaped challenge. And the usual alternative which is offered treats research as providing enlightenment, rather than tools to be applied or even seeds to be planted. However, there are different versions of this enlightenment model, as we saw in Chapter 2. Some commentators advocate what we might call 'strong enlightenment', one example of which is 'critical' enquiry. This treats research as producing theory, in the form of a comprehensive perspective that serves as a basis for transformative action: on the part of the working-class, women, and/or subordinated groups of other kinds (see Fay 1987). In a similar way, sociology has also sometimes been regarded as providing a perspective which offers an enlightened basis for political action or state policy.[16]

On this strong interpretation, the enlightenment model implies an equal or greater role for research in relation to practice than the engineering model: it is concerned not just with means but also with the goals of practice. Moreover, while it starts from a discrepancy between the 'world' of the practitioner and that of the researcher, it is nevertheless one-worldist in a deeper sense. It treats this deviation as ideological, and as open to and requiring remedy: the practitioner is to be emancipated and brought to an understanding of the world as revealed by research; or, in more dialectical formulations, transformation of the two 'worlds' is to be effected, producing a comprehensive overcoming of the distinction between appearance and reality.

So, many of the terms we use to talk about the relationship between research and practice – 'application', 'implementation', 'dissemination', plus some uses of 'enlightenment' – either deny differences in horizontal perspectives or, where these are recognised, treat them as eradicable and their eradication as desirable. However, as we saw earlier, there is a rather different view of the role of research knowledge in relation to practice which is closer to multiple-worldism, and therefore presents that relationship as more complex than either the engineering or the strong enlightenment model suggests. This is what was referred to earlier as the moderate enlightenment model.[17] From this point of view, what research can provide is simply resources that practitioners may find useful. But whether they will find them useful, in which ways, and what the effects of using them will be, involves a large element of contingency. In the context of this model, the talk is sometimes of research findings being 'translated' into action, a metaphor which implies a very different relationship between research and practice from that assumed by the other metaphors we have discussed. We saw earlier how Taylor regarded multiple worlds as characterised by different 'languages'; and this clearly implies the need for translation.[18]

The translation metaphor and its implications

In using this metaphor, much depends on how we interpret the concept of language. Thus, when people talk about research findings being translated into practice, they may nevertheless still be operating closer to a one- than to a multiple-world view: seeing translation as relatively unproblematic (for example, see Clarke 1998). The implied model here is of a common real world which languages carve up in much the same way as each other, simply using different names for the same parts. Yet, in fact, we know that the vocabularies of languages divide the world up somewhat differently; indeed, we can see languages as collections of resources that have been shaped by the practical activity in which their speaker communities have engaged in the past, and therefore as reflecting distinctive features of that activity pattern. And this is likely to be even more true of different horizonal perspectives. Thus, the different 'languages' of research and other kinds of practice reflect differences between these forms of activity, leading to differences in what is given priority, in what is thematised in any situation, in the descriptive frameworks used to identify objects, in what is taken to be inferrable from any description (because different explanatory schemas may be used) and, therefore, in what is treated as reliable knowledge. And all of these differences stem from diversity in relevance structures, which derive in turn from differences in what is taken to be the core task.

What this implies is that different worlds may be more or less distant from one another, and that relating research to practice involves dealing with this distance in some way. What one-worldism claims is that this must be done either by the researcher becoming 'realistic' or 'street-wise' and moving into the world of practice so as to supply what is required there, or by practitioners being emancipated from the false world they currently inhabit into the true reality conceptualised by research. As we noted earlier, this implies substantial change on one or other or both sides. By contrast, the metaphor of translation suggests a way of dealing with the distance between the two worlds that leaves them separate and largely intact; just as two languages continue to exist despite translations between them.[19]

We can illustrate this by looking at another important interchange between research and other forms of practice. It is a feature of translation between two languages that it can go in both directions. And the same is true of translation between 'worlds'. Thus, not only can the results of social research be translated into the terms of various forms of practice, but social researchers often use information from the people they study as a resource in their work; and, in doing so, they engage in a process of translation – interpreting informants' accounts for the purposes of their own 'world' of research.[20] And this process illuminates what is involved in translation between 'worlds'. Thus, on one side, there is a sense in which informants need to be 'trained' or socialised into knowing what would and would not be relevant to the researcher, though the best informants may need little of this because their personal orientations are similar to that of the researcher in relevant ways.[21] On the other side, the researcher does not want an informant who looks at the world entirely in research terms. James Spradley provides an illustration. He refers to Bob, an informant he worked with in the course of his study of tramps. Bob had spent four years on skid row, but he was also a Harvard graduate, and had gone on to do postgraduate work in anthropology. Spradley recounts:

> On my next visit to the treatment center I invited Bob into my office. We chatted casually for a few minutes, then I started asking him some ethnographic questions. 'What kind of men go through Seattle City Jail and end up at this alcoholism treatment center?' I asked. 'I've been thinking about

> the men who are here' Bob said thoughtfully. 'I would divide them up first
> in terms of race. There are Negroes, Indians, Caucasians, and a few Eskimo.
> Next I think I would divide them on the basis of their education. Some
> have almost none, a few have some college. Then some of the men are
> married and some are single'. For the next fifteen minutes he proceeded
> to give me the standard analytic categories that many social scientists use.
> (Spradley 1979:53)

In part, the problem for Spradley here is that the informant is employing
categories that are not central to his research focus. But there is a deeper
problem as well: the informant is filtering his experience through sociological categories in a way that not only pre-judges what would and
would not be relevant but also formulates what he judges to be relevant
in a way that makes any exploration of it difficult or impossible. What
this highlights is that while research involves a process of mediation
between the 'worlds' of the people being studied and the 'world' of the
researcher, this process requires the maintenance of distance as well as
contact: it requires the researcher to move conceptually backwards and
forwards, nearer and then further away. Lofland talks of the ethnographer needing to operate in two worlds (Lofland 1972:97, 108–9). He also
reports a sense of betrayal because, however much the ethnographer may
appear to participants to have joined their 'world', he or she remains
located in the 'world' of the research, a 'world' which has different
priorities from theirs. This is also the reason why researchers cannot
avoid those they study often reacting against the accounts provided in
research reports (Becker 1970:chs 7 and 8).[22]

It is important to note the implications of our argument here for what
it is that research produces. If the metaphor of translation is correct, social
scientists cannot claim to provide an account of the world that is in some
sense a universalistic replacement for the parochial perspectives of the
people they study. It may well be that they discover facts about the
environment in which people act, or about people's own activities, which
show errors in the latter's perspectives. But there is no sense in which
research offers a single, overarching true account of the world by contrast
with the partial accounts of participants. The view offered by research is
also partial and perspectival, necessarily so.[23]

Of course, the language metaphor we are relying on here can be
interpreted in a way which suggests that communication between those
in different worlds is actually impossible. Language is seen by some as
constitutive in character – as *constructing* the world that is experienced.
And this can be taken as ruling out the possibility of translation between
languages. Indeed, this view can be found in the context of discussions
of the relationship between research and the perspectives of the people
studied. Here, research is seen as distorting those perspectives, as
pretending to cross what is in fact an unbridgeable gulf.[24] Yet we know
that translation between languages *is* possible, even though it is generally

acknowledged that something may be lost in translation (it is also possible, of course, that something may be gained!). And much the same seems likely to be true of translation between 'worlds'.

Indeed, the metaphor of translation has the advantage that it counters any tendency to treat multiple worlds as if they were unrelated to one another. Not only are some other forms of practice and their exponents part of any 'world' generated by a particular activity, but also links with some of those other forms of practice will usually be built into it. For instance, the output of research is always directed towards some audience. And in this context it is important to remember that, in communicating with others, we do not simply translate our thoughts into terms that we hope they will understand. Rather, we send messages that we believe will be relevant to them in one respect or another. And the other side of this is that messages are read with a view to their intended relevance; indeed, this is often crucial to understanding the content of a message (Sperber and Wilson 1986). So, in writing research reports, researchers must anticipate the relevances of the target audience to some extent.

This means that researchers necessarily try to communicate what they have found in a form that is going to be understandable by others who do not share their 'world'. This is true even if the target audience is fellow researchers working in the same field. While they will share a common world to a great extent, their 'worlds' will still differ in some respects; reflecting both the fact that the boundaries of research fields are diffuse and that there are sub-groups within any field who pursue different approaches. And the further away from one another the fields are in which two researchers work, the more translation will be required in communications between them. This is one reason why replication can be problematic (Collins 1975). Of course, researchers will also sometimes seek to communicate with a broader audience than this. Thus, the rationale of much research involves the notion that it will feed into discussion within 'public spheres' in which many different types of participant are involved. And here the target audience will necessarily be rather unspecific in character.

Against this background, any move to render academic research closer to the world of one group of practitioners may lead to its products being less relevant for other groups. It seems likely that there is a trade-off involved here. It follows from this that the relative autonomy of academic research may be essential if it is to serve a wide range of audiences. Of course, this also means that different types of 'translation' of the research findings, designed for different audiences, will be required, with no single correct translation being ideal for everyone (Crystal 1987). Furthermore, the greater the distance between the world of research and the form of practice concerned, the more work that will have to go into the provision of any usable translation, and perhaps also the greater the range of relevant alternative translations that could be produced.

What this underlines is the fact that communications vary in the degree to which they are targeted at a specific audience with known character-istics. This is a point which Bernstein conceptualised in his distinction between universalistic and particularistic modes of speech (Bernstein 1971). So, what research produces can be universalistic, in the sense of having general relevance, even though it can never replace the perspec-tives developed to pursue other activities.

This highlights the fact that communication is never one-sided. The potential audience for any research must attend to its message and put in some work to interpret its meaning and (even more) the significance which it carries for the activities in which they are involved.[25] This relates to a point that Crystal makes about translation between languages. He reports that 'on the whole, most translators work *into* their mother tongue (or language of habitual use)' (Crystal 1987:344). And, of course, metaphorically speaking, this is what researchers do in their use of informants. However, this suggests that the task of translating academic research into implications for practice should fall primarily to practi-tioners, or to a select few of them who can act as mediators. Of course, audiences will vary in their capability and willingness to do this, for a whole variety of reasons: how much effort it involves, what the likely payoff is estimated to be, what time and energy they have available, etc. It is assumed by the model of evidence- or research-based practice that practitioner audiences will be, or ought to be, highly capable of making, and motivated to make, use of research findings. But this need not be so. Indeed, that model tends to overlook the diversity of sources on which forms of practice draw (and draw with good reason, in their own terms at least), and the essential role that experience and judgement play within them (see Chapter 2).

What the multiple-world model suggests, then, is that differences in orientation between researchers and other practitioners will remain, despite attempts to obliterate them. Furthermore, the extent to which the products of research are found useful by various kinds of practitioner, and *how* they are found useful, will always remain rather unpredictable; in other words, there is an inevitable degree of contingency involved in the relationship between research findings, practical 'implications' and effects. Given that tailoring research to one group of practitioners is likely to render it less relevant to other groups, there is an argument for academic research which is designed to produce universalistic knowledge, in the sense of knowledge that is potentially relevant to diverse audiences operating in different worlds who must themselves do much of the work of 'translation'. Indeed, this may be essential if research is to feed into discussions within the 'public sphere'. There may be tension, then, between research intended to service the expertise of pol-icymakers and practitioners, on the one hand, and that intended to provide resources for public discussion of policy and practice, on the other.[26]

The sources of one-worldism

Recent criticisms of educational research for failing to serve policymaking and practice are premised on the idea that it operates in the same world as these other activities; or that, if it does not, it ought to do so. This criticism has led to suggestions for reform whose aim seems to be to erase the boundaries between all these activities: to integrate them into a single process of research-development-policy-and-practice. Given the internal heterogeneity of research, the implications of this will vary for different researchers. To some extent, what is proposed is a shift from scientific to practical research.[27] However, even practical research is primarily concerned with the production of sound knowledge, albeit within the context of assumptions characteristic of the practice(s) it serves. So there is still the potential for conflict. Indeed, this is recognised by the British government itself in the way that, when funding research directly, its departments use contracts which give them the right to prevent publication or even to rewrite the findings.[28]

So, from the point of view of multiple-world theory, while it may be possible to bring research into closer proximity with some of the other 'worlds' to which it relates, this will never produce isomorphism; and in most cases it will involve substantial changes to research, or to the other kinds of practice, or to both. Moreover, any gain in the relevance of research to one activity is likely to be bought at the cost of lower relevance to others. This is obscured by some of the most influential ways of conceptualising the relationship between research and practice, such as the engineering model and the metaphors of application, implementation, and dissemination associated with it. They assume a single world in which the activity of research feeds directly and smoothly into practice. Any failure in this respect is taken to indicate a defect in the way in which one or other activity is being performed. Similarly, while the strong enlightenment model recognises the way in which research and other forms of practice generate different 'worlds', it treats any deviation of practice from what would be rational in theoretical or research terms as dysfunctional; though it also allows the possibility of seeing particular forms of research as irrelevant, on the grounds that they have no practical value in the political struggle, or that they are ideological (see, for example, Mies 1991). The implication of both these models, often, is that practice must be redefined in research terms. This is the central message of action research, for example. But in the field of education the recent emphasis has been on the need for research to be transformed in order to facilitate evidence-based practice on the part of teachers and policymakers.

The significance of this needs to be underlined. The pressure for the reform of educational research is not coming primarily from practitioners – for example from teachers – but rather from government agencies and 'education managers'.[29] Moreover, it has arisen against the background of attempts to reform the education system through the establishment of central controls and guidelines – the National Curriculum, key stages, the literacy and numeracy hours – and various means of monitoring the performance of teachers and schools – the publication of examination results and league tables, value-added measurement schemes, SATs, and OFSTED inspections.

Managerialism

What is being demanded of educational research, then, is not just, or even, that it serve teaching but, rather, that it serve the project of transforming the education system into a more 'transparent' public management organisation. This reflects the influence of what is often referred to as managerialism.[30] Central to this is the idea that management is a generic form of practice, a notion which emerged and flourished in industrial and commercial sectors in the mid-twentieth century. Where, before, the management of an organisation had usually been carried out by the owner or by someone who had worked within it in other capacities, this came to be no longer the case. A labour market for managers emerged, with much mobility not just within sectors but across them, and the number of managers increased exponentially. As part of this, management came to be seen as requiring specialised occupational training; training which underlined the *generic* character of the knowledge and skills involved.

There are no doubt multiple causes of this change, but among them might be included: the increased size of organisations in both the private and public sectors, the greater competition resulting from globalisation, the growth of consumer organisations and pressure groups, the increasing role of the mass media in commercial and political life, and the scope for upward mobility and increased control offered by managerialism to members of some occupational categories.

A feature of the past 20 years has been the spread of managerialism from the private to the public sector. And, closely associated with this, forms of quasi-market have been introduced *within* organisations and organisational sectors, designed to simulate 'the discipline of the market' that is assumed to operate outside. This has involved particularly dramatic change for the public sector, where organisations did not previously operate within an environment that approximated closely to the market model and where more collegial forms of organisation had prevailed.

Earlier, we made the point that there is not simply one form of practice to be contrasted with research. And the above account provides a way of seeing what is happening to educational research as part of changes in the relationships among other kinds of practice; in particular, between educational administrators and managers, on the one hand, and teachers, on the other. We suggest that this is at least as important as any secular shift to a new mode of socially distributed knowledge production (on which see Gibbons et al. 1994).

Managerialism, research and the modernist intellectual

In many ways, managerialism is an imperialistic form of practice, preoccupied with incorporating others within its own world. Moreover, like other occupational ideologies it draws on research as part of its rationale. This connects with a point we made earlier: about the heterogeneity not just of other forms of practice but also of research itself. And some forms of research are similarly imperialistic, in the sense that they are intended to provide a replacement for 'folk knowledge'. To put it another way, they are one-worldist, and see research as documenting the world within which all activity is properly located. It has often been argued that these forms of research are complicit with the modernist project of subjugating nature, including human nature.[31] Furthermore, while there seems to be increasing recognition of the futility of any attempt to achieve total control over non-human nature, pressure for collective control over human social life seems, if anything, to be growing; for example, with demands that both private and public sector organisations maximise their performance in terms of multiple 'e's: economy, efficiency, effectiveness, equity, excellence, etc. (see Mayne and Zapico-Goni 1997:5).

There is a tendency to see this concern with performativity as a feature of Right and Centre politics, and as implicating quantitative rather than qualitative research. Yet, as Bauman has pointed out, the aspiration of modernist intellectuals *generally* has been to become legislators; to engage in the reconstruction of society along rational lines. This is true not just of influential versions of sociology but also of some 'critical', feminist and other approaches on the Left. They claim to offer a comprehensive picture on the basis of which practitioners of one kind or another can rationalise a currently irrational world.[32] What we are suggesting, then, is that there is an affinity between managerialism and those forms of research which are one-worldist in character; whether linked to the engineering or to the strong enlightenment models. In the field of education, the most obvious example of research which aids managerialism is that concerned with school effectiveness. Nevertheless, much other research, for example feminist and 'critical' work on equal opportunities and social justice, has also been designed to support policies that will bring practice into line with performance criteria (see, for example, Gewirtz 1998).

Yet, as multiple-world theory would predict, the fit between these kinds of imperialistic research and managerialist practice is far from unproblematic. Thus, while school effectiveness research has been heavily criticised by other educational researchers for its 'political opportunism' and 'discourse of performativity' (see, for example, Slee and Weiner

1998), it has also shown the limits of 'the school effect' and revealed the weaknesses of many of the policies and administrative procedures employed in the managerialisation of education, notably league tables and OFSTED 'research' (see, for example, Mortimore and Goldstein 1996).

Bauman traces the idea of the intellectual as legislator back to the kind of state power developed in the *ancien régime* in France, and greatly expanded and developed during the French Revolution and the Napoleonic period. He argues, for example, that:

> The social-intellectual movement recorded in history as the 'age of enlightenment' was not (contrary to the Whig version of history) a huge propaganda exercise on behalf of truth, reason, science, and rationality; neither was it a noble dream of bringing the light of wisdom to the confused and oppressed. Enlightenment was, instead, an exercise in two distinct, though intimately related, parts. First, in extending the powers and the ambitions of the state, in transferring to the state the pastoral function exercised previously (in a way incipient and modest by comparison) by the Church, in reorganising the state around the function of planning, designing and managing the reproduction of the social order. Secondly, in the creation of an entirely new, and consciously designed, social mechanism of disciplining action, aimed at regulating and regularizing the socially relevant lives of the subjects of the teaching and managing state. (Bauman 1987:80)

This seems a curiously apt characterisation of what lies behind recent education reform in Britain, since the mid-1980s. And it is within this context that the proposals to reform educational research can be understood. The underlying complaint is that this research does not have the character needed for it to play the role demanded by 'the teaching and managing state'; sometimes euphemised as 'the learning society' (see Ransom 1998). Whether it can ever play that role, in a practical rather than a merely ideological sense, is open to serious question. After all, managerialism is perfectionist and anti-pluralist: it neglects not just the limited power of organisational management, but also the plural (and often irreconcilable) values that underpin human life. Under the guise of an exclusive concern with effectiveness and efficiency, instrumental and even commercial goals are promoted above all others. By contrast, research almost inevitably reveals the contingency and conflict that are characteristic of social life, and the diversity of perspectives to be found within it.

We suggest, then, that the existence of multiple 'worlds' is an inevitable feature of the divisions of labour built into human social life. Attempts to 'modernise' these differences out of existence are not only likely to fail but will have consequences for the effective pursuit of the activities concerned. In short, if current efforts to reform educational research in universities push ahead in the direction proposed, this research will be not so much 'socially distributed' as reconstituted entirely into practical research – or perhaps even into little more than a public relations resource available to policymakers and education managers.

Notes

1. These criticisms of research are not necessarily applied in a blanket fashion. Some research may be held up as a model by which to criticise the rest. On the notion of 'interactive social science', see Caswill and Shove (2000).
2. It is worth noting that there has been some debate about the relative status of *theoria* and *praxis* in Aristotle's philosophy. See Ackrill (1981:ch. 10, especially pp. 138–41).
3. Garfinkel's more recent work, and the writings of some other ethnomethod-ologists, challenge this distinction. See Lynch (1988 and 1993).
4. Scott and Shore (1979:appendix) adopt a similar view about the relationship between academic sociological research and policymaking.
5. Nisbet and Broadfoot (1980) document the long history of such attempts at reform.
6. In fairness to Schütz, it should be noted that he had to work hard to provide the resources for his philosophical work. Escaping from Germany in the 1930s, and having no university teaching qualification, he had to work full-time in a banking firm in the United States. On his struggle with his 'two lives', see Grathoff (1989).
7. This is true whether what is involved is patronage or commercial exchange, different though these two models of the relationship are. For a useful discussion of patronage, see Turner (1990).
8. On the concept of trajectory, see Maines (1991).
9. This is not an entirely straightforward matter, and furthermore the term has come to acquire all sorts of other meanings: see van Peursen (1977:182–3 and *passim*). For other discussions of the concepts of 'horizon', 'world', and 'lifeworld', see Kuhn (1940), Landgrebe (1940), Carr (1977) and Luckmann (1970). We elaborate on the meaning of the terms 'world' and 'horizon' here in ways that are not always consistent with this literature. Also relevant is interactionist work on social worlds: see Clarke (1991).
10. As this quotation indicates, Husserl retains the idea that science is superior to many other perspectives in being 'instrumental in a broader range of application', and he also sees phenomenological philosophy as enjoying an even more fundamental universality.
11. These two strategies are, of course, central to social research, especially that of an ethnographic or qualitative kind. One of the problems with horizons is that for much of the time we are not aware of the limitations they involve: these are below the level of our consciousness. This provides one of the rationales for ethnographic research.
12. In Schütz's terms they arise from changes in relevances, and he provides a useful typology of these. See Schütz (1970), and Schütz and Luckmann (1974).
13. Herein lies one of the sources of conflict between research and other forms of practice, given the commitment of research to expand the field of knowledge. This is a conflict that was discussed by Nietzsche in his essay 'On the uses and disadvantages of history for life' (Nietzsche 1874).
14. It is perhaps worth emphasising that we are not suggesting that different 'worlds' or perspectives are incommensurable in the sense that there is no scope for reasonable argument among those participating in different ones. The concept of horizon avoids such epistemological relativism, though it also

suggests that mutual understanding may often be very difficult to achieve, and agreement on the right course of action sometimes impossible.

15. Another metaphor sometimes employed is that of 'impact' (see, for example, NERF 2000:9). This is even more mechanical in character. The implication seems to be that a given effect is built into a research study, so that we can identify its value by direct observation.

16. See, for instance, Gouldner (1973:ch. 4) and Finch (1986); and for a discussion of this see Hammersley (1999b).

17. This is the version of the enlightenment model presented by Taylor (1973).

18. Our use of the term 'translation' here is rather different from that which has become popular in the field of science and technology studies: see, for example, Latour (1987).

19. Of course, in the long term languages will be affected by the translations that are made; and the same may be true of 'worlds'.

20. Our late colleague Peter Foster highlighted the relevance of this point for us, and made very important contributions to our thinking about this and other matters.

21. See, for example, Whyte's discussion of the qualities of his informant Doc (Whyte 1955:appendix).

22. This sense of betrayal may be especially great where participants expect the researcher to supply findings that are useful to them in return for access.

23. Though, for the reasons explained earlier, the *validity* of any truths produced is not relative to the perspective.

24. This seems to be implied in some contributions to the postmodernism debate in anthropology: see Clifford and Marcus (1986).

25. On the distinction between meaning and significance, see Hirsch (1967).

26. This is an issue that is largely overlooked by Gibbons et al. (1994), in their advocacy of Mode 2 research. While they stress the increased 'social account-ability' of this kind of work, they do so within the context of an implicit social theory which seems close in character to normative functionalism, in which the differential power of those involved to shape what counts as research and knowledge, what is investigated, what findings are and are not reported, etc. is largely neglected. And, most important of all in our view, they neglect the different goals which that power is used to pursue.

27. On this distinction, see Foster et al. (1996:32-4) and Chapter 6.

28. See *The Guardian*, Higher Education, 29 October 1998, and Cohen (2000). These restrictions are not new, see Pettigrew (1994) and Norris (1995).

29. And from one or two influential educational researchers associated with these sources.

30. The seminal work is, of course, Burnham (1945). On more recent develop-ments, see Mayne and Zapico-Goni (1997:8-9).

31. The classic source is Horkheimer and Adorno (1944). For an outline of their argument, see Jay (1973:ch. 8).

32. Foucault's critique of the role of intellectuals in relation to Leftist political movements parallels Bauman's critique of intellectuals and the state. In the words of Poster, Foucault argues that 'the intellectual's assertion of univer-sality easily becomes an alibi for grasping power; knowledge and power are locked in a *mésalliance* which can be traced back to Plato's philosopher-king' (Poster 1974:41).

Chapter 4

If the Social World Is How Qualitative Researchers Say It Is, What Impact Can their Work Have on Policymaking and Practice?

There is currently increasing pressure on social and educational researchers to make their work have greater impact on policymaking and practice than it has previously achieved. Moreover, it is becoming clear that this has implications not just for the 'dissemination' of research findings but also for the *kind* of research that is to be done. It is significant in this context that a very substantial proportion of recent British research on education is qualitative in character. And qualitative work was picked out for particular criticism in James Tooley's evaluation of the field (Tooley 1998). Moreover, David Hargreaves' critique of educational research (Hargreaves 1996) implied the need for more experimental or quasi-experimental research, on the model of evidence-based medicine, where randomised controlled trials are treated as the gold standard (see Cochrane 1972).

Perhaps as a result, recent official pronouncements about educational research seem to prioritise quantitative rather than qualitative research. An example is the Economic and Social Research Council's (ESRC) funding programme on 'teaching and learning'. Despite recognition that a range of forms of enquiry will be required, the main emphasis seems to be on quantitative research. In a section of its web site that discusses 'capacity building', qualitative work is only mentioned in one bullet point (whereas quantitative research is mentioned in three out of five), and even here it is described as needing to be 'articulated' or 'combined' with quantitative investigations (Economic and Social Research Council 2000).

The implication of all this is that qualitative research is believed to be unable to 'deliver' the sort of findings that are required for evidence-based practice. Further signs of this belief – in the context of social research generally – are to be found in David Blunkett's speech to the ESRC in early 2000. He states,

> One of our prime needs is to be able to measure the size of the effect of A on B. This is genuine social science and reliable answers can only be

reached if the best social scientists are willing to engage in this endeavour. We are not interested in worthless correlations based on small samples from which it is impossible to draw generalisable conclusions.

It is not clear whether, in these terms, qualitative work could ever count as 'genuine social science' though the Secretary of State does add: 'We welcome studies which combine large scale, quantitative information on effect sizes which will allow us to generalise, with in-depth case studies which provide insights into how processes work' (Blunkett 2000:paras 56–7). At best, here, qualitative research is given a secondary – and subordinate – role; perhaps only as a supplier of illustrative material. Furthermore, the main emphasis on quantitative work is reinforced later when Mr Blunkett comments: 'There is a danger of too much concentration on the micro-level – what is the point of research which becomes narrower and narrower, with small groups of people responding to each other's writing in esoteric journals, read only by themselves and relevant only to themselves?' (Blunkett 2000:para 21). Here, 'concentration on the micro-level' seems to be a synonym for qualitative work; the assumption being that any study of a small number of cases will only be of interest to a small number of people – that only statistically generalisable findings can have general relevance.[1]

In this context, it is interesting to note that Ann Oakley, who was once widely regarded as an advocate of qualitative work, has now become in the eyes of some critics 'a quantitative tyrant, a missionary of logical positivism' (Oakley 2000:21). Since the early 1990s she has been arguing for the importance of randomised controlled trials in a variety of fields, including education. She has also recently been involved in establishing the Evidence for Policy and Practice: Information and Co-ordinating Centre, at the Institute of Education, University of London. In her book *Experiments in Knowing*, like David Blunkett, she presents qualitative research as playing (at best) a subordinate role to quantitative evaluations. Moreover, at one point she writes:

> It is important to do the kind of research that will provide the best evidence possible about what works. *Whether* something works is here the primary question, the question of greatest interest to most practitioners and policymakers. *How* something works, and theories or behavioural models which might underpin the relationship between intervention and effects, are secondary questions. (Oakley 2000:310)[2]

It is evident from this that what is driving the increased emphasis on quantitative method is a highly instrumental attitude towards the value of social and educational research. Hodgkinson has argued that David Blunkett's ESRC speech assumes an 'engineering' view of the relationship between research and practice, and so makes positivist assumptions about the nature and function of social research (Hodgkinson 2000). Like Auguste

Comte, the Secretary of State believes that the main task of such enquiry is to provide information that will facilitate the governance of society; this consisting of knowledge about determinate causal relationships. Hodgkinson comments: 'for Blunkett, the entire enterprise of social science is therefore encapsulated in the following: how does society "work", and how can we best "engineer" it?' (ibid.:3.1). The task of research becomes 'to "discover" the knowledge required by politicians to enact the necessary interventions' (ibid.:3.3). This is close to Comte's idea that science produces predictions which can form the basis for state policy; the assumption is that the whole point of research is the production of knowledge which has practical application (see Charlton 1959:35–6).[3]

Now, some qualitative researchers might insist that qualitative work *can* inform decisions about 'what works', perhaps even in ways that do not subordinate it to quantitative method. However, I want to suggest here that there is a fundamental incompatibility between qualitative enquiry and the instrumentalism which guides much current criticism of educational research. As already noted, that instrumentalism rests on an 'engineering' view of the relationship between research and practice; whereas, I will argue, there is an important sense in which a qualitative approach implies an 'enlightenment' view of that relationship – albeit one particular version of it. Specifically, I will argue that there is a conflict between the image of society built into the engineering model – and its close associate, the medical model – and the image of human social life which emerges out of much qualitative research.

The image of social life built into the engineering and medical models

The engineering model has, of course, been subjected to a great deal of criticism (see, for example, Bulmer 1982 and Finch 1986). What I want to highlight here is that it relies on an image of society as a machine, in which all the various parts of a national society are treated as designed to serve one another, and as capable of being re-engineered so as to maximise the performance of the whole. This is the basis for what has become a standard argument in current political discourse: that there needs to be continual improvement in the performance of all institutions, so as to ensure national success, or even survival, in the global economy. And, from this point of view, the task of the researcher is to provide information that is of direct use for this kind of social engineering.

Also employed in recent discussions have been medical analogies. One played an important part in Hargreaves' influential critique of educational research (Hargreaves 1996). He contrasted this research adversely with research in medicine, implying close correspondence in key respects between the work of teachers and of doctors. And he employed another medical analogy in a much earlier paper, which deals with the uses of qualitative research. Referring to the failure of educational reforms, he writes: 'our attempted grafts (and various forms of major or minor surgery) merely arouse the "antibodies" of the host which undermine our attempts to play doctor to an educational patient' (Hargreaves, 1978:20). More recently, he has referred to 'healthy' and (by implication) 'unhealthy' staff subcultures in schools. He comments:

> Healthy subcultures among a school staff do not challenge the school leaders' right to manage nor the right of other colleagues to take a different point of view. Resistance groups [that is, 'unhealthy' staff subcultures] are *counter*-cultures, who are actively subversive of management and intolerant of differences between subcultures. Such a group saps the morale and commitment of the supporters of change, and exasperates the leader(s).

He concludes: 'The most effective method of countering the resistance group is simply stated: get rid of them or at least the most active and vocal ones' (Hargreaves 1999c:60).

Despite important differences, there are strong similarities between metaphors treating social phenomena as machines and as organisms. As with machines, the various parts of an organism are designed to serve one another, whether by Creator or by evolution. And, once again, there is a role prescribed for someone to monitor performance and to intervene where parts are going wrong, or are not performing as well as they should be. From this perspective, the task of the social researcher is along the lines of the sports physician, who is concerned with devising means to enhance the performance of the athlete, including identifying what is unhealthy for the surgeon to cut it out.[4]

So, both the engineering and medical models treat societies – or, on a smaller scale, particular institutions, organisations or groups – as functioning wholes. In other words, they rely on a kind of functionalism, whereby each part is to be understood and judged in terms of its contribution to the operation of the whole. And both models define the role of researcher as concerned with monitoring and improving social functioning. On this functionalist perspective, there seems to be a smooth continuity between research, on the one hand, and policymaking or practice, on the other. In playing its proper role in society, the first feeds – or ought to feed – directly into the second.

Of course, use of the mechanical and organismic metaphors is by no means unknown even within qualitative research. The most notable example is the use made of the organismic metaphor by early British social anthropology (see Evans-Pritchard 1951:ch. 3). However, that metaphor has been subjected to sustained criticism, and in the past 50 years most qualitative researchers have rejected the whole tendency to treat societies as functioning wholes. Instead, they have employed a number of alternative metaphors for thinking about social life: as an arena in which conflicting groups battle and/or negotiate (conflict, negotiated order, or social world theory); as a theatre, or set of theatres, in which actors perform (dramaturgy); as a field in which different individuals and groups carry on their activities in a variety of changing relationships (the ecology of games); as having the character of stories (narrative theory, of various kinds), etc.[5]

In the next section I want to examine what I take to be key ideas about the nature of social life that inform qualitative research, and that are at odds with the functionalism I have identified as characteristic of the engineering and medical models. Before I go any further, however, I should note the dangers involved in generalising about qualitative research. Denzin and Lincoln (1994) have claimed that it has travelled through at least six different 'moments'. Whatever one thinks about their account (see Atkinson et al. 1999 and Hammersley 1999a for criticism), it is certainly true that the field of qualitative research is now highly fragmented in terms of approach; and that it has always displayed tensions and variation in perspective. Nevertheless, I am going to risk making some general claims about the social imagery on which it relies.

The image of social life in qualitative research

A first – relatively banal, but not unimportant – point is that because in recent years qualitative enquiry has tended to focus at the micro level, there has not been much temptation for qualitative researchers to assume that the key unit for social analysis is the national society, in the way that functionalism and some other macro theories have often done. Instead, qualitative researchers have usually emphasised the diversity within national societies, as well as the constructed character of boundaries between them (see, for example, Cohen 1986). Moreover, with current recognition of the role of globalisation – and of the local constraints, the opportunities, and the varied responses it generates (on which, see Burawoy et al. 2000) – any notion of national societies as distinct and well-integrated entities becomes of doubtful value. An approach which recognises different and overlapping forms of organisation operating at various levels within and across national boundaries seems necessary.

A second point is that the functionalist model assumes a standard commitment to the national society, or to particular social institutions, on the part of members. This commitment is sometimes simply taken for granted, but in more developed sociological accounts it is treated as a product of the socialisation of members into relevant values and norms. In short, societies and institutions are not only viewed as characterised by *structural* integration, but also this is seen as produced by *social* integration.[6] It is assumed that all the various parts of a society have been designed to work together and serve the whole, and that this is established and maintained by a consensus about the roles played by these various parts, whether institutions or particular roles.

An important consequence of treating structural integration as a defining feature of societies, on analogy with machines and organisms, is that it is also taken to be an ideal. As a result, this type of functionalism is normative in two senses: it emphasises the role of conformity to norms (to rules and regulations) in producing structural integration; and it treats social and structural integration as a normative standard in analysing societies and institutions. Here we have the smuggling in of values that has often been highlighted in critiques of sociological functionalism.[7] It is this which gives the impression that functional analysis can lead directly to diagnoses of what is wrong, and to recommendations about what should be done to remedy or improve the situation; hence its fit with the engineering and medical models.

Many, though not all, qualitative researchers have rejected not only functionalism but also the kind of 'correctionalism' that often follows from it; which treats the task of social science as to identify and remedy social problems. Instead, they have adopted what Matza refers to as an *appreciative* stance (Matza 1969).[8] This requires a different starting point from correctionalism. We must begin not from societies or institutions as systems but from the activities of human beings. Moreover, those activities are viewed not in behaviourist terms, as automatic products of prior learning, but as artful productions, as exemplifying some form of practical rationality. Indeed, their rationality is a starting assumption: a key analytic task is to discover the rationality in what, from a conventional point of view, may be regarded as irrational. The most obvious example of this is attempting to understand the rationality of various kinds of social deviance; and this was, indeed, the context in which Matza developed his notion of appreciation. However, it can equally be applied to understanding the negative responses of some practitioners in the health and education systems to what the present government calls 'modernisation'. Rather than dismissing these practitioners as 'forces of conservatism' or as participants in a 'culture of mediocrity', the aim would be to try to understand why they react in the way that they do (see, for example, Woods et al. 1997).[9]

It is important to underline the sharp break with correctionalism here. That point of view starts from some implicit or explicit notion of how the situation studied ought to be, and whatever departs from this is treated as defective, as a causal product of ineffective socialisation and/or of ineffective integration of social institutions. By contrast, the aim in qualitative research, I suggest, is to try to understand people's behaviour as necessarily making sense within the context in which it occurs. Indeed, it is emphasised that *all* behaviour *only* makes sense in context. Matza comments: 'A basic difficulty with the correctional perspective is that it systematically interferes with the capacity to empathise and thus comprehend the subject of enquiry' (Matza 1969:15). There is no need to accept the reference to empathy here in order to take the general point. And I suggest that what follows from this point is an insistence on the need to separate the task of description and explanation from that of moral and political judgement.[10]

A fourth point is that qualitative researchers often question the degree of structural integration that actually exists in modern societies. Of course, even functionalists recognise that there is sometimes a lack of integration between the various parts of society at particular times, but (in effect) they treat this as abnormal in a 'medical' as well as a statistical sense. By contrast, qualitative researchers treat it as normal in both senses: they resist any evaluation, and retain an open mind about the *degree* of structural integration to be found. Indeed, some of them question the viability of the concept. Even aside from the question of which level of social organisation is to be taken as the focus, we can ask: by what criteria are we to judge when one part of society is working well with another? There is plenty of room for disagreement, and even for quite different evaluative frameworks; though this does not rule out the possibility of reasonable judgement or even substantial consensus. Moreover, this is a matter of practical, value-based – not scientific – judgement (see Foster et al. 2000).

Equally important, underlying the ideal of structural integration is a strong notion of social causality, whereby a fixed relationship can be expected to be regularly displayed between particular causes and particular effects. This is what we might call the regularity theory of causation: it requires that there are recurrent patterns of action occurring in society in which instances of type A cause instances of type B. Now, qualitative researchers have usually been very cautious about the notion of causality. To go back to Matza, he distinguishes between hard and soft determinism, arguing for the latter (Matza 1963); and later he seems to abandon even this weak version of causal determinism (Matza 1969). And, even where they have not rejected it, qualitative researchers have generally adopted a very different view of causality from the regularity model.

A recent example is provided by Howard Becker (Becker 1992 and 1998). He presents a natural history or narrative model of social causation, arguing that it is a *process* in which there is *contingency*; in the sense that it can lead down different paths to a variety of possible outcomes. Conversely, the same outcomes can sometimes be reached by very different routes. Becker points out how difficult it can often be to explain an outcome without understanding the path by which it was reached, using the example of someone's decision to have a sex change operation (Becker 1998:26–8). Many years ago Sally Macintyre provided a similar analysis of the contingencies involved in becoming what would today be called a 'lone parent' (Macintyre 1977).

From this point of view, rather than specific causes regularly generating the same outcomes, causal factors always operate on existing states of affairs and do so at different points in time, with the result that outcomes are not determinate and predictable, at least not in any strong way. There is a variety of routes that events might follow from any starting position, depending not just on the particular factors that operate but also on the sequencing and timing of their operation.[11]

It is not difficult to see that in a world characterised by this sort of causality the engineered society is a hopeless ideal. One can never start with a blank sheet, and the outcomes of action are rather unpredictable because of the effects of contingent factors (not just because of our inadequate knowledge). At best what is involved is a set of open systems, rather than a single closed one; and the elements of these systems are continually threatening to, and often actually do, go off in different directions. Furthermore, the more complex and long term the course of action that is planned, the less likely that the goal will be realised without a great deal of adjustment along the way, and perhaps even change in the goal itself. Furthermore, this adjustment and change may not be a matter of conscious decision, but rather a process of 'drift' of which the actor is largely unaware (Matza 1963).

So, this narrative or path model of causality does not support the notion of structural integration as likely to be the norm, even in a statistical sense. I can illustrate this by appealing, once again, to the sociology of deviance; the area of social enquiry where Becker's work is best known (Becker 1973). From a functionalist perspective, the role of punishment is to deter further deviance: it is a mechanism which re-establishes structural integration. However, sociologists of deviance have shown that punishment can amplify deviance; an idea that has been applied to the way in which teachers deal with pupils in the classroom (see, for example, Hargreaves et al. 1975). Labelling can amplify deviance in two ways. First, it changes the circumstances of the offender's life, for example by making it more likely that a pupil will be identified as the culprit in future incidents, irrespective of what role they actually play in these. Secondly, it changes his or her sense of self. Following punishment, being a 'troublemaker' often becomes much more central to the identity of the person than it was before. For both these reasons, the chances of engagement in further deviance may be increased, not reduced. Moreover, this process of deviance amplification often involves the creation of a subculture which valorises a particular form of deviance; and this subculture may draw others into deviance, thereby producing amplification at the collective not just the individual level. It is important to stress, however, that the argument is not that labelling and punishment *always* produce deviance amplification, only that they *can* do so. Much depends on the temporally structured complex of events within which they take place.

Another, perhaps even more fundamental, point is that for most qualitative researchers action is based on interpretation: it involves people *making* sense of the world. This throws potential doubt on the idea that prior socialisation can predetermine social coordination or integration. In other words, people do not simply respond in automatic ways to the situations they face. Rather, they try to make sense of those situations, and they act on the basis of what sense these situations make to them.

One of the most striking versions of this argument comes from ethnomethodology, which points out that the application of any value, or even of specific rules, to particular situations always involves judgement. Thus, Garfinkel rejects models of society that present people as 'judgemental dopes' who are simply programmed to act out roles (Garfinkel 1967b:67). And ethnomethodology sets its task as to explain how, despite the fact that prior socialisation cannot guarantee structural integration, social life is orderly in many respects; in the sense of being intelligible and even to some degree predictable.

By contrast, other interpretative sociologists have laid stress on the *variety* of ways in which people make sense of the same situation, suggesting that, because of this, some level of disorder and even conflict is inevitable. Diverse perspectives are a feature of how human social life *is*: it can never be rendered machine-like or organism-like in any strong sense, not even under totalitarian regimes. Under such regimes, people distance themselves from, and develop secondary adjustments to, commands and rules; even when they do not engage in direct resistance.[12]

In short, qualitative researchers typically view conformity to social structural requirements as less widespread than mechanical or organismic metaphors assume. Moreover, where it *does* occur, they treat it as generated by diverse motivations, and/or as a product of local *work* (rather than as emerging automatically or naturally from the operation of the whole society or institution). These points are summarised in Figure 4.1.

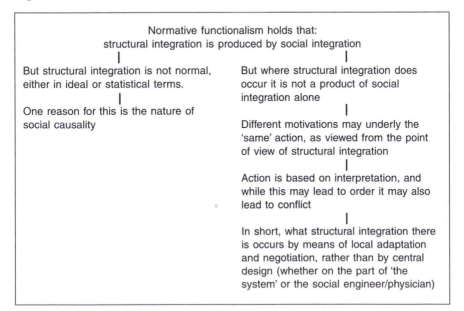

Figure 4.1 Qualitative doubts about normative functionalism

In my view, these ideas coming out of qualitative research about the nature of social life, are sound, and they carry important implications for the role of all social enquiry in relation to policymaking and practice. They count against any idea that social researchers can function in the way that technicians or medical personnel are often believed to do: identifying problems and prescribing remedies for them on the basis of research evidence; thereby simultaneously demonstrating their own 'value for money'.

Alternatives to the engineering or medical model

The engineering model has traditionally been contrasted with the enlightenment model. The latter sees research as rarely having immediate and determinate effects on practice, for example by providing solutions to specific problems. Rather, it has an impact by shaping how practitioners view the world, and thereby how they conceptualise problems. Indeed, it may even show that there are problems of which practitioners are unaware; or demonstrate that what was thought to be a problem is not one, or is not of the kind assumed. Thus, Weiss argues that: 'Social science provides an angle of vision, a focus for looking at the world. It is a source of illumination on the rich details and tangled interrelations in that world. Whatever else it may or may not do, it serves a global function of enlightenment' (Weiss 1977:17). Moreover, she and others have shown that empirically this is closer to the way in which social research has actually influenced policymakers: there is little evidence of it operating in the way that the engineering model suggests (Weiss 1980). And advocates of the enlightenment model have usually argued on this basis that the engineering model involves unrealistic or inappropriate expectations.

However, as I indicated in Chapter 2, the notion of enlightenment is open to diverse interpretations, and some of them are not as different from the engineering model as they at first appear. Indeed, there is a problem with the very term 'enlightenment'. In particular, it could be taken to imply that research supplies the light which enables practitioners to do their work, suggesting that without it they would be, and previously have been, in the dark. Many researchers may be tempted to accept this view, especially in relation to policymakers: it is not uncommon for researchers to see policymakers as prejudiced, as relying on conservative assumptions, as incompetent, etc.[13] But this deficit model is misleading. It is not far from the dope theory of human beings that I mentioned earlier. It denies the practical rationality of actors. And it ascribes a level of superiority to research knowledge that would be difficult to defend.

What this problem with the enlightenment model points to is that there can be variation in the nature of the enlightenment that research is taken to provide, and also differences in view about whether it is the *only* source of illumination. One aspect of this concerns variation in the comprehensiveness of what is supplied: whether research provides specific items of knowledge or a whole worldview. Moreover, this dimension cross-cuts the distinction between engineering and enlightenment models. Figure 4.2 outlines this.

I will not spend much time discussing the engineering model row of this diagram. At one extreme, we have the researcher setting out to answer specific questions from some client. An obvious example would be a great deal of work in opinion polling and market research. At the other extreme is the kind of approach represented by Lewin's action research, where scientific method is taken as a model for rational action of other kinds (see Lewin 1948:ch. 13 and Marrow 1969).[14] However, what is involved here is, at most, a difference of degree. Thus, the researcher as moderniser usually also provides specific items of knowledge along with a new way of thinking. Conversely, there is a sense in which even the supply of specific information or techniques always carries with it some perspective on the world, and an associated mode of operation; so that to one degree or another it remakes or reconfigures the world in which it is used. This is the import of some recent work in the sociology of technology (Woolgar 2000).

Turning to the distinction between the two versions of the

	Supplying specific items or bodies of knowledge, or specific techniques	Supplying a whole theoretical framework, worldview, and/or mode of operation
Engineering model	The researcher as aide, setting out to produce specific information that meets the requirements of policymakers and other practitioners	The researcher as moderniser, supplying a 'scientific way of thinking' to replace the folk or craft methods that have previously been employed
Enlightenment model	The researcher as 'specific intellectual' supplying facts and/or arguments that can be used to challenge the status quo.	The researcher as public intellectual, providing a perspective that offers a new theoretical under-standing of society to replace the ideological view built into what currently passes for common sense

Figure 4.2 A dimension cross-cutting the contrast between engineering and strong enlightenment models

enlightenment model included in Figure 4.2, this needs more elaboration, though once again we are probably dealing with a matter of degree. Here I have made use of terminology which is to be found in some recent discussions of the role of the intellectual: the distinction between the public, grand or universal intellectual, on the one hand, and the specific intellectual, on the other (see Jennings 1997). This relates to a difference in what is supplied; though it also partly concerns variation in the power or authority of the researcher as against practitioners, including political activists.

So, in the bottom right-hand cell of Figure 4.2, we have the researcher as public intellectual.[15] This relies on what I have referred to elsewhere as the strong enlightenment model (see Chapter 2). The most influential examples of this approach are Marxism and what has come to be called the 'critical' tradition – based in part on critical theory, but also informed by feminism and anti-racism.[16] In this model, a distinctive perspective on the world is supplied by the researcher, designed to replace or at least transform what is viewed as commonsense ideology.

Now, what I want to point out is that this strong enlightenment position shares the functionalism which I identified as underpinning the engineering model. It has been cogently argued by Cohen, and others, that Marxism relies on a functionalist image of society (see Cohen 1978; see also Hargreaves 1982 and Hickox 1982). While there are differences among Marxists in their societal imagery, most retain some notion of capitalist society as a system composed of parts that serve the whole. And many critical researchers hold a similar view of society (see Harvey 1990). Thus, some colleagues and I have shown that much critical research in the field of educational inequalities relies on social reproduction theory. This is derived from Marxism, and is clearly functionalist in character. It *assumes* that schooling, like other parts of the system, functions in such a way as to reproduce the existing, unequal social order (Foster et al. 1996: 165–70). Of course, Marxists and critical researchers differ from non-Marxist functionalists in their *evaluation* of the functioning of extant society, and about the potential (if not always about the prospects) for change to a different type of system. But this takes place within an overall commitment to functionalism, at least in the minimal sense of that term I outlined earlier.

What I am suggesting, then, is that there is an important correspondence in image of social life between the engineering model and at least one version of the enlightenment model. Moreover, this lays the basis for some similarity in their conceptions of the role of social research in society. One of the models associated with Marxism is the party intellectual; and, in some key respects, there is a close parallel between this role and that of government adviser, which is associated with the engineering model. Indeed, if and when the party served by the intellectual comes to power even the superficial differences may disappear. For both these roles, the task is to produce knowledge that will promote particular practical purposes: in other words, to assist with achieving politically defined goals. Of course, by no means all Marxists have been party intellectuals. But even in the case of 'fellow-travelling' intellectuals who maintain autonomy from political groupings, as exemplified by Jean-Paul Sartre for much of his life, there is usually close identification with the cause. And, very often, given the absence of any commitment to value neutrality, what is written and said is shaped by assumptions about the interests of that cause.[17]

Of course, *some* critical researchers reject *any* kind of 'constructive' role in relation to 'power', whether the power of a government or of an opposition party. For them, the task of research is to criticise, and thereby to destabilise, the status quo; irrespective of the shape or shade of the current socio-political regime. Alongside this, and sometimes under the influence of postmodernism, in recent times many critical researchers have renounced any claim to produce a grand theory or worldview that can provide a basis for change to a new type of society. Meta-narratives are frequently rejected as themselves oppressive – not least as legitimating oppression by public intellectuals, including those on the Left.[18] In terms of Figure 4.2, what I have just described is a move from the bottom right-hand to the bottom left-hand cell: to the researcher as specific intellectual.

There is a variety of versions of the specific intellectual.[19] Some of these seem, at times, to reject the functionalist model of society; as, for example, in the case of Foucault's Nietzschean conception of power, or of Lyotard's appropriation of the Wittgensteinian idea of language games. However, on my reading, neither of these authors abandons the reproduction model completely; it remains in the background and continues to guide their thinking. Indeed, sometimes post-structuralist and postmodernist thought seems to take the reproduction model to the ultimate extreme, in which even resistance is portrayed as necessarily a product of the system and as serving to maintain it (Bogard 1990).

As with the French sources of the idea of the specific intellectual, its Anglo-American reception has also tended to involve retention of the reproduction model.[20] An example is to be found in the work of Stephen Ball. In an article entitled 'Intellectuals or technicians?', which effectively contrasts the engineering and enlightenment models, he outlines what he takes to be the proper function of the educational researcher. While he criticises the reproduction model at one point (Ball 1995:257–8), he does not abandon it. Indeed, he presents an account of the way policy or engineering science functions which seems to accept that, along with associated institutional processes, it can turn society into a machine.[21] He argues that the study of education operates as:

> a disciplinary technology, part of the exercise of disciplinary power. Management, effectiveness and appraisal, for example, ... work together to locate individuals in space, in a hierarchical and efficiently visible organ-

isation. In and through our research the school and the teacher are captured within a perfect diagram of power; and the classroom is increasingly one of those 'small theatres', in which 'each actor is alone, perfectly individualized and constantly visible' (Foucault, 1979, p.200). It is thus that *governmentality* is achieved through the minute mechanisms of everyday life and the application of 'progressive' and efficient technical solutions to designated problems (Foucault, 1979, p.20). (Ball 1995:262–3)

The implication seems to be that educational research, at least of a certain kind, participates in the exercise of massive control over the fine detail of people's lives. The image is of their being trained to behave in ways that predictably serve the dominant requirements. Here, disciplinary technologies and ideological subjection play much the same explanatory role as prior socialisation did in normative functionalism; and, once again, society is portrayed as having a very high level of structural integration.[22]

Ball contrasts the proper role of the researcher with that of technician, which is associated with policy science. The researcher should be concerned with the production of theory, whose function, Ball claims, is 'destructive, disruptive and violent'; it offers 'a language for challenge, and modes of thought other than those articulated for us by dominant others' (ibid.:266). Thus, it allows us to work: ' "on and against" prevailing practices of ideological subjection' (ibid.:267). In other words, the researcher is to be a 'semiotic guerrilla' (ibid.:268).

In effect, here the concept of functionality is retained from the engineering model, but its value is inverted. Where, under the engineering model, the task of the researcher was to facilitate the smooth running of the social machine, for Ball it is to throw spanners in the works. Yet the underlying model of society is much the same. And I think this is true of many accounts of the role of the specific intellectual.

So, I am claiming that both versions of the enlightenment model included in Figure 4.2, linked to the grand and specific models of the intellectual respectively, are at odds with the image of social life that I suggested comes out of much qualitative research. Given this, the latter must imply a different model of how research can relate to practice. This is what I referred to in Chapter 2 as the moderate enlightenment model. However, in some ways, this terminology may be misleading because it suggests that the difference from strong enlightenment is only a matter of degree; whereas there is an important substantive difference in social imagery involved. In order to emphasise this here, I will give this fifth model a new title: the cognitive resources model (see Figure 4.3).

The cognitive resources model assumes a much weaker and less determinate relationship between the products of research and policymaking or practice than the other four models. It insists that there are no practical implications *built into* the descriptions, explanations, and theories produced by research. Such implications can only be derived by

	Supplying specific items or bodies of knowledge, or specific techniques	Supplying a whole theoretical framework, worldview, and/or mode of operation
Engineering model	The researcher as aide, setting out to produce specific information that meets the requirements of policymakers and other practitioners	The researcher as moderniser, supplying a 'scientific way of thinking' to replace the folk or craft methods that have previously been employed
Enlightenment model	The researcher as 'specific intellectual' supplying facts and/or arguments that can be used to criticise the status quo	The researcher as public intellectual, providing a perspective that offers a new theoretical under-standing of society to replace the ideological view built into what currently passes as common sense.
Cognitive resources model	The researcher as contributor to bodies of knowledge which may be used as a resource by practitioners, but only as and when they judge appropriate, and with consequences that are far from completely pre-dictable	

Figure 4.3 The engineering, strong enlightenment, and cognitive resources models

adding value premises. Moreover, it is assumed by this model that research will not be the only source of cognitive resources on which practitioners rely. The idea is rejected that research can provide a replacement for, or transformation of, knowledge deriving from practical experience; an idea which is shared in common by those versions of the engineering and enlightenment models in the right-hand column of Figure 4.3. At most, the knowledge produced by research can only provide a corrective; and practitioners' judgements concerning whether to change their assumptions about the world on the basis of research findings are necessarily complex, and are not solely a matter of the validity of those assumptions; at least, not as judged in research terms. All of this implies that the effects of research on policymaking or practice will not be predictable or, usually, very dramatic.[23]

Conclusion

In this chapter I have argued that built into the engineering and medical models – which underpin current pressure for educational research to be more directly useful to policymakers and practitioners – is a kind of functionalism. This treats national societies or social institutions as functioning wholes, and their parts are analysed in terms of how well they contribute to the operation of the whole. I suggested that this image of social life is at odds with the ideas associated with much qualitative research. Qualitative researchers do not usually focus primarily at the national level. Instead their work emphasises other levels and forms of social organisation. They question the regularity conception of causality that seems to underlie functionalism; with its idea that society is characterised by a high degree of structural integration generated by a high level of social integration. Indeed, when not denying the existence of *any* kind of causality in the social world, qualitative researchers adopt a rather different conception of it; for example one which stresses the way in which causal factors operate at different points in time, generating contingent courses of events, which can lead to a variety of outcomes. Even more fundamentally, they emphasise the role of interpretation in social interaction, and in some cases this is seen as leading to a plurality of perspectives and to conflict. So, structural integration is not regarded as automatic, or even as normal in a statistical sense; and when it does occur it is not produced simply by social integration, but by processes of adaptation and negotiation, in other words by local work on the part of particular social actors.

In the second half of the chapter I argued that the usual contrast between the engineering and enlightenment models is more complicated than it is usually taken to be. I suggested, initially, that we can identify two versions of each of these models, varying according to whether what is supplied is specific information or a comprehensive theory or worldview. Furthermore, I argued that the two forms of the enlightenment model that this picks out both share the functionalism of the engineering model. In response to this, I outlined a fifth model, one which matches the assumptions that I identified as associated with qualitative research, assumptions which I believe to be sound. I referred to this as the cognitive resources model, suggesting that it not only captures the way in which social research currently influences policymaking and practice, but also implies that no major transformation of this relationship is likely to be possible. In other words, my argument is that researchers cannot be technicians, legislators or revolutionaries. And I suggest that the sooner this is recognised the better it will be for all concerned.

Notes

1. It is important to note, here, that it is not just qualitative research that does not provide statistically generalisable findings; neither does experimental research.
2. In an endnote Oakley recognises that this is only true where the primary concern is with 'effectiveness', but her whole book privileges that primary concern.
3. It is perhaps worth quoting from Charlton's discussion: 'Comte is a scientist in a hurry, and his desire for quick results leads him to accept easy results. In the last resort, he prefers false laws to no laws at all' (Charlton 1959:42). David Blunkett and other advocates of evidence-based practice seem likely to be subject to the same temptation.
4. Bulmer notes how the models of engineer and doctor operate more or less as substitutes within the literature on the uses of social research (Bulmer 1982:43). And, indeed, the medical model was also drawn on by Comte: in places he sees the sociologist as the doctor of society, diagnosing social ills and giving prescriptions, see Charlton (1959:47).
5. On conflict theory, see for example Bailey (1969) and Cohen (1974). On negotiated order theory, see Strauss (1978). On social arena or social world theory, see Clarke (1991). The key proponent of dramaturgy was, of course, Goffman (see Goffman 1959 and 1975). On community as an ecology of games, see Long (1958). Evans-Pritchard moves in the direction of seeing social life as narrative history, but others have taken this further. See, for example, Shotter and Gergen (1989).
6. The distinction between structural and social integration is a modification of that between system and social integration found in Lockwood (1964). This distinction, though not the terminology, comes from Marxism. For an elaboration, in the context of 'analytical dualism', see Archer (1996).
7. For various criticisms of normative functionalism, see Demerath and Peterson (1967). The role of values in functionalist analyses was recognised by some of its proponents, see Fallding (1963).
8. Interestingly, Matza argues that some functionalism also has an appreciative element: those accounts which show the functionality of what is denounced from a conventional, moralistic perspective – such as organised crime and prostitution (see Matza 1969:31–7).
9. The phrases 'forces of conservatism' and a 'culture of mediocrity' were used by the Prime Minister of Great Britain, Tony Blair, in speeches in the late 1990s.
10. This is an area where, in my view, some recent qualitative research has departed from a basic and important principle (see Hammersley 1998b and 2000c:ch. 5).
11. This view of causation is not unique to qualitative researchers. A version of it was put forward by Stephen Jay Gould in his account of evolution (see Gould 1989). Furthermore, it would be accepted by many quantitative researchers. However, as Becker points out, currently available quantitative techniques for causal analysis cannot take this temporal character of causation into account; though there are some sociologists seeking to develop alternative models that will do so (see, for instance, Abbott 1992 and 1998).

12. Goffman's work on total institutions is relevant here (see Goffman 1961:60–5 and *passim*).
13. There are elements of this, for example, in Finch's discussion of the relationship between qualitative research and social and educational policy (Finch 1986).
14. I have suggested that something similar to this second view informs some later versions of action research in the field of education, albeit drawing on a very different notion of research rationality (see Hammersley 1993).
15. For recent discussions of the perils of the public intellectual in the second half of the twentieth century, and responses to them, see Goodson (1999), Fuller (1999) and Smyth and Hattam (2000).
16. By no means all critical researchers adhere to the strong enlightenment model, as we shall see.
17. See Sartre (1949), Judt (1992) and Weightman (1993). See also Watson's discussion of English intellectuals' responses to knowledge about Soviet work camps (Watson 1973).
18. It is important to remember that post-structuralism and postmodernism in France were in large part reactions against Marxism, usually from the ultra Left (see Dews 1986).
19. See, for example, Foucault and Deleuze (1972) and Kristeva (1977). On this aspect of Foucault's work, see Jennings (1997). On Lyotard's view of the role of the intellectual, see Readings (1991).
20. Often it seems to be used as a new language in which to present that theory, one whose obscurity serves as a way of not facing up to the problems associated with Marxism. A curious feature of the Anglo-American reception of post-structuralism and postmodernism is its tendency to neglect French critiques (many of which have been translated, for example Ferry and Renaut 1990 and 1997) and even the critical Anglo-American secondary literature (see, for instance, Dews 1987); and to ignore the quite different intellectual trends that have prevailed in France for the past 30 years (see Lilla 1994).
21. On the notion of policy science, see Fay (1975). This conforms closely to the engineering model.
22. In one place Foucault characterises power as 'a machine in which everyone is caught up' (Foucault 1980:156). This is quoted by Merquior (1985:114), who also discusses the spurious distinction drawn by Foucault and his defenders between a disciplinary and a disciplined society. Of course, Foucault recognises that power not only constrains but also enables, and that it generates resistance; but there is little coherence or clarity in his account of the operation of power (Merquior 1985:ch. 8). Brenner reinforces this, arguing that Foucault's work displays a form of functionalism. He quotes Elster to the effect that there is a tendency 'to see every minute detail of social action as part of a vast design for oppression' (Elster 1982:454–5, quoted in Brenner 1994:700). Curiously, Ball has shown elsewhere that policies do *not* have determinate effects, that they are reinterpreted and negotiated over the course of their implementation (Bowe et al. 1992; Ball 1994). And this account is compatible with the assumptions I have suggested are implicit in qualitative research; whereas his discussion of the role of policy science in disciplining society is not.
23. It is a peculiar irony of intellectual history that the most devastating critique of the engineering and strong enlightenment models was written by an author who is often blamed for inspiring the new public management that currently threatens social research (see, for example, Ball 1997:259). In *The Counter-Revolution of Science: studies in the abuse of reason*, Friedrich Hayek criticises

the kind of positivism put forward by Comte, describing it as 'the religion of the engineers' (Hayek 1952). He argues that it misunderstands both the nature of social science and the character of the social world. Furthermore, the image of society Hayek adopts is not far from the one I have suggested is embodied in much qualitative research. He emphasises the role of subjective factors and the sense in which social order emerges out of the activities of individuals. At one point, he comments that the 'presumptuous aspiration that "reason" should direct its own growth' is a direct outcome of 'a misunderstood or misapplied rationalism which fails to recognize the extent to which individual reason is a product of inter-individual relationships' (ibid.:90–1). And he is very resistant to mechanical and organismic metaphors in thinking about society. Of course, for him the market is the central social institution, and he attributes to it a unique capacity to generate innovation and maintain freedom that few qualitative researchers would accept; and rightly so. Nevertheless his ideas deserve attention rather than instant dismissal. Interestingly, one writer has described Hayek's thought as bordering on postmodernism, in the sense that he questions 'both the Cartesian individualism commonly exhibited in neoclassical economics and the holistic social theory characteristic of traditional Marxism' (Burczak 1994:37).

Chapter 5

Diversity or Control in Educational Research?

One way of formulating the issues raised by current attempts to reform educational research in England and Wales is in terms of a contrast between the principles of control and diversity.[1] The proposed reforms are designed to exercise central, and external, control over educational research in order to remedy its faults; many of which are believed to result from a lack of accountability. By contrast, some critics of the reforms have argued that what is involved is an attack on diversity of approach in educational research; and they see diversity as a positive not a negative feature (see, for example, Thomas 1998; Lomax 1999 and 2000; Hodkinson and Garratt 2000; Hodkinson 2001).

In fact, for many researchers today, the very formulation of the dispute as one between exercising control and valuing diversity may well indicate, unequivocally, which side we should be on. After all, who could be against diversity, and who would be in favour of control? Yet this is misleading. The contrast between diversity and control does not match that between political virtue and vice; nor is it an opposition between just two, mutually incompatible, perspectives.

It is not unreasonable, in principle, to argue that in a situation of scarce resources expenditure should be coordinated so as to maximise the benefit. Similarly, it is not obviously false to claim that – because public funds are being spent on research, and because research can have both positive and negative consequences for public welfare – social and educational research ought to be subjected to democratic control. There is nothing unacceptable about the principles appealed to here; what is at issue is whether they can, and should, be applied to this case.

Equally important, the arguments on the other side – against central control of research, and/or for diversity in methodological approach – can vary considerably in character. One argument is that diversity should be celebrated as part of a more general valorisation of 'difference'. Indeed, some would treat this as characteristic of a properly ethical attitude towards the world, and/or as following from what they see as the function of research in amplifying the voices of the marginalised.[2] Alternatively, it can be argued that toleration of diversity is essential if intellectual progress is to be facilitated: the seeds of new ideas must be allowed to grow, and it is through discussion of competing ideas that true and false ideas are identified.[3] A third possibility is that opposition to central control of research may rely on the arguments of economic neo-liberalism, perhaps even leading to the recommendation that research be left to the freedom of the market.[4]

So, the contrast between control and diversity is not a straightforward matter. Moreover, disputes about this issue border on what might be called the political philosophy of enquiry. In this chapter I want to present a line of argument against the exercise of central control over educational research which is close to the second of the three positions outlined in the previous paragraph. In doing so, I will draw on a classic source which makes an explicit appeal to political philosophy. Moreover, this arose initially out of a context where, as at the present time, attempts were being made by government to 'organise' research; though, then, the target was the work of natural scientists. I am referring to an article entitled 'The republic of science', written by the chemist and philosopher Michael Polanyi (Polanyi 1962). In this he puts forward a particular model of the operation of scientific communities, one which suggests that external or central control can only damage the progress of scientific knowledge. At the same time, as we shall see, his model does not imply that academic autonomy requires us to tolerate, even less to celebrate, all diversity in approach to research. Instead, it raises more specific questions: control *by whom*; and on what *grounds*?

Polanyi on the nature of the scientific community

As the word 'republic' in the title of Polanyi's article indicates, he draws an analogy between the social organisation of scientific communities and the political organisation of states.[5] It is not clear which of the many meanings of 'republic' he is drawing on here; though the main implication seems to be that the scientific community must be self-governing. It is likely that he associates the idea of a republic with the emergence of commercial society and liberal politics in the seventeenth century, perhaps as a parallel to 'the republic of letters'.[6] This may explain why another analogy plays an even more important role in his argument: that between the way scientific communities operate and the manner in which economic markets work.

Polanyi's article arose out of his opposition to early attempts to establish central coordination of natural science in Britain in the late 1940s and early 1950s. These attempts were influenced by the ideas of an important group of natural scientists in the inter-war period, led by J. D. Bernal. This group were impressed by what they took to be the successful model offered by the Soviet Union of gearing science to social ends. In his book, *The Social Function of Science*, Bernal pointed to one of the key lessons of the first half of the twentieth century: that while science could bring great benefits, it could also be used for evil purposes. In addition, he argued that the haphazard and uneven way in which science had developed in the West, under the influence of the profit motive and the capitalist state, had resulted in the neglect of many areas of research and application which would be of immediate value to human welfare – in favour of 'the more profitable physical and chemical sciences' (Bernal 1939:xiv). Bernal also pointed out how, as the scale of scientific work had grown, the organisation and administration required to make it efficient had not developed at the same pace: so that, in his view, a concern with the freedom of individual scientists had to be combined with a concern for increased efficiency (Bernal 1939:xiii). His conclusion from all this was that natural science needed to be brought under collective, democratic, state control. However, he did not see this as imposing constraints on scientists, because he believed that there is a necessary affinity between science and progressive social change.[7] He writes:

> For those who have once seen it, the frustration of science is a very bitter thing. It shows itself as disease, enforced stupidity, misery, thankless toil, and premature death for the great majority, and an anxious, grasping, and futile life for the remainder. Science can change all this, but only science working with those social forces which understand its functions and which march to the same ends. (Bernal 1939:xv)

Pressure for more central control over natural science was also stimulated in the late 1940s and early 1950s by the experience of the war economy in Britain, by the role of scientists in devising new military technologies, such as radar, and also by their work in developing operational research to facilitate military planning. Another factor was the growing amount of public funds being spent on research in the natural sciences, and the increasing costs of some kinds of research, especially in physics.

However, the attempts to coordinate natural science in the early 1950s were not successful; perhaps because of the emergence of the Cold War, and the fact that central control of science came to be associated with totalitarianism (following the Lysenko Affair).[8] In part, this outcome may also have been a result of the efforts of another group of scientists, opposed to the first group, who labelled themselves the Society for Freedom in Science. Polanyi was a member of this group (see McGucken 1978). He argued that the Soviet model was not one that should be followed: that it involved a distortion of science, and reflected a more general suppression of individual liberty (see Polanyi 1940, 1946 and 1951; Baker 1978).

Now it is important to note that Polanyi did not deny the practical contributions that scientists can make to national and commercial goals when employed to do so. But he *did* deny that such work could replace, or was a model for, basic science. He argued that this work consisted of the *application* of scientific ideas, most notably in the development of technologies. In other words, for Polanyi, applied science and technology are distinct from basic science, *and are parasitic upon it*. And Polanyi argued that while external or central control may be appropriate in the development of technology, it is not appropriate in basic science.[9]

He argues that, in science, decisions about what to research and how to research it must be made by individual researchers, rather than being laid down by any external agency or even by some central board of scientists. Furthermore, he insists that the outcome of such decisions is not chaotic, but rather represents a spontaneous form of social organisation. He contends that while scientists work independently 'freely making their own choice of problems and pursuing them in light of their own personal judgement [they] are in fact cooperating as members of a closely knit organisation'. This coordination takes place through what he calls 'adjustment of the efforts of each to the hitherto achieved results of the others' (Polanyi 1962:54).

This is where the parallel with the market arises, since markets also involve mutual coordination of individual initiatives. Polanyi's argument here is analogous to Friedrich Hayek's defence of the market against central economic planning (see, for example, Hayek 1978:ch. 14). Hayek argues that no one has all the information that would be necessary to know how production resources should be allocated in order best to satisfy consumer needs. The great strength of the market, he claims, is that it is a self-organising system which, because decision-making is locally distributed, allocates resources in such a way as to maximise collective satisfaction.

In much the same way, Polanyi argues that no single scientist, even less any non-scientist, has the overall knowledge necessary to determine satisfactorily general priorities about what should be investigated, when, and how. By contrast, the aggregate effect of individual scientists making decisions about these matters for themselves, affected as it is by what their colleagues are doing in the same and adjoining areas, serves to drive science forward in the most productive manner possible. Polanyi writes: 'Such self-coordination of independent initiatives leads to a joint result which is unpremeditated by any of those who bring it about. Their coordination is guided as by "an invisible hand" towards the joint discovery of a hidden system of things' (Polanyi 1962:55).[10]

To illustrate his argument, Polanyi uses another analogy: that of trying to do a jigsaw puzzle which has a very large number of pieces. The most efficient way of pursuing this task is to divide the pieces among many individuals, so that every person has a relatively small number. They will then be able to find the appropriate place for each of their pieces as and when this arises. By contrast, any kind of central coordination, for example requiring individuals to work on particular parts of the jigsaw, will be less efficient – and, indeed, may make completion of the jigsaw impossible.

Polanyi argues that the kind of autonomous and spontaneous organisation he outlines was what had facilitated the unprecedented advancement of science in the nineteenth and twentieth centuries. He comments: 'though it is easy to find flaws in their operation, [these principles] remain the only [ones] by which this vast domain of collective creativity can be effectively promoted and coordinated' (Polanyi 1962:61).

It is necessary to be clear about the nature of Polanyi's analogy between science and the market. What he proposes is not an application of the market model to science. He argues that the market is only one form of spontaneous social organisation by mutual adjustment, and that the scientific community is another (Polanyi 1962:71). In fact, he suggests that the research model may be more appropriate than the market model for organising public services (Polanyi 1962:65). Certainly, despite his opposition to communism, he would have had little sympathy with the suggestion that research should be funded entirely via the market (see Polanyi 1940:14–15).

A closely related element of Polanyi's position is that, in his words: 'Any attempt at guiding scientific research towards a purpose other than its own [which he takes to be the production of knowledge for its own sake] is an attempt to deflect it from the advancement of science'. He comments: 'You can kill or mutilate the advance of science, you cannot shape it. For it can advance only by essentially unpredictable steps, pursuing problems of its own, and the practical benefits of these advances will be incidental and hence doubly unpredictable' (Polanyi 1962:62). Thus, Polanyi argued against both central and external control of science, and in favour of the autonomy of individual scientists, who are to exercise local control on the basis of internal criteria to do with likely validity, promise of future discoveries, etc.

The implications of Polanyi's model for the organisation of educational research

It seems to me that Polanyi's model captures something important about how research communities work.[11] Attempts to exert central control over research run into the same fundamental obstacles as Eastern European efforts to operate command economies did in the middle decades of the twentieth century. These foundered on the problem that inadequate knowledge inevitably governed the attempts to specify production targets from the centre, and that local intelligence came to be exercised solely in meeting, or (often) simply in *appearing* to meet, central commands (see Nove 1969). The result was not just inefficiency, but frequently a failure to serve basic needs. And the parallels between this form of economic organisation and current attempts in the West to manage the public sector in terms of 'performance indicators', 'targets', 'external audit', etc, ought to be underlined.

Of course, even if Polanyi's account of what is required for natural science to flourish is accepted, it may be denied that this model applies to educational research. There are three arguments that could be used to support this denial. First, Polanyi was writing about the natural rather than the social sciences. Secondly, his concern was with basic rather than with applied work, and educational research falls into the latter category. Thirdly, the educational research community does not currently operate in a sound manner, and external intervention is necessary to correct this.

The first issue can be dealt with relatively quickly. It is not clear that even a sharp distinction between the character of natural and social science would count against the applicability of Polanyi's model to the latter. Even if we see the fundamental methodological approach of social research as quite different from that of natural science, for example as interpretative or hermeneutic in character, we may still regard the relatively autonomous operation of academic communities as central to the production of knowledge about the social world. The only exception would be a view of social and/or educational research as essentially applied or practical in character; and there are, of course, those who distinguish educational research from social science precisely on the grounds that it is immediately committed to the improvement of education (see, for example, Bassey 1995 and Pring 2000).[12] Here, though, the first argument against the relevance of Polanyi's model merges into the second.

In assessing the second argument, much depends on what we mean by 'applied' or 'practice-oriented' enquiry, and about its relationship to basic research. As I have already indicated, Polanyi saw basic science as primary, and the application of its results as technology. Such a view is rather unfashionable today. The tendency is towards blurring or denying the distinction between basic and applied research, or reformulating them as competing versions of science. An influential recent example of the latter is the distinction between Mode 1 and Mode 2 research put forward by Michael Gibbons and his colleagues in their book *The New Production of Knowledge* (Gibbons et al. 1994).

For these authors, Mode 1 research is the traditional academic model, more or less as Polanyi represents it. By contrast, Mode 2 research has the following characteristics:

1 It is focused on solving problems arising in particular practical contexts. The aim is to generate a solution or a product, rather than simply to contribute to a body of knowledge.
2 It takes place via team work, teams being 'non-hierarchical' and 'essentially transient'.
3 It is transdisciplinary in orientation. The research teams are interdisciplinary; and, while disciplinary knowledge is drawn on, what is most important is the knowledge, understanding and techniques accumulated through experience in doing Mode 2 research.

4 Accountability in Mode 2 research is practical in character, involving users as well as researchers. And market considerations can be crucial: its products are likely to be judged at least in part by whether they are 'competitive' and 'cost effective'.

In many respects this notion of Mode 2 work amounts to a relaunch of applied research, increasing its status and denying that it is dependent on basic research. It is presented as a competing form of research organisation that is more in tune with emerging social conditions than Mode 1.

In my view, these authors are right that there is a kind of enquiry which is different in character from basic scientific work, and that is not simply an adjunct to it. I will refer to this as 'practical research' (see Chapter 6). However, they are wrong to present this form of enquiry as superior to Mode 1; especially since they do not provide any explicit argument for its superiority. Instead, they advocate it implicitly, on the grounds that it is a growing tendency across many fields of research, and that it fits wider social trends towards a 'knowledge economy' (see also Gibbons 2000). This is what is sometimes referred to as a historicist justification: a form of argument which implies that the highest, perhaps sole, value is adaptation to changing historical circumstances. And it is not difficult to identify the weaknesses, and dangers, of this form of argument: it can be used to justify whatever mode of thinking or form of social organisation comes to prevail.[13]

Historicism also seems to be a frequent element of arguments for the central coordination of educational research. It is to be found, for example, in the National Educational Research Forum's (NERF) consultation paper designed to set up a national strategy for educational research in England and Wales. Here, changes in the nature of the economy are said to have created new challenges for the education system, and it is the task of 'research and development' to assist educational policymakers and practitioners in meeting these challenges (NERF 2000). Here, again, what are lacking are specific arguments in favour of what is recommended. Even aside from the factual accuracy of the implicit sociological analysis, we must ask: why should historical trends be treated as inevitable, or current social demands be accepted as legitimate?

Moreover, unlike Gibbons et al., the authors of this consultation paper fail to draw a clear distinction between scientific research, on the one hand, and practical research, on the other; being preoccupied with what they refer to as educational 'research and development'. For me, the crucial difference between these two kinds of research is their audience, and the different weight and operationalisations they give to validity and relevance as criteria in assessing research findings. What is essential to scientific research is that the results of any individual study are judged by fellow researchers before being accepted as sound knowledge. As a result, the first audience for research reports must be academic colleagues: only what are taken by them to be well-established findings from such enquiry should be communicated outside the research community via research reviews (on which, see Chapter 7). Moreover, from this perspective, collective assessment by researchers must involve 'organised scepticism' (Merton 1973:chs12 and 13), by which I mean a tendency to err on the side of rejecting what is true rather than of accepting as true what is in fact false. One implication of organised scepticism is that scientific research will often be unable to provide specific kinds of information that policymakers and practitioners desire, at least at the time when they need it. By contrast, providing such information (where this is accessible) *is* the main task of practical research; but this necessarily means that the validity of the findings cannot be subjected to the same kind or level of assessment as in scientific work.

It is important to emphasise that I regard practical and scientific research as of equal value – and indeed as complementary – *but also as non-substitutable*. Neither can perform the task of the other effectively. Thus, I can see no cogent reason for assuming that *all* educational research should be practical in character; which seems to be the implication of the NERF consultation paper, and of current government policy towards educational research in England and Wales. Why should educational institutions be out of bounds for scientific enquiry? Indeed, the products of such enquiry should form one important resource on which practical educational research can draw.

Now, of course, it could be argued that recent government efforts to reform educational research are designed not to abolish scientific research on educational processes and institutions, but to stimulate more and higher quality *practical* research. This is a laudable aim.[14] And even if it is accepted that the Polanyi model is appropriate for scientific educational research, its appropriateness could be denied in the case of practical educational research. After all, this must be closely geared to the requirements of policymakers and practitioners, and so they should play a key role in setting the agenda.

I think this is true, but with a couple of qualifications. First, some recognition is required of the expertise involved in doing practical research; and expertise implies considerable autonomy of judgement on the part of researchers, notably over how to investigate what has been identified as a priority and over what can and cannot be investigated with reasonable chance of success. The second qualification is that the notion of education as a profession (or a collection of professions) implies substantial local autonomy, rather than central government control. Thus, it seems to me that while practical educational research should be under external control (in terms of the setting of the research agenda), it should not be under *central* control: it should serve individual educational practitioners, organisations and interest groups as well as policymakers, with different studies addressed to different audiences. In this context, the current attempt to exert central control over educational research must be seen as part of the larger project, pursued by governments in Britain since at least the early 1980s, of increasing central control over the education system; a project which, on some views, amounts to deprofessionalisation of both teachers and researchers (see Chapters 1 and 3).

Let me turn, finally, to the argument that the educational research community has not been functioning properly, and that external intervention is necessary in order to correct this. It is probably true that a substantial proportion of educational researchers in Britain today would accept that all is not well with their field; and many social scientists might take the same view of the social sciences more generally. But their diagnoses of the problem, and therefore the remedies they propose, would vary considerably. Furthermore, one can recognise that a field of research is not operating in the way that it should, and yet deny that external intervention is likely to remedy the situation. After all, those who are currently seeking to reform academic educational research do not hold to a conception of it that is at all close to Polanyi's model. Instead, they are concerned with increasing its practical payoff.

My own view is that there are indeed very serious problems with the current state of educational research. And I believe that, to a large extent, these actually stem from the fact that it does not operate in a manner which approximates to Polanyi's model. In particular, there has been a growing tendency to supplement or override judgements about the likely validity of conclusions with concerns about their practical and political assumptions or implications. In part, this has stemmed from pressure coming from outside agencies to make research more relevant to current policy concerns or to educational practice. Equally important, though, has been the increasing tendency of many educational researchers themselves to believe that their work should serve practical or political goals directly, rather than simply producing knowledge relevant to those goals. A number of factors have led to this. One is institutional: many educational researchers are also involved in teacher education, and regard the main function of educational enquiry as to serve this activity. Another factor is the influence of very diverse trends of thought which all emphasise the instrumental character of knowledge; for example, the evidence-based practice movement, Deweyan or Rortian pragmatism, and 'critical' approaches to social research. A more recent influence in the same direction is postmodernism, with its sceptical challenge to the very possibility of knowledge as conventionally understood; which threatens to undermine the idea that the goal of research can be to produce knowledge. All of these intellectual trends have encouraged a reformulation of the notion of validity in partially or totally instrumental terms.[15]

Another important consequence of these external and internal pressures has been to reinforce the idea that the results of each single piece of research must be of direct relevance to policymaking or practice, and should be formulated in such a way as to be accessible to a practitioner audience. This undermines the division of labour that is essential to scientific research (see Hammersley 1992:138–9). Moreover, it is often based on an exaggerated sense of what research can provide, in the short term and perhaps even in the longer term. A crucial element of Polanyi's model of mutual adjustment was that individual scientists make judgements about what to study not just in terms of the likely scientific value of the results but also according to *feasibility*. And this is one reason why it is important that judgements about priorities are made by individual researchers located in the relevant research field, rather than by a central committee or forum. Feasibility cannot be judged in global terms. Moreover, judgements about it are likely to be distorted by any pressure to produce 'actionable' knowledge. In my view, the problem with much educational research today is that it is far too ambitious in its stated aims and in its knowledge claims. Sometimes, what it attempts is impossible given the current level of knowledge and the resources available. Worse still, it often pretends to have been successful when it has not been.[16]

In summary, then, I do not believe that external intervention is likely to resolve the problems facing the educational research community at the moment. Indeed, I think it probably follows from Polanyi's position that external intervention is never likely to improve matters, at least as regards *scientific* enquiry, since this contradicts the character of research communities as republics. In political history, external interventions have rarely led to the preservation of this form of government; generally speaking, they have resulted in the establishment of empires. So, judged in the light of Polanyi's model, the current defects of the educational research community can only be remedied by educational researchers themselves. Moreover, this will require increased, not reduced, autonomy from outside interests and pressures.

Returning to the theme with which this chapter began, however, it is important to add that Polanyi's model does not imply a celebration of diversity in approach among scientific researchers. Nor does it suggest that a research community must tolerate those who reject, or seek to reformulate, the task of research. This is because the model does not recommend an *absence* of control, but rather the exercise of *internal* and *local* control. In other words, researchers, both as individuals and in playing gatekeeping roles within their community, must engage in public evaluation of research products in terms of the goal of producing sound knowledge; and those evaluations must form the basis for decisions about what research should and should not be funded, what findings should and should not be published, and what published findings should and should not be accepted as sound knowledge. Moreover, while there may be legitimate disagreement about the standards in terms of which research proposals or findings ought to be judged, toleration should not extend to views which assume immediate goals other than the production of knowledge.

Some readers may see this as revealing that Polanyi's model is authoritarian in its implications. But this would not be a sound criticism, even if 'authoritarian' were to be defined in a way which would apply to any but the most libertarian regime. This is because the criticism involves a performative contradiction. Thus, to argue that diversity of approach in educational research should be celebrated simultaneously implies rejection of approaches which claim there are universal standards by which research should be judged. In supporting diversity, Hodkinson and Garratt recognise the problem, commenting that they 'risk a paradox' (Hodkinson and Garratt 2000). But, in fact, what is involved is a *contradiction* not a paradox; and it is a contradiction that is *committed* not risked. This is because while, in principle, they attribute unlimited value to diversity in methodological approach, in practice they limit their tolerance only to those other approaches which also declare unlimited tolerance.

Furthermore, these authors justify the principle of unlimited tolerance on the grounds that it will advance our knowledge about educational issues. Yet this would only be true of diverse approaches which are nevertheless all directed towards that goal; whereas they wish to allow pursuit of other immediate goals. They claim that:

> If being a researcher is to search for new 'truths' or new 'meanings', be they seen as realist discoveries, interpretive constructions, postmodern deconstructions, collaborative emancipations, transgressive actions or something other than any of these, then a questioning mind is a self-evident, defining characteristic. One thing research cannot be is closed and unquestioning. (Hodkinson and Garratt 2000:12)

Here they treat closedness as an all-or-nothing matter; and not just in degree but also in kind. Yet one can be more or less open; and it is possible to be comparatively open in relation to some kinds of proposal, while closed in relation to others. Moreover, as already noted, Hodkinson and Garratt's own position shows that it is impossible *not* to be closed in *some* respect. So the issue is not openness versus closedness but rather: to what should the research community have a relatively open attitude, and to what ought it to be more closed?[17]

Interestingly, Polanyi argues that science is necessarily *relatively* closed, not only in terms of its commitment to the sole immediate goal of producing knowledge, but also as regards the acceptance of new knowledge claims (see, for example, Polanyi 1946:15–17 and *passim*). He recognises that this involves risks, but argues that considerable caution about accepting new ideas is essential to the operation of research communities:

> scientific opinion may, of course, sometimes be mistaken, and as a result unorthodox work of high originality and merit may be discouraged or altogether suppressed for a time. But these risks have to be taken. Only the discipline imposed by an effective scientific opinion can prevent the adulteration of science by cranks and dabblers. In parts of the world where

no sound and authoritative scientific opinion is established, research stagnates for lack of stimulus, while unsound reputations grow based on commonplace achievements or mere empty boasts. Politics and business play havoc with appointments and the granting of subsidies for research; journals are made unreadable by including so much trash. (Polanyi 1962:61)

Thus, Polanyi argues that the scientific community is characterised not by an absence of authority, by a celebration of diversity in approach or conclusion, but rather by the local exercise of authority – in which researchers make judgements about what does and does not amount to the production of sound knowledge.[18]

Conclusion

In this chapter I have explored the implications of a particular model of the operation of scientific communities for current attempts to reform educational research in England and Wales. In his article 'The republic of science', Michael Polanyi argued that the flourishing of science requires considerable autonomy on the part of researchers in determining what is to be investigated, when, and how. He concluded that, in the case of natural science, attempts at central control would obstruct or distort the growth of scientific knowledge.

I have suggested that Polanyi's model counts against current attempts to exercise central coordination of educational research; for instance, through the establishment of a forum which would identify priorities, specify quality criteria, and enforce these. Even if the aim is to turn all (or most) educational enquiry into practical research, it is not clear that the result would be beneficial. In practical as in scientific research, what are the most appropriate methods and what is the quality of the findings cannot be *determined* by the application of some general code, laid down from the centre. Researchers must make local judgements about these matters in light of the goal of producing knowledge. Moreover, while practical research may need to be under *external* control – in relation to what is investigated and when – it should not be under *central* control, even in these respects.

For me, Polanyi's model has further significance, in that it shows that defence of the autonomy of research communities does not depend primarily on claims about abstract rights to academic freedom or on the valorisation of 'difference'. Indeed, as I have emphasised, while his model rules out both external and central control, it sees the exercise of *internal* and *local* control as an essential feature of scientific communities. Where an emphasis on the celebration of difference, or at least the unlimited toleration of diversity, might imply that all voices should be heard, and perhaps even be given equal status, Polanyi's picture of the research community implies that researchers must judge their own and others' work rigorously in terms of its contribution to the advance of knowledge; and that they should deny status and resources to ideas that do not survive those judgements. The resulting picture of the research community is not one in which we must let 'a hundred flowers blossom' (Mao Zedong 1972:302–3), but one where gardeners routinely eliminate weeds, even while accepting that their judgements are always fallible.[19]

I am not suggesting that academic educational research currently matches the model of the scientific community that Polanyi puts forward. It does not. The point is simply that attempts to reform it via central control will make the situation worse, not better. Indeed, in my view, its defects stem largely from the way in which it has been pushed, both by external demands and by the concerns of many researchers, to try to make its findings of immediate practical or political relevance. To use the fashionable currency of medical analogy: far from being an antidote to the disease, the policy of central coordination is a version of the illness. It will make the patient's condition worse, and may even prove fatal.

Notes

1. This was the way it was formulated by the organisers of the conference at which an earlier version of this chapter was given. For background information about recent attempts to reform educational research, see the Introduction.
2. See, for instance, Usher's discussion of the ethics of Levinas and Derrida and their implications for educational research (Usher 2000).
3. One version of this idea is to be found in John Stuart Mill's defence of intellectual freedom. On Mill's argument, see Edwards (1988).
4. This seems to be the position of James Tooley, whose critique of educational research (Tooley 1998) has, nevertheless, been used as part of the argument for central coordination. For Tooley's views, see Tooley (1999:178).
5. This analogy was later taken up by others: see, for example, Weinberg (1978), Ziman (1978) and Fuller (2000).
6. In fact, there was considerable discussion in the eighteenth century about the compatibility between republicanism and commercial society: see Pocock's discussion of Adam Smith (Pocock 1975). Interestingly, in an earlier discussion of 'the republic of science', Polanyi appeals to Rousseau's notion of the general will: see Polanyi (1946:16 and 64). He seems to see this as similar to Smith's 'invisible hand'.
7. On the origins of this idea in Marxism, see Polanyi (1940:1–3).
8. This was not, of course, the end of the struggle: see Wilkie (1991).
9. For Polanyi, of course, the republic of science is international, and for that reason too cannot be tied to the goals of any nation-state.
10. Polanyi's view of the nature of local decision-making is quite complex. He argues that:

   while scientists can admittedly exercise competent judgement only over a small part of science, they can usually judge an area adjoining their own special studies that is broad enough to include some fields on which other scientists have specialised. We thus have a considerable degree of overlapping between the areas over which a scientist can exercise a sound critical judgement. And, of course, each scientist who is a member of a group of overlapping competences will also be a member of other groups of the same kind, so that the whole of science will be covered by chains and networks of overlapping neighbourhoods. ... [And] through these overlapping neighbourhoods uniform standards of scientific merit will prevail over the entire range of science. (Polanyi 1962:59)

11. I cannot offer support for this contention here, but arguments for a model of this kind are provided elsewhere. See, for example, Hammersley (1992 and 1995a); and Foster et al. (1996). What also cannot be discussed is the question of how far Polanyi's model applies even to *natural* science. This was a point of disagreement between him and Bernal. And the problem becomes more obvious in the context of what Ravetz (1971) calls 'industrialised science'.

12. Some versions of hermeneutic philosophy, such as that of Gadamer, also seem to imply that social enquiry should be concerned with what might be called 'living truth': with how to live our lives. This would imply that it should have a practical orientation.

13. The problems with this form of argument have been explored in the context of Marxism. See, for example, Merleau-Ponty (1973) and Lukes (1985).

14. However, it is worth noting that the current attempt to make educational research more practical is being pursued by redirecting the already severely limited funds earmarked for scientific research in this area. Occasional acknowledgements of the value of 'blue skies' research (to be found in Hargreaves 1996, in Blunkett 2000 and in NERF 2000) do not alter this fact. The result of the proposed reform will be that it becomes even more difficult, if not impossible, to get funding for research on education which cannot claim to have direct practical benefit. At the very least, those researchers who are unwilling to pretend that their research makes a direct contribution to the UK's economic competitiveness, the effectiveness of public services and policy, or the quality of life – to use the ESRC's version of the priorities – or to 'the improvement of educational standards' – to use the government's criterion (Clarke 1998) – will simply be starved of funds. One long-term effect of this will be to undermine growth in our understanding of the social and psychological processes which shape education.

15. For an assessment of these trends and their effects, see Hammersley (2000b).

16. Evidential support for this argument in relation to one area of educational research can be found in Foster et al. (1996). In my view, though, the same point applies to many others.

17. This is analogous to the point that the commitments of political liberalism are not purely formal but necessarily involve some, albeit perhaps minimal, conception of the good life. See Larmore (1987).

18. It should be noted that, in his work as a physical chemist, he was himself the victim of false scientific opinion, which refused to accept the validity of some of his findings for 20 years (see Prosch 1986:109). As Prosch points out, as a result, for many years, he could not even teach his theory to his own students, or at least could not present it as well established.

19. Policy towards the arts and sciences, to which the quotation from Mao relates, is one area in which his emphasis on the close relationship between theory and practice (see Mao Zedong 1972:205–6) did not operate. Indeed, as I noted earlier, the impetus for central control of science, to which Polanyi was responding, came from communism. A contradiction between rhetoric and reality is, however, by no means limited to communist regimes.

Chapter 6

Varieties of Social Research:
A Typology

For a long time, social and educational research methodology was dominated by the model of the natural sciences; though interpretations of this paradigm varied considerably, as did judgements about how far it could be approximated in studying the social world. Closely associated with the natural science model was the distinction between basic and applied work. Applied research was generally treated as of lower status; but, within the social sciences at least, there was always a tension built into this status hierarchy. The tension arose partly from the fact that, often, more funds were available for applied than for basic research. Indeed, the eventual practical contribution of basic research frequently had to be emphasised for it to be funded. Equally important, though, most social scientists themselves have had a dual commitment; not just to science but also to facilitating improvement or change that would remedy social problems.

In recent years, this tension between basic and applied work has increased within the social sciences, as a result of both internal and external trends towards greater emphasis on the application and impact of research. Many researchers have come to stress that enquiry is necessarily value-laden, and some have argued that it should be geared directly towards achieving desirable political or practical goals.[1] Externally, there have been growing demands that publicly funded research make a demonstrable contribution to society: to national and local policymaking, to professional practice and/or to commercial enterprise. Following the Rothschild Report, applied research came to be interpreted as requiring a clear contractual relationship between funders and researchers (Rothschild 1971). Moreover, while Rothschild denied the appropriateness of this contract model for basic research, even in the social sciences (Rothschild 1982), it has come to be applied more and more widely. For example, it seems to be the basis for the British government's current attempt to reform academic research on education, including that funded through the Higher Education Funding Councils and the

Economic and Social Research Council (see Clarke 1998). Furthermore, there are growing signs that this approach is to be extended to other areas of social research (see Blunkett 2000). Of course, commitment to basic research has by no means disappeared within social science, or among those who fund it. Indeed, very often what is demanded is that social and educational research meet the requirements appropriate to both kinds of enquiry.

However, in my view, this is unrealistic – these two sets of requirements are often incompatible. So, my aim in this chapter is to clarify the different forms that social and educational research can legitimately take, and what separates them. The distinction between basic and applied modes of enquiry captures some of the relevant diversity. Furthermore, it is worth underlining that this distinction does not deny that basic research has sometimes led to practical or technical applications, or that applied work can stimulate theoretical ideas. It refers exclusively to variation in the immediate goal of research projects, rather than purporting to provide an exhaustive description of their social contribution or functioning. And, likewise, my focus in this chapter will be on the immediate goals of different kinds of research. However, I will argue that the basic/applied distinction does not provide an adequate way of understanding the variety of forms that social enquiry can take. I will begin by addressing some of the problems associated with this distinction, and then outline an alternative typology.

Basic and applied research

There are several respects in which the distinction between basic and applied research is unsatisfactory. One problem is the way in which these terms are typically used in an ad hoc way to identify contrasting points on what is seen as a continuum; running from (at one end) research designed directly to meet practical requirements for information to (at the other) enquiry whose relationship to practical concerns is remote or uncertain. An effect of this ad hoc usage is that the meaning of the two terms varies according to the particular contrast being drawn; and this introduces much uncertainty into their interpretation, especially where the contrast remains implicit.

More fundamentally, I want to question the idea that this distinction represents a scale; and to suggest, instead, that there is a fundamental difference in orientation between research aimed at providing information of direct relevance to practical activities, and that which is designed to contribute to a body of disciplinary knowledge. The dichotomous nature of the distinction has been obscured, I suggest, by the longstanding tendency to believe that basic and applied orientations can be integrated or combined; on the presumption that pursuit of social improvement and of knowledge are one and the same, or at least are very closely related (and mutually compatible) activities (Hammersley

2000b:ch. 1). Once we abandon this assumption, and there seems to be little justification for upholding it, there is no reason to believe that knowledge will always be 'usable' or that using it will always have good effects (see Chapter 2).

Closely associated with this is the problem that the metaphor underlying the distinction between basic and applied research is defective. It implies the production of a foundation of knowledge from which instructions for appropriate action can be derived and applied. This ignores the disjunction between the factual – and usually rather abstract or general – knowledge produced by basic science, on the one hand, and the prescriptive and more concrete information requirements of practical and technical activities, on the other. Along with this, the metaphor neglects the role that other sources of knowledge, as well as experience and judgement, play in successful practical action. These are important even in a field like engineering, which is often used as a model for the 'application' of social research.[2] Even engineering is not simply the *implementation* of natural science knowledge (see, for example, Davis 1998). Furthermore, judgement and contextual knowledge are of still greater significance in occupations where the 'material' dealt with is people; as in medicine, social work, education, management, social policy, etc. In short, the basic/applied distinction treats application as an adjunct to the production of disciplinary knowledge, and therefore involves no clear characterisation of applied work as an independent activity; and this defect is especially significant in the context of social and educational research (see Gouldner 1965).

A further problem is that a two-term distinction does not capture all the relevant variation within social enquiry. Recognition of this has led to the introduction of intermediate terms, notably 'strategic research'. However, this phrase comes from a different typology, relying on a different metaphor: 'strategic' contrasts with 'tactical', rather than with either 'basic' or 'applied'. As a result, it is unclear what the proper relationship of this third term is to the basic/applied metaphor. Moreover, introducing it leaves that original metaphor in place.

A final problem is that, as I noted earlier, what is involved in the basic/applied distinction is not simply a terminological matter but a status hierarchy; with basic research usually seen as of higher status than applied work – at least by researchers. Recently, there are signs of this status hierarchy being inverted (see, for example, Gibbons 1994). However, inversion does not solve the problem. Whatever function status judgements serve, and one cannot *legislate* parity of esteem, they often get in the way of identifying legitimate diversity. It is important that we recognise the different forms of social and educational research, understand that our judgements of their relative value are dependent on the evaluative criteria we employ, and realise that the appropriateness of different sets of criteria depends partly on purpose and context.

Scientific and practical research

In place of the distinction between basic and applied research – though occupying much of the same referential space – I propose one between scientific and practical enquiry.[3] In this usage, the term 'scientific enquiry' refers to research that is designed to contribute to a body of disciplinary knowledge, so that the immediate audience is fellow researchers, though the ultimate aim is to produce knowledge, communicated through reviews of research findings in particular fields, that will be a resource for anyone with an interest in the relevant topic. By contrast, practical research is geared directly to providing information that is needed to deal with some practical problem, so that here the immediate audience for research reports is people with a practical interest in the issue; notably, but not exclusively, policymakers and occupational practitioners of the relevant kinds.

Central to this distinction, and directly related to variation in the primary audience, are differences in the validating mechanisms involved in, and the criteria of assessment appropriate to, these two types of research. In scientific research there is collective evaluation of knowledge claims by a research community, on the basis both of the body of knowledge this community currently takes to be valid and of the evidence offered in support of the claims. Moreover, this process of evaluation tends to operate in such a way as to err on the side of rejecting as false what may be true, as against accepting as true what is in fact false.[4] While this mode of operation maximises the chances of producing sound knowledge (though it cannot guarantee it), the disadvantage is that it renders the process of knowledge production very slow, with the result that it cannot usually meet the deadlines which surround policy-making and practice. There is another implication too. This is that the topics investigated must be of relatively general character, otherwise they would not be of interest to an international community of researchers.

Of course, those engaged in practical research are concerned to ensure that their findings are valid as well. But they differ in how they operationalise this criterion, and in the weight they give to it by comparison with relevance. First, in assessing validity the practical researcher need not, and usually will not be able to, restrict his or her assumptions to those which are treated as valid by the appropriate research community. This arises from the fact that practitioners are the main immediate audience, and most practitioner communities operate on a wealth of assumptions that have not been validated by scientific work. Indeed, they could not do otherwise; partly because of the slowness of scientific knowledge production, but also because they are dealing with particular phenomena in specific locales that have not usually themselves been subjected to scientific investigation. In other words, practitioners operate within perspectives that are organised around practical concerns, and which draw on personal and collective experience of the activity concerned. Furthermore, in this context, practical assessments of acceptable levels of probable validity tend to vary according to the costs associated with different kinds of error: where the practical cost of an error is likely to be high, judgements will be stringent; but where the likely cost is low, they may not be.

The second difference is that practical researchers place a lot more emphasis on the direct *relevance* of what they produce to current policy or practical concerns, compared with scientific researchers. And there is usually a trade-off between meeting the requirement of immediate relevance and the amount of time and resources available for checking the validity of findings. One reason for this is that, as already noted, the emphasis on relevance requires the practical researcher to take over many lay assumptions that would not be accepted in a scientific context.[5] Another reason is that the production of the research findings needs to be timely: they need to appear when the issue with which they are concerned is near the top of the relevant agenda, or can be moved up it.

It should be clear from this that there is a divide between pursuing scientific and practical research. They involve somewhat different goals and different immediate audiences; and the most effective approach to each generally involves serious costs from the point of view of the other. Thus, trying to do both kinds of research simultaneously will often result in the requirements of neither being well satisfied.

So, to summarise, in place of the distinction between basic and applied research, I suggest one between scientific and practical research. This avoids some of the problematic features of the conventional distinction I noted earlier; in particular, the reliance on a misleading metaphor. And it has the advantage of pointing to crucial variation within the field of social research over intended audience and the way that its findings are, or ought to be, assessed. However, what I have proposed does not deal with the failure of a two-term distinction to capture all the relevant heterogeneity within the field. Some further distinctions are required within each category, and I will outline these in the next section.

Further distinctions

Within scientific research it is possible to distinguish between what I will call theoretical and substantive work. Theoretical research, as its name indicates, is concerned with the pursuit of theory; conceptualised here as knowledge of *general relationships* among *types* of phenomena, usually of a *conditional* character. In these terms, theory takes the form: if specified conditions are met, then X will produce Y, other things being equal.[6] Substantive research, by contrast, is concerned with producing *descriptions* and *explanations* of *particular* social phenomena: that is, of phenomena that exist, or have existed, at particular places and times, albeit sometimes over long periods and across wide areas. Thus, substantive research might be concerned at the micro level with explaining how a particular decision was made within a committee, or at the macro level with describing the nature of globalisation as a feature of human societies in the late twentieth century. Very often, substantive scientific research focuses on perennial issues that are of practical or political importance; but, by contrast with practical enquiry, it is not concerned with meeting immediate requirements for information about these on the part of particular audiences. Furthermore, to a greater degree than practical research, it will use the products of theoretical work as resources for framing its descriptions and explanations.[7]

It is equally important to draw distinctions within the field of practical research. Here, first of all, we can distinguish between work that is commissioned to produce a specified type of information on the basis of a detailed contract, on the one hand, and, on the other, the situation where researchers have more autonomy in what they produce, even though their audience is still lay rather than academic.[8] For instance, evaluation studies can vary considerably in how independent a role the evaluators are able to play. In some cases they are restricted to operationalising project goals and measuring the extent to which these have been achieved. In other cases, the scope of the evaluation is more open, allowing evaluators to choose appropriate assessment criteria, to decide what to focus on, and even to change criteria and/or focus over the course of their work. This can be labelled as a distinction between contract-based and autonomous practical enquiry.

Equally significant is the distinction between research which is designed to serve the needs of some particular group of practitioners or of some organisation, and that which is addressed to a wider range of audiences. In every field there is usually an array of groups having some interest in or involvement with its central issues. These include: members of various occupations; individual clients and their families; organised client groups; professional associations and trade unions; regulatory authorities; national, local and specialist media; government-sponsored agencies of relevant kinds; government departments and ministers. Often, practical research will be concerned with feeding information to many or all of these audiences, rather than just one. Indeed, researchers may play a proactive role in identifying and highlighting problems, for example by exploring clients' attitudes towards the service they receive or the attitudes of the wider public towards some controversial issue. A strong justification can be framed for this type of work as furthering democratic participation in decisions that are of public importance. I will label research designed to meet the needs for information of a particular group 'dedicated practical research'; and that which addresses a wider range of audiences 'democratic practical research'.[9]

These two distinctions within practical research cross-cut one another, giving four ideal types, though instances of them will not occur with equal frequency (see Figure 6.1).

These distinctions refer to dimensions rather than to dichotomies.

	Commissioned on the basis of a contract to produce specific information	Autonomous role in producing practically relevant information
Designed to meet the specific needs of some particular group of policy-makers or practitioners	*Contract-based, dedicated, practical research*	*Autonomous, dedicated, practical research*
Aimed at a wider range of practitioner audiences	*Contract-based, democratic, practical research*	*Autonomous, democratic, practical research*

Figure 6.1 Types of practical enquiry

Nevertheless, trade-offs may be involved; so that research which seeks to find a position midway between one or another type may compound the problems that it faces, and render unclear what mode of assessment should be applied.

Conclusion

In this chapter, I have argued that the conventional distinction between basic and applied research involves some serious problems. In its place, I have suggested a distinction between scientific and practical research. I outlined the distinguishing features of these two kinds of work, relating primarily to the criteria by which, and ways in which, knowledge claims should be assessed. The same standards of assessment apply to both – validity and relevance – but these are given differential weight and vary in how they are interpreted in the two contexts. In addition, I considered some variations in the form that research can take *within* these two main categories. This involved distinguishing between theoretical and substantive scientific research; and between contract-based versus autonomous, and dedicated versus democratic, practical research (see Figure 6.2).

It is important to emphasise both the differences and the complementary strengths and weaknesses of these various kinds of research. For instance, practical research offers findings that are likely to be more directly relevant to dealing with social problems. However, it does this at greater risk of error compared with scientific work, due to the absence of sustained collective assessment of knowledge-claims by a research community.[10] Similarly, contract-based practical research maximises the

Scientific enquiry		Practical enquiry	
The immediate audience is fellow researchers		The immediate audience is practitioners and policymakers of various kinds, as well as others who have a practical interest in the particular issue	
The aim is to contribute to a cumulating body of knowledge about some aspect of the world		The aim is to provide knowledge that will be of immediate practical use	
Findings are assessed primarily in terms of validity; with a preference for erring on the side of rejecting as false what is true, rather than accepting as true what is false		Findings are assessed in terms of relevance and timeliness as well as validity, with the latter being judged on the basis of lay as well as research-based knowledge	
Theoretical scientific research	*Substantive scientific research*	*Dedicated practical research*	*Democratic practical research*
The aim is to develop and test theoretical ideas: to produce knowledge about general causal relationships	The task is to provide descriptions and explanations of particular cases relevant to perennial issues of human concern	The goal is to provide information that is needed by a specific group of policymakers or practitioners at a particular time	The purpose is to provide information that will be of use to anyone concerned with a particular, currently pressing, issue
		Contract-based, practical research	*Autonomous, practical research*
		This type of research is commissioned on the basis of a contract to produce specific information	Researchers play an autonomous role in producing practically relevant information

Figure 6.2 A typology of social research

usability of the findings by a particular group of practitioners, but at the risk of overlooking significant issues that more autonomous enquiry might have uncovered. The crucial point is that there are always losses as well as gains in choosing one type of research over another; and that each type has value.

Failure to recognise the variety of forms that social and educational research can take, and their relative strengths and weaknesses, is one source of the difficulties researchers often face in deciding how best to pursue their work. Equally important, it generates much of the criticism that this work attracts. Criticism arises, in part at least, from the impossibility of satisfying, simultaneously, all the criteria by which research findings can be judged. Distinguishing among different types of enquiry should also be of value for those involved in funding or using social research. It facilitates judgements about what sort of work would best serve particular purposes, and what can and cannot reasonably be expected from any particular study. Above all, it warns against attempts to privilege one kind of research over all others.

Notes

1. For discussion of these views, see Hammersley (2000b:ch. 1).
2. For discussion of the 'engineering model', see Chapters 1 and 4.
3. My aim here is to restrict the scope of the term 'science', on the grounds that overextension of it is a kind of cultural imperialism, and is one of the reasons for the widespread public reaction against science.
4. This refers to a key norm governing academic communities, what Merton refers to as 'organised scepticism' (Merton 1973b:chs 12 and 13; see also Hammersley 1992:ch. 2). In practice, the influence of this norm varies considerably across research communities. The view that scientific research involves collective assessment of knowledge claims is central to several contrasting philosophical accounts; notably, those of Popper, Polanyi and Kuhn. There has, nevertheless, been some criticism of the claim that there are scientific norms, see Stehr (1978).
5. I am not denying that practical research can usefully challenge practitioners' assumptions; but it is important to note that whether raising questions about a set of assumptions is desirable, on any particular occasion, depends on practical considerations, not just on academic judgements about the validity of those assumptions.
6. For a discussion of the various meanings that can be given to 'theory', see Hammersley (1995b).
7. For further explication of this distinction between theoretical and substantive work, see Foster et al. (1996:32–4).
8. This is close to Gouldner's distinction between 'engineering' and 'clinical' forms of applied social research (see Gouldner 1965).
9. For explicit justification of this latter type of research in the field of educational evaluation, see MacDonald (1974) and Simons (1987:44–52). The way these authors formulate the justification seems to throw doubt both on the value of practical enquiry of other kinds and on that of academic research. However, the argument need not take this form; and, in my view, there is no more reason for formulating it this way than there was previously for taking basic

research as the only legitimate type of enquiry. Furthermore, scientific research can also be justified in terms of its democratic contribution, even though this is indirect.

10. This is a matter of general tendency, rather than being true in every case. And how likely it is to be true depends on the extent, and strength, of the threats to validity applying to the knowledge claims. Furthermore, where the distinction between these two types of research is weakly maintained or non-existent, so too will be the difference in the likely validity of their findings.

Chapter 7

A Review of Reviews: Structure and Function in Reviews of Educational Research (written with Peter Foster)

One response to the current crisis in educational research has been greater emphasis on the importance of disseminating research findings. Indeed, there has been much discussion among educational researchers about how best to make the products of their work more widely available.[1] This is a desirable goal, in many ways. However, it is by no means a simple or straightforward matter.

Sometimes, the idea is that the findings of every study should be widely publicised and 'applied'; however, in our view, this is not appropriate. It presupposes a conception of research as a process of individual discovery, whereby the researcher sets out to investigate some phenomenon and, by using rigorous methods or getting into direct contact with it, brings back knowledge. Now, while this model may be appropriate for relatively simple and uncontroversial kinds of knowledge, it is not sufficient for pursuit of the sort of knowledge with which educational research is usually concerned. Nor does it match the way in which natural scientific research communities operate. There, assessments of reported findings, including attempts to replicate them, are a crucial part of the process of producing knowledge. Thus, it is generally only when such assessments have reached a broad consensus that valid knowledge is felt to have been achieved. Social and educational researchers often argue, quite rightly in our view, that the phenomena they study are more complex and more difficult to investigate than those with which most natural science deals. Given this, it seems to us that in social and educational research even less reliance can be placed on the results of single studies. Communal assessment of their validity is essential and, even where experimental replication is not possible, further investigation will often be required before they can legitimately be accepted as valid. For this reason, and given that the distinctive claim to authority of scientific conclusions is that they are less likely to be false than those from other sources, it is important that what is communicated to lay audiences by researchers has gone through this process of collective assessment and validation (Goldstein and Mortimore 1997; McIntyre 1997a).[2]

From this point of view, the main channel of communication between researchers and lay people ought to be reviews of whole fields of research, rather than reports of single studies. While such reviews have long been a feature of the educational research scene, it is arguable that in Britain they have not been as central as they should have been.[3] Nevertheless, recently, an increasing number of reviews of educational research in particular fields have been published, many specifically concerned with improving the communication links between educational researchers and practitioners. We regard this as an important and welcome development, and it provided the stimulus for this chapter. In it we consider some of the issues raised by reviews of research, and especially those directed at lay audiences. These arise both for those who write reviews and for those who use them. We will organise our discussion under four main headings: initiating reviews, defining the field, coverage and treatment of relevant research, and drawing conclusions.[4]

Initiating reviews: by whom, for whom, and for what purpose?

Reviews of research can take a wide variety of forms. In part, this reflects the fact that they can be initiated in different ways. In crude terms, some are generated mainly from within the world of educational research, while others originate elsewhere. For example, the review of research on primary teaching produced by Caroline Gipps seems to have been initiated and produced by her without sponsorship outside the London Institute of Education (Gipps 1992). By contrast, the report of the 'three wise men', which covers much of the same ground, had its origins within the UK government, and two of its authors were drawn from outside the field of educational research (Alexander et al. 1992).[5]

However, if what we are interested in is who determines the shape of a review, this contrast between the initiation of reviews inside and outside the world of research is too simple. While commissioned by an outside agency, the production of a review may sometimes be left largely in the hands of the reviewer. Conversely, internally generated reviews may seek outside sponsorship for publication, and this can have an effect on their character. So, the influence of external and internal factors is complex. Indeed, there may sometimes be a problem in distinguishing between what is internal and what is external. One reason for this is that many educational researchers also play practitioner roles (for example in teacher education), so that the reviews they produce are shaped by factors both internal and external to educational enquiry. Another reason is that educational research is sometimes seen as directly geared to educational improvement (see, for example, Bassey 1995); and this raises the whole question of where the boundary around it ought to be drawn.

We can illustrate some of these complexities by looking in a little more detail at the case of the report of the 'three wise men' (Alexander et al. 1992). This had a complex history. The initial suggestion for it seems to have come from Tim Eggar, a junior minister in the Department of Education and Science, as it then was. However, the proposal was taken over and modified by Kenneth Clarke, the Secretary of State for Education, partly as a result of influence from the right wing of the Conservative Party and from the National Curriculum Council (Alexander 1997:ch. 10).

Clarke's announcement of the commissioning of the report made clear his commitment to the reform of primary school pedagogy, and also the direction in which he believed this should go. In other words, there was a very clear anticipation of what the conclusions of the review would (or should) be: recommendation of a more 'traditional' approach (DES 1991). As Alexander reports, this was part of a 'winter initiative' designed to stake out the battleground on which the government hoped to win the approaching election (Alexander 1997:ch. 10). It is fair to assume that Kenneth Clarke (and perhaps even his officials) were not familiar with much of the research literature, but he was aware of the results of the final report of the Leeds evaluation produced by Alexander (1992) and with the reports produced by Her Majesty's Inspectorate (HMI); and these were interpreted as pointing in the same general direction as his own opinions, opinions widely shared within the Conservative party and voiced by much of the media. And it seems likely that the 'three wise men' were selected so as to enable the report to serve its intended political function. However, Alexander had different concerns. His aim was to use the opportunity presented by an officially sponsored review to convey the results of recent educational research to practitioners. And what he took to be the practical implications of this research represented a much more nuanced view of education than that being promoted by the right wing press and the government; one in which fitness for purpose and the consequent need for professional judgement on the part of teachers were central. This view was shared by a number of other researchers in the field who stressed the value of direct forms of teaching, but who nevertheless recognised the actual and proper diversity of styles necessary in primary classrooms (see also Gipps 1992).[6]

This example illustrates the fact that even where there is external sponsorship of a review and appointment of reviewers, researchers and the research community may still play an important role in shaping its purpose and character; albeit under considerable external pressure and with only partial success. It underlines the complexity of the motives frequently involved in the production of reviews, the negotiative and sometimes even coercive relationships between sponsors and reviewers, and how these features can affect the eventual product.

Reviews may also vary in their intended audience.[7] Here again we can begin with a contrast: between reviews addressed to other researchers, and those directed outside the world of research to people who have an interest (in both senses of that word) in the area. We explained earlier why we believe that reviews perform an essential role in communicating scientific research results to policymakers, managers, and practitioners. But it is also worth noting that reviews of research in a particular field can be of great value for researchers working in this and neighbouring areas. Reviews may update researchers' knowledge of relevant literature, clarify issues, indicate topics for further work, and give some sense of the priority among these. While all researchers in a field need, recurrently, to make their own sense of it, the systematic thought and effort that go into producing a written review may well enable individual researchers to improve their awareness of how different parts of the field link together and of where its growth points lie. The value of such reviews for researchers takes on particular significance when we recognise that fields are not clearly bounded and are related to one another in complex ways, so that even an experienced researcher in a particular area may find that a review of it supplies new information or new insights.

Who is the intended audience will, of course, affect the nature of the review. But, here again, the matter is rarely simple. Even when there is a specific target audience, it is unlikely that this will be the sole acknowledged one. Writers do not have control over whom their audience will be, and are usually only too aware of that fact. Indeed, they are likely to anticipate that some kinds of people will read what they write who are not part of the main target audience. Sometimes, on realistic expectations, such 'sideline' audiences may make up most of the actual audience; and, even where they do not, they will probably still be taken account of by those producing the review; for example because of the consequences that a negative response from them could have. Thus, even if the intended audience is non-researchers, the reviewer will nevertheless be aware that fellow researchers are also likely to read the review. And, given that the opinions of these colleagues will probably matter to the author, and could have material consequences, they are likely to be borne in mind, thereby shaping the review to some extent. Indeed, it could be argued that this is as it should be; that it exerts a precautionary restraint on the reviewer, keeping him or her honest in research terms. Equally, though, researchers as a sideline audience may distract the reviewer from providing what would be most helpful for policymakers and practitioners. What this highlights is that there is considerable scope for tension among the demands of different intended, potential, and likely audiences.

We can illustrate the fact that the anticipated audience for a review is often diverse by looking at two OFSTED-sponsored reviews (Gillborn and Gipps 1996; Reynolds and Farrell 1996). According to their back covers, these are both intended 'to make published research findings more accessible to teachers and trainee teachers'. However, despite this stated target audience, if we examine the body of these reviews we find evidence of a concern with other audiences as well. Indeed, Reynolds and Farrell's *Worlds Apart?*, which focuses on international comparisons of educational performance and the light these throw on the British education system, seems to be directed more at educational researchers and policymakers than at teachers. The emphasis is on the value in research terms of the kind of work that is being reviewed: 'comparisons of different countries have potentially much use for researchers in England: they offer a chance to see factors in systems which do not exist in our own culture and the possibility of developing an answer to the question of "what factors travel, and why" ' (Reynolds and Farrell 1996:6). This contrasts somewhat with Gillborn and Gipps' *Ethnic Minorities* review, which is, in some respects, more clearly directed at practitioners, especially teachers but perhaps also policymakers. For example, at one point Gillborn and Gipps note that they cannot include every study and they comment: 'We have chosen to focus on issues that directly influence pupils' achievements, especially where they relate to education policy, schools, and matters that teachers might wish to address as part of their work' (Gillborn and Gipps 1996:7). However, here too researchers and funders of research also seem to be included in the audience. Thus, in the press release from OFSTED about this review, three of the recommendations refer primarily to researchers, one to schools and one to policymakers and managers. And the review ends by discussing implications for future research as well as for policy and practice: a number of gaps are identified around which 'a research agenda could be compiled' (ibid.:80).[8]

Even apart from the role of sideline audiences, it is important to remember that there is not one single, well-defined, and internally homogeneous professional audience, but rather multiple, overlapping publics whose boundaries and characteristics are ill-defined. Very often, a research review will be targeted mainly at a particular cluster of these, for example at teachers or policymakers in a particular sector of the education system. But, even so, the intended audience is likely to be heterogeneous in significant ways. For example, what was probably the target audience for both Gipps' review and the report of the 'three wise men' – primary school teachers – is diverse in a variety of respects: not just as regards commitment to traditional versus progressive teaching (not a single dimension anyway), but also for example in terms of early and later years teachers, specialists in different subjects, differences in seniority and managerial level, etc.[9]

There will, then, always be some uncertainty for producers of reviews about exactly whom their audience will be, and they cannot usually afford to define the acknowledged audience very narrowly. For this and other reasons audience considerations will have as complex a relationship to the character of the reviews produced as do the constraints involved in initial sponsorship.[10] The impact of audience on the shape of a review is also likely to be complicated because there are different ways in which the anticipated responses of audiences can be responded to: this may lead to some things being said and other things not being said (and these effects can operate on a large or a small scale, and on central or peripheral matters); it can shape *how* points are made, for example with or without qualifiers or through the use of modal formulations; it can lead to distancing strategies or attempts to avert possible interpretations that are not desired, etc.

An example of the way in which reviewers may adjust to the anticipated reaction of an audience is to be found in the *Ethnic Minorities* review. Its title refers to 'the achievements of ethnic minority pupils'. But this bears a less than straightforward relationship to the research that is reviewed. Indeed, 'the underachievement of ethnic minority pupils' would have had a closer fit to most of it. The research, and the review itself, are not much concerned with explaining why some ethnic minority groups outperformed ethnic majority pupils in some areas. This success is noted; but, not unreasonably, the focus is very much on those areas where ethnic minority achievement is less than that of the ethnic majority.[11] And, indeed, the authors describe the task of section 2 of their report as looking at 'the achievement of ethnic minority pupils at different points in their educational careers, focusing in particular on the issue of "under-achievement" ' (Gillborn and Gipps 1996:7). But, as the quotation marks indicate, they also express concern about the word 'under-achievement', on the grounds that 'it is a relatively crude term, relating to differences in group averages. It has long been misunderstood as implying that some groups are better or worse than others' (ibid.:1). It seems, then, that while the main focus is indeed on underachievement on the part of ethnic minority groups, in the sense of lower average achievement levels, the term 'underachievement' is avoided or qualified in order to discourage readers from assuming that differential average performance is to be explained by deficiencies on the part of ethnic minority pupils; or from assuming that the authors are committed to such an explanation. Here, the authors seem to be anticipating the likely responses of various parts of their audience and seeking to counteract them.[12]

Despite all the complexities of audience effects, it is probably still worthwhile to keep in mind the polar opposites of a review targeted at fellow researchers and one aimed at lay audiences, since these tend to place somewhat different requirements on the reviewer. At the very least, the differences relate to the kind of language that is appropriate, the amount of information of various kinds that needs to be supplied, what pre-existing attitudes can and must be assumed, and also the textual organisation of the review (for example whether an 'executive summary' is provided). There may also be differences in the extent to which emphasis is given to critical methodological assessments of studies, on the one hand, and to the more positive task of summarising the current state of well-established knowledge, on the other.

Finally, in this section, we must consider the purposes for which reviews of research are initiated. Here too we can reasonably expect some diversity. We shall assume that the *immediate* purpose of any review is to supply accurate research-based information that is relevant to a public issue and/or to a practical problem. But there is considerable scope for variation in how this task is interpreted. To illustrate this we can identify two extremes. At one pole, would be a review which takes as its framework the research that has been published in a field within a given period and seeks to convey the results in a way that represents the current consensus among researchers. At the other extreme is a review which starts from some policy or practical problem and draws from the research literature whatever it is believed might be useful to practitioners for dealing effectively with this. These are, of course, pure types, but as we shall see they identify one important dimension of variation to be found in reviews.

There are other, less immediate, motives that can stimulate and influence the production of research reviews, besides a concern with the provision of relevant information. Some of these may come from outside the researcher role, narrowly defined. As in the case of the report of the 'three wise men', the aim of some of those involved in the initiation of a review may be to endorse a particular policy. Equally, there may be a concern, on the part of sponsors and/or reviewers, to promote up the political agenda the issue on which the review focuses by emphasising its importance. There is evidence of this kind of motive at the beginning of the *Ethnic Minorities* review. Gillborn and Gipps start by outlining the context of the review, pointing out that 'More than a decade has passed since the last major review of the educational experiences and achievements of ethnic minority pupils', that new research findings and methods have emerged, and that massive educational reforms have occurred in the interim. And they conclude the opening section of their summary: 'During this period issues of "race" and equal opportunity have tended to slip from policy agendas: this review demonstrates the need for this to change' (ibid.:1). It seems from this that there was a concern with reasserting the importance of educational inequalities among ethnic groups as an issue, a concern which perhaps arises from the authors' role as educationalists, rather than specifically as educational researchers (though, as we have noted, this distinction is by no means universally accepted, or drawn by everyone in the same place).

Motives other than a concern with making information publicly available can also arise directly out of the researcher role itself. For example, a review of research may be used to try to demonstrate the practical value of research so as to underline the need for funds, or to push a particular topic up the agendas of funding bodies, especially at a time when finance for research is scarce. Thus, it seems clear that the

Worlds Apart? review was partly concerned with promoting research on international variation in educational achievement and school effectiveness. Early on in the report, the authors comment that 'the true power of education, researchers have begun to think, may only be shown by internationally based research' (Reynolds and Farrell 1996:5). And it is striking that earlier forms of comparative educational research are dismissed as 'frankly inept' (Reynolds and Farrell 1996:53). In this way, both the potential of comparative research, and the failure of previous work of this kind to realise it, are emphasised.[13]

In this context, we ought to note that since researchers are likely to be aware that potential funders form part of the audience there may be a tendency to present research in general, or particular kinds of research, in a favourable light; perhaps even to exaggerate the likely validity of findings or the potential for future breakthroughs, and to play down the significance of methodological problems.[14] Thus, we need to be aware of the extent to which research reviews may be designed to serve as advertisements for research.

However, the fact that all manner of motives may underlie the production of research reviews on the part of sponsors and authors does not in itself mean that the accounts of research findings produced are distorted, or that the reviews will not serve a useful purpose. The implication of our discussion in this section is simply that both writers and readers of research reviews need to pay attention to the effects of sponsorship and authorship, of intended and anticipated audiences, and of the different purposes reviews can be intended to serve. To one degree or another, and in various ways, these will affect the nature of the review that is produced.

Defining the field: the role of factual and value assumptions in providing a framework for research reviews

In the previous section we contrasted two principles on the basis of which reviews could be constructed: so as to represent the current state of knowledge in a particular field of research, or in order to provide resources designed to address a particular policy question. In the field of education this contrast is not as sharp as it would be in some others, since policy issues are one of the main axes around which its research fields are constructed. Nevertheless, even here there may be some tension between what are seen as the demands of policy or practice, on the one hand, and what is available in the research literature, on the other.

We can illustrate this by looking again at the two OFSTED reviews. *Worlds Apart*? takes as its focus international comparisons of levels of educational achievement involving England and/or Britain. This was a highly topical issue at the time the review was produced, and remains so. It was argued by many that international comparisons, especially with the 'tiger' economies of East Asia, highlight the failure of the British or the English education system to meet industry's workforce needs. However, at the same time, the scope of this review is largely determined by the evidence available from the international surveys that have been carried out, rather than by the policy concern itself. One striking consequence of this is that in practice the focus is narrowed to mathematics and science. These are the curriculum areas where most surveys have been done, and as the authors point out those in other areas are subject to serious methodological difficulties (Reynolds and Farrell 1996:2, 11, 13).

This creates some ambiguity within the report: is the aim to draw inferences about comparative educational achievement in general on the basis of evidence about mathematics and science, or are the conclusions intended to be restricted to levels of achievement in these two subject areas? On the one hand, the title of the review implies a general comparison, as do the headings within it. And at one point the authors refer to their focus as 'how different countries perform educationally' (ibid.:1). On the other hand, Reynolds and Farrell seek to justify their restricted focus not just on methodological grounds but also on the basis that 'mathematics and science are universally recognised as the key skills needed in a modern industrial society, and particularly in the new "information age" economies' (ibid.:1). This suggests that the more specific focus of the two is intended, and that this is believed to be justified on the grounds that these subject areas are the most crucial ones for economic success.

This tension within *Worlds Apart?* also highlights the way in which identification of a body of research to be reviewed introduces assumptions. While there are conventional identifications of different fields which guide the production of reviews to some extent, these are themselves constructions (even if not arbitrary ones), may be controversial and are likely to have fuzzy boundaries. In adopting a particular definition of a field, the reviewer is, in effect, making a decision about how the field of educational research is to be carved up and the divisions formulated. This can be illustrated by a difference between Gipps' review of research on effective primary teaching and the report of the 'three wise men'. Gipps devotes a separate section of her review to 'the contribution of theory and theorists'. She argues that while this contribution does not lie in any one theory's 'ability to give us all, or indeed any, of the right answers, . . . [theory offers] a range of insights which we can use to build up an understanding of the science *and* art of teaching within the complex classroom setting' (Gipps 1992:8). In effect, she uses psychological theory as a background against which research on classroom teaching and learning can be understood. By contrast, Alexander et al. cite none of the literature of psychological theorists and refer to it only at one point, and then simply in order to contrast 'Piagetian theories' with the findings of 'more recent studies', to the detriment of the former (Alexander et al. 1992:18). These authors seem to play theory off negatively against the realities of empirical evidence and practice. So, implicit in these two reviews are rather different ideas about the nature of research and about the boundaries of the field.

Underlying any definition of a research field, conventional or otherwise, then, is a set of relevances which guide what is and is not to be included; and these are not always a matter of consensus, and (even when they are consensual) are not fixed but may change over time. Given this, the boundaries around the focus of a review, and the reasons why the area has been defined in the way that it has, are important matters that may need to be addressed, and are aspects of reviews about which readers will sometimes need to ask questions.

In the case of *Worlds Apart?*, for example, there are questions that could be asked about how the field was defined, whichever of the two rationales discussed above is intended. If the goal is to document the comparative success of different countries in educational terms, we ought to consider on what grounds results in mathematics and science can be taken as typical of those in other subjects. And it should be noted in this context that there is a significant difference between the results for these two subjects. If, on the other hand, the focus is specifically on achievement in mathematics and science, we might raise doubts about whether these subjects are actually 'universally recognised' as 'the key skills', as well as about whether they *are* the key skills, and also about whether ' "information age" economies' represent a distinctive type of society, one that is currently predominant or will be in the future. And *both* rationales seem to depend on the factual assumption that schooling is a major factor in determining economic competitiveness. Implicitly throughout, and sometimes explicitly, economic success on the part of the Pacific Rim nations is treated as arising from the superior performance of their educational systems in preparing children for participation in the economy. But how strong is the evidence for this assumption (see Robinson 1997:17–21)? And how strong does it need to be to provide the basis for a review?[15] There are also value assumptions that seem to be involved in the way that the focus of this review is framed, for example to the effect that the main goal of education should be to contribute to national economic competitiveness, or at least to economic growth.

Similar issues arise about the way in which the field is defined by the *Ethnic Minorities* review. One concerns the fact that Gillborn and Gipps' focus is on achievement levels measured by examination and test results, and on factors affecting variation in these. While this kind of educational achievement certainly has significance – in that it may play an important role in occupational recruitment, and thereby in the fortunes of ethnic minority groups in the labour market – it does not necessarily tell us whether ethnic majority and minority children are receiving an adequate education in other respects. Moreover, what adequacy amounts to here might be an issue about which there is considerable disagreement. This could relate to the question of whether what would be an appropriate education is the same across ethnic (and, especially, religious) lines.[16] But there are also questions which could be raised about how well examination and test results measure the quality of education received by pupils in general.[17]

Another aspect of the way in which value assumptions inform the way that the *Ethnic Minorities* review defines its field concerns the identification of inequalities. This depends on assumptions about what would and would not be *equitable*, and there are different interpretations of this (Foster et al. 1996; Hammersley 1997b). The equity principle that is adopted by Gillborn and Gipps is equality of group outcome. But, while they note that this is 'hotly contested' (Gillborn and Gipps 1996:10), they merely state their position rather than providing supporting argument to show why it is more appropriate than other definitions of equality. And the danger of this is that readers will draw the questionable inference that it is the only legitimate interpretation of equity, or that research has validated or can validate it. On the other hand, we should note that introducing what is inevitably likely to be a rather complex discussion about alternative conceptions of justice could blunt the impact of a review on the intended audience.

Gillborn and Gipps might also argue that the assumptions about equality on which they rely are taken for granted within the research community. This is probably true, but it raises two interesting issues. One is the question of how narrowly or widely the relevant research community should be defined. This will often make a considerable difference to what assumptions are accepted. The other issue concerns the role of reviewers. Should they simply report what is a matter of consensus within the relevant field of research, or ought they to stand back from this and examine the assumptions which structure the research they are reviewing, perhaps raising critical questions about them? Of course, even if this proactive role is seen as desirable, it is likely to have consequences for the length and complexity of the reviews produced, and these too are factors that are relevant to a review's likely impact on practitioners. It also raises questions about the sense in which the review is accurately representing the field of research to which it relates.

So, both factual and value assumptions are involved in the way in which the focus of a research review is structured, and this generates a number of issues: what presuppositions are and are not justified in the structuring of research reviews? How should these be handled? In particular, when do they need to be made explicit? And is it necessary for them to be supported by argument where they are controversial, or can they simply be adopted as working assumptions? Is discussion of these presuppositions required when they are a matter of substantial consensus within the relevant research field and/or among policymakers and practitioners? Do the answers to the previous questions vary between factual and value assumptions? And, finally, what weight should be given to the likely consequences for the practical impact of reviews of the different decisions that can be taken about these matters?

Coverage and treatment of the relevant research

It is rare for a review to cover all of the research relevant to a particular focus, at least in the same level of detail. In some areas, the amount of research available for review makes this out of the question. But the fact that, as we noted earlier, the boundaries of any field are socially constructed, fuzzy, and open to potential dispute, may make it impossible even in principle. Nevertheless, reviews do vary substantially in the range of literature they cover, and in the relative coverage given to different studies. We can see this by comparing the OFSTED *Ethnic Minorities* review with two earlier ones concerned with the education of ethnic minority children (Taylor 1981 and Tomlinson 1983). Taylor's 1981 review, which focuses exclusively on the education of 'West Indian' children, is quite explicit about the principles by which studies were to be included. And, as far as one can tell, virtually every study falling within her definition of the field is discussed, albeit in varying detail.[18] There is rather less discussion of the principles of selection in Tomlinson's review, but she too is virtually exhaustive in coverage. By contrast, the authors of the OFSTED review indicate that they have been fairly selective, though the only information provided about the criteria used is the brief statement quoted earlier – that the focus is on 'issues that directly influence pupils' achievements which relate to education or school policy or matters that teachers might want to address as part of their work' (Gillborn and Gipps 1996:7).

There are a number of different aspects of selectivity in research reviews.[19] One relates to the timescale which the review covers. The aim may be to document current reality, although in one sense reviews are always out of date. A concern with contemporary relevance is especially likely in reviews that are directed at a practitioner audience. For this reason studies carried out before a particular date, as well as more recent ones that are historical in the sense of referring to the situation before that date, may be excluded. This would rule out descriptive information that is dated, though not necessarily explanations and theories appearing (or relating to situations) before the relevant period. Of course, there are senses in which explanations and theories can themselves date. One reason is the cumulation of knowledge. Studies may be rendered obsolete by subsequent work which supersedes them in some way, either by showing that they are in error or by developing them in such a manner as to leave no remainder worth mentioning. Equally, theories and explanations may date as a result of political changes which affect their value relevance.

This is highlighted by another contrast between the earlier reviews of research on the education of ethnic minority pupils and that of Gillborn and Gipps. Both Taylor and Tomlinson cover research on a wide range of factors that could affect the performance of ethnic minority pupils, both those relating to home and local community and those to do with schools. Gillborn and Gipps, on the other hand, concentrate almost entirely on factors internal to the education system, with particular emphasis on school processes. To a large extent, this reflects a shift within the field of research they are reviewing. This was a response, in part, to the arguments of earlier reviewers that more work needed to be done on the treatment of ethnic minority pupils in schools. But, more importantly, it relates to a wider change in cultural climate that has affected educational research in many fields. It is striking that before the 1970s the effects of home background on pupils' achievement was a central pre-occupation of educational policymakers and researchers, whereas there is now an almost exclusive focus on the role of schools.[20]

This shift in focus is not the result of research evidence conclusively disproving the substantial causal effect of external factors – while school effectiveness research has established that 'schools can make a difference', it has also acknowledged the substantial role played by extra-school factors (see, for example, Gray et al. 1990). Rather, this shift is the result of a change in view about where the responsibility for educational failure lies. On the political Right this has involved increased emphasis on the accountability of public institutions, and on the Left this emphasis has been combined with a growing tendency to reject any explanation for pupil failure which could be interpreted as 'blaming the victim'. It is striking, though, that none of the recent reviews we have discussed has explicitly located itself in relation to this change. In the case of the OFSTED *Ethnic Minorities* review, one could be forgiven for assuming that the emphasis on school rather than home and community factors was a product of research evidence rather than of ideological change.[21]

Another criterion, besides time period, that might be used in selecting studies for inclusion, or in deciding the extent to which they are discussed, is methodological. Studies whose findings are very questionable as a result of likely error or bias might reasonably be excluded or given no more than a mention. As we noted earlier, this was one of the reasons why Reynolds and Farrell excluded surveys of achievement in areas other than mathematics and science. However, it is rarely possible to rank studies in an unequivocal way in methodological terms, given the trade-offs frequently involved in research and the fact that the comparative significance of methodological defects is not easy to determine. And, of course, this is made even more difficult by current disagreements about methodological matters, and specifically about criteria of assessment, among social and educational researchers (Hammersley 1992; Smith 1993; Altheide and Johnson 1994; Schwandt 1996). This suggests, perhaps, that reviews need to make clear the extent to which methodological selection criteria were employed and what these were.

A closely related issue is the treatment of methodological problems and cautions in reviews. Problems are likely to arise even in relation to the conclusions of the best studies. But how much discussion should be given to them, and what salience should be accorded to any resulting qualifications about the validity of those conclusions? Should this differ between reviews directed at researchers, on the one hand, and those aimed primarily at policymaker or practitioner audiences, on the other? If methodological issues are played down, this may give a misleading impression of the reliability (in the common-sense meaning of that term) of the research findings reviewed. But, on the other side, it may be argued that, in order to gain attention and influence, research results must necessarily be presented with minimal qualification and caution. There are difficult issues involved here that relate back to the purposes of reviews of research, and to the way in which they are intended to bridge the two quite different worlds of research and practice. (See Chapter 3.)

The reviews we have looked at vary quite sharply in their treatment of methodological matters. Two of them, the report of the 'three wise men' and Gipps' review of research relevant to effective primary school teaching, give virtually no attention to methodological considerations. The OFSTED *Ethnic Minorities* review gives some attention to these, *Worlds Apart*? rather more.[22]

Gillborn and Gipps mention methodological problems only briefly in the 'Summary' that opens their review. And this is representative of much of the rest of it. The main exception is the section dealing with 'Educational progress and school effectiveness', where a range of problems is mentioned in the opening paragraphs as regards quantitative studies of school effectiveness, concluding with the following statement: 'The issues are complex and raise vital questions about what research can and cannot tell us. There is no simple solution to these dilemmas, but they should be kept in mind when considering statistical work of this kind' (Gillborn and Gipps 1996:39). And, in the remainder of this section, there are repeated references to methodological problems. This contrasts with the discussion of qualitative research that follows. While two methodological issues are mentioned at the beginning of this, these seem to be formulated as less serious than the 'dilemmas' to which there is 'no simple solution' addressed in the previous section. Indeed, the discussion concludes as follows: 'Despite these weaknesses, qualitative research frequently offers a more revealing perspective, highlighting patterns of experience and achievement that are not visible in quantitative studies' (Gillborn and Gipps 1996:49). The only other reference to methodological problems associated with qualitative research is a brief discussion of the work of Foster, whose findings conflict with those of other qualitative studies in the field and with the conclusions the reviewers themselves draw. His work is criticised for demanding 'absolute proof' and for defending teachers.[23] Clearly, here, the reviewers have exercised some discretion in their treatment of methodological issues, but there is little explicit discussion of the grounds for the judgements they have made or of the controversy surrounding those issues. On the other hand, providing this would have increased the length and complexity of the review, and perhaps thereby reduced its overall usefulness.[24]

Reynolds and Farrell (1996) open their review with a substantial discussion of methodological issues that relate to the central body of the literature they are concerned with. They do not disguise the seriousness of these problems, commenting that the field is 'a minefield of debate, assertion and evidence' (Reynolds and Farrell 1996:1). The problems relate both to the extent to which differential performance within and across countries has been measured effectively, and to the difficulty of showing any relationship between specific features of education systems and differences in outcomes. In discussing particular surveys, however, Reynolds and Farrell make little further reference to methodological concerns: they summarise the main findings of each one without providing any judgement about how confident we can be about their validity. Only at the end do the reviewers return to methodological problems, and there they suggest that these are unlikely to affect the soundness of their conclusions.[25]

So, reviewers necessarily make judgements about the relative validity of research findings, and about how these should be presented. They must also decide how much space to give to discussion of methodological problems relating to different types of study. And the decisions they make will not necessarily be uncontroversial. One question that arises here is how far the treatment of methodological issues should reflect the judgements of the particular reviewer(s), that of researchers in a particular area, or the educational research community as a whole. Another is how explicit reviewers ought to be about the grounds for their judgements, and to what extent they should inform readers about disagreements within the field. Do researchers have a responsibility to educate non-researchers about methodological cautions in the interpretation of research results, and indeed of any other source of evidence? Or is their task simply to make the best judgements they can about the validity of the various findings and to convey these to practitioners?

A final issue to do with coverage concerns the extent to which research reviews restrict themselves to published research findings or introduce unpublished primary data or unpublished secondary material. Many of the reviews discussed here take the second option. For example, in preparing to draft the 'three wise men report', Alexander wrote to researchers in the field asking for information about work in progress, and while the impact of this on the review is difficult to judge it may have been substantial. In the case of *Worlds Apart?* the unpublished material, from the authors' own research, was used to support their explanation for the comparative underachievement of pupils in British schools. In the *Ethnic Minorities* review primary data from local authority ethnic monitoring play a major role. Here the aim was to provide more recent information about achievement levels than was otherwise available.[26] From the point of view of presenting a coherent and up-to-date picture there is clearly much to be said for these uses of unpublished material. However, if the main task of a reviewer is to represent the broad consensus among researchers in the field about what are and are not sound factual conclusions, the use of such material is questionable. This is because it has not been through any public process of collective assessment. As a result, lay readers are reliant on the judgement of the reviewer alone. This undercuts what we argued earlier was one of the advantages of research reviews as a means of disseminating research results. But, even if this argument is sound, how is it to be weighed against the possible value of such unpublished material for practitioners and policymakers?

In this section we have dealt with the way in which reviews cover the relevant research field. We noted that they vary in how explicit they are about the criteria of selection used, and this may imply variation in the degree to which criteria are applied systematically. The criteria likely to be involved include time period and methodological quality, and there is some scope in relation to both for variations in judgement on the part of reviewers about what to include and what to exclude. We also looked at the treatment of methodological issues, an area where there are significant differences in treatment across the reviews we have discussed. Finally, we noted how some reviews include unpublished material and we raised the issue of the desirability of this.

Drawing conclusions

It is common for reviews that are addressed to lay audiences to draw practical conclusions, but this is done with varying degrees of explicit-ness. At one end of the spectrum, the report of the 'three wise men' is strongly evaluative in its discussion throughout, and makes explicit recommendations which are presented as deriving directly from the evidence reviewed. In some of the other reviews, practical recommendations are less explicit and/or less specific. Thus, the final section of *Worlds Apart?*, entitled 'The next steps', simply encourages educationists to look beyond geographical boundaries to see what they can learn, and to experiment; though there are clear indications of more specific recommendations earlier in the review – in favour of more whole-class teaching, and of trying to ensure that all pupils reach a minimum standard.

At least two issues arise about the drawing of practical conclusions. One relates to the question of how closely any factual conclusions must stay to the findings of the studies reviewed. Should the reviewer simply summarise those findings, or can generalisations be formulated that go beyond them? In other words, how much interpretative licence should a reviewer exercise? Of course, reviewing research reports always involves selection and summary: in reducing the results of whole studies to a few sentences the reviewer makes decisions about what is and is not important about each investigation. Considerable discretion is involved here. But judgement is also involved in how the results of multiple studies are weighed and their general drift summarised.[27]

Reviews also vary in the extent to which they shape the material they discuss into an overall narrative line. At one extreme, we have the research review as digest, while at the other end of the spectrum are reviews where a clear-cut and practically relevant argument is developed throughout, perhaps reinforced by an executive summary placed at the beginning. The reviews we have discussed vary in terms of where they are located along this dimension. That by Gipps (and those of Taylor and Tomlinson) are the ones closest to the digest form, while those of the 'three wise men' and of Gillborn and Gipps are nearest to what we might call the narrative model. In the case of the report of the 'three wise men', for example, to a considerable extent there is a story line about declining standards in literacy and numeracy and the role of progressive ideas in producing this.[28] A similar narrative line structures the OFSTED *Ethnic Minorities* report: underachievement is again the focus, in terms of the extent to which some ethnic minority groups achieve at a lower level than the ethnic majority. However, there is a difference between these reviews in the relationship of the narrative frame employed, and the conclusions reached, to the storylines found in the studies reviewed. In the case of the 'three wise men' report, while some researchers had come to emphasise the value of direct teaching, the overall argument presented in the report is not to be found in most of the studies cited. By contrast, in the case of the *Ethnic Minorities* review, many of the studies Gillborn and Gipps discuss were guided by much the same narrative line that they adopt. Thus, the conclusion the reviewers draw – that discrimination in schools against black children continues to cause underachievement – conforms to that of a large proportion of the studies reviewed.

Another issue concerns whether reviews should provide evaluations and/or prescriptions at all, or should restrict themselves solely to factual conclusions. There is no doubt that policymakers and practitioners look to research reviews for practical implications, and they may well expect reviewers to 'make these explicit'. Another way of conceptualising what is involved in this is to see research reviews as offering 'translations' of the findings of research into practical recommendations. It might be assumed that researchers are well placed to do this because they are 'bilingual', given that many of them are not only researchers but also educational practitioners. However, more is involved in deriving practical recommendations than simply making the implicit explicit, or translating from one form of discourse into another. Factual information cannot, in itself, tell us what should be done. Practical recommendations also depend on value assumptions or commitments.[29]

Of course, it might be argued that in many areas there is general agreement about the relevant value issues. After all, few people would be against maximising reading and numeracy levels in British schools, or against maximising the achievement levels of ethnic minority pupils. However, while there may be agreement at a general level about the desirability of particular aims, considerable disagreement can arise over the priorities among educational goals, and about how those aims are best achieved. Practical recommendations involve costs, including opportunity costs. In a situation of scarce resources, which is the norm, judgements have to be made about what should be traded off against what. There are also questions about what is feasible. Hindess has pointed out the tendency in the past for arguments about public policy to assume that the state has more power to change things than it has (Hindess 1987), and this tendency seems to be especially prevalent in the field of education today.

There is, then, usually room for disagreement about the value issues that underlie practical recommendations in the field of education. And some would argue that, because of this, drawing conclusions that are evaluative or prescriptive in reviews goes beyond the authority of research (Foster et al. 1996 and 2000). However, even from this point of view, it may be legitimate for researchers to make *conditional* evaluations and prescriptions. These have the form: given commitment to this goal, then policy or practice meets or falls short of what is required in the following respects; or, given this goal and these particular value concerns about means, the following course of action would be desirable. In these terms, while research cannot tell us what is right or wrong about current policy or practice, it may be able to show that what actually occurs does or does not match the goals of practitioners or policymakers. Similarly, reviews can indicate what might be necessary in order to achieve a particular goal, or at least what courses of action lead in that direction; and this can be done without assuming the overall priority of the goal or the feasibility of its achievement in present or foreseeable circumstances.

Making evaluations or prescriptions, whether practical or conditional, places certain responsibilities on reviewers. As far as evaluations are concerned, for example, it needs to be quite clear in terms of what criteria a policy or practice can be shown to have succeeded or failed. There also needs to be evidence that what success or failure has occurred did in fact result from the policy or practice involved, not from some extraneous factor (what is and is not extraneous, of course, being relative to the criteria). Similarly, in relation to prescriptions, the assumptions being made about goals and means need to be made explicit.

Where evaluations and prescriptions are offered in research reviews, these do not usually take an explicitly conditional form; nor is the kind of information outlined above always included. This is most obviously true of the report of the 'three wise men'; and this despite its being labelled 'a discussion paper'. The other reviews are less explicitly evaluative and prescriptive, but the same issue arises to some degree. Thus, the OFSTED *Ethnic Minorities* review concludes that 'colour-blind policies' have failed and should be abandoned. And the authors argue that there should be systematic ethnic monitoring, the implication being that teachers and others must work to eliminate any underachievement by minority groups that this reveals. This practical conclusion is presented as if it followed unproblematically from the evidence reviewed. Yet it is not clear how the term 'colour-blind policies' is being defined, when (and how effectively) they were implemented, what the time period was over which their effects were evaluated and (if they have failed) why this happened. There are also questions that are not addressed about the role of ethnic monitoring itself (Ahmad and Sheldon 1991; Foster 1994).

One of the reasons why the assumptions underlying practical recommendations are not spelt out may be the fact, noted earlier, that many educational researchers also play practitioner roles. This opens up the possibility that the conclusions are based not just on research evidence but also on practitioner expertise. And, indeed, it could be argued that if researcher/practitioners were not to interpret the practical implications of research evidence as reviewers, this would be done by non-researchers in ways that are detrimental to educational progress. Certainly, it is true that research reviews enter an arena in which there are already many voices offering practical evaluations and prescriptions, appealing to experience and common sense, and even to research evidence, in order to press their claims. In such an arena, it might be argued, it is essential for reviewers to make clear what they see as the practical implications of research findings.

It is undoubtedly true that the character of public debates about educational and other matters is a long way from any idealised version of academic discussion, and researchers must take account of this if their work is to have any impact. It should be noted, though, that relying on an appeal to practitioner expertise is open to challenge (see, for example, Hargreaves' characterisation of non-research-based practitioner knowledge: Hargreaves 1996:7–8). It is also worth questioning whether the value issues involved in the 'translation' of research findings into practical recommendations can ever be entirely 'professionalised'. There is a danger that research reviews which draw practical conclusions will effectively close down discussion of those issues, and this may have negative consequences for attempts to enhance the quality of educational provision as well as for the development of reflective educational practitioners.

Summarising the questions we have raised: how far must reviewers restrict themselves to outlining the results of research, as opposed to drawing more general conclusions? And is it legitimate for them to offer practical evaluations and prescriptions based on such conclusions and/or on professional expertise? Or are only conditional evaluations and prescriptions acceptable? And, if evaluations and prescriptions are to be made, what information needs to be provided about the basis on which they rely? Finally, what are the implications of decisions about these matters for the public image of research and for its impact on policy and practice?

Conclusion

In the course of our discussion we have raised a variety of issues that need to be taken into account by both writers and readers of research reviews, and indeed by the educational research community as a whole. There is a cluster of concerns relating to the initiation of reviews: notably about their sponsorship, audience, and purpose. There are also questions to be raised about the way in which the field to be reviewed is defined. We drew attention here to the role of factual and value assumptions, and raised questions about the extent to which these need to be made explicit and justified. The coverage and treatment of relevant research also involves decisions – about the salience to be given to different studies and the manner in which they are treated – and we highlighted the significance of the criteria guiding these decisions. These relate to the time period the review is to cover, the effects of changing value relevances and methodological considerations; and all of them involve scope for differential judgement. Finally, we looked at the nature of the conclusions drawn from reviews. One obvious issue here relates back to the question of audience: whether the conclusions presented are about further research or about policymaking and practice. And, in relation to the latter, there is the question of what type of conclusion can legitimately be drawn, of the extent of the authority of research over practice and of the proper relationship between research and professional expertise of various kinds.

In recent years there has been a growing amount of attention given to the texts produced by researchers, especially but not exclusively those of qualitative researchers. Atkinson has argued that this is an essential component of the reflexivity that ought to be a central feature of any researcher's orientation (Atkinson 1992). Since reviews of research serve an important function in showing how the products of research relate to practical concerns, and perhaps also in shaping their use by policymakers and practitioners, reflexivity ought surely to be extended to include them. At the very least, it is essential to recognise that reviews can take a variety of forms, and that they are structured by different interpretations of the role of the reviewer in relation both to the field of research and to that of policymaking and practice.

Notes

1. See, for example, the discussions in the British Educational Research Association newsletter *Research Intelligence* during 1995 and 1996.
2. It is important to note that our concern in this chapter is with scientific, or academic, not with practical research (see Chapter 6 for this distinction).

3. It is perhaps significant that there is no British equivalent of the *Review of Educational Research*, published by the American Educational Research Association. However, there is currently a proposal within the British Educational Research Association for a journal fulfilling something like this role (see McIntyre 1997b). Furthermore, an Evidence for Policy and Practice: Information and Co-ordinating Centre (EPPI Centre) has recently been established at the Institute of Education, University of London, which has the task of overseeing the development of systematic reviews of the educational research literature. For a critique of the concept of systematic review, see Hammersley (2001b).

4. We have chosen to focus on a small number of recent reviews, though we will also make reference to some older ones. Our aim was not to achieve a representative sample, but rather to select reviews that allowed fruitful comparison.

5. Jim Rose was HM Chief Inspector of Primary Schools and Chris Woodhead was then Chief Executive of the National Curriculum Council. Only Robin Alexander was an experienced educational researcher.

6. Alexander records what happened when it became clear that he was pursuing a different line (Alexander 1997:ch. 10). See also Woods (1996:152–3). For another account of the role of the educationist in policy formation in this period, see Galton (1996).

7. For a useful discussion of different types of review, aimed at different audiences, see Bassey (2000). For highly divergent interpretations of the nature and function of reviews, see Eisenhart (1998), Meacham (1998), Schwandt (1998), Lather (1999), Livingston (1999).

8. In personal communications, both authors of this review indicated that, to a considerable extent, it was designed for an academic audience.

9. For evidence about the differential reception of the report of the 'three wise men', see Wenham (1994) and Woods and Wenham (1995).

10. Of course these two factors overlap. Sponsors will usually be at least a sideline audience; and an important one – given that they may be able to block publication or distribution of the review. And, even if they cannot, a negative reaction on their part could affect future funding.

11. There is one section, of two pages, that deals with understanding the success of ethnic minority pupils, but there is very little research which the reviewers can draw on here: Gillborn and Gipps (1996:58–9).

12. Interestingly, the report nevertheless came in for some criticism for its focus on underachievement, see Pyke (1996).

13. Something similar may be present in Gillborn and Gipps' emphasis on the contribution that *qualitative* research can make to an understanding of educational inequalities (Gillborn and Gipps 1996:48–59).

14. Such a tendency is likely to be reinforced by the anticipated response of lay audiences: they will probably be seen as wanting clear-cut findings whose validity is certain, and that carry direct implications for practice.

15. The recent dip in the fortunes of Asian economies underlines the importance of these questions.

16. This is an issue which is foregrounded by the review's rejection of a 'colour-blind' approach, on which see below.

17. There is a history of argument to the effect that both examinations and testing have anti-educational effects because they do not measure true learning and thereby discourage it. For an early example in relation to exams, see Herbert (1889).

18. Taylor produced a series of reviews covering all the main ethnic minorities:

see also Taylor and Hegarty (1985), Taylor (1986 and 1988).

19. Some we will not discuss are geographical and linguistic. Reviews may focus exclusively on research dealing with a particular country or area of the world. Equally, reviews will often be restricted to the literature in a single language, often English.

20. This is illustrated by the parallels between the two OFSTED reviews we are discussing here. Both focus on comparative levels of educational achievement, in one case between *countries*, in the other between *ethnic groups* within a single country. Furthermore, in each case much of the public relevance of the review hinges on 'underachievement'. In the case of *Worlds Apart?*, the concern is the underachievement of pupils in the English/British education system. With the other OFSTED review, it is the underachievement of some ethnic minority pupils within that system. Finally, in both reviews, the explanations appeared to concern intra-school processes.

21. This is compounded by the lack of any specific reference to the earlier reviews in this field.

22. In her much longer review, Taylor (1981) provides even greater in-depth discussion of methodological problems, both in general and in relation to some specific studies.

23. We might take this opportunity to note that the criticisms here are inaccurate. Foster does not propose 'absolute proof' as a requirement, only validity 'beyond reasonable doubt'; see Hammersley (1995:ch. 4). And it is in these terms that Foster's work questions the validity of qualitative studies on which Gillborn and Gipps rely in this section: see Foster (1990, 1993a, 1993b and 1993c), Foster et al. (1996).

24. As it was, OFSTED forced them to cut down the length of the final draft, and also challenged them to justify the value of qualitative research in the field (Gillborn: personal communication).

25. This is a stance which is controversial. See Bracey (1996), Stedman (1997a and 1997b), Baker (1997) and Bracey (1997); and also a recent exchange about the value of school effectiveness research (Elliott 1996; Sammons and Reynolds 1997).

26. More recently, Gillborn and Mirza have provided further evidence of this kind (Gillborn and Mirza 2000).

27 There is also a question about the *means* by which general conclusions ought to be drawn from a body of research findings. Should this be done informally, or does it require some more systematic approach, such as meta-analysis (Glass et al. 1981)? Of course, the latter is controversial even in relation to quantitative research, and is hardly developed at all in the context of qualitative work (Noblitt and Hare 1988). None of the reviews we have discussed uses meta-analysis, but this may be an area that is ripe for future development.

28. See Hammersley and Scarth (1993). This storyline does not exhaust the message, and there are various subtleties introduced, such as the idea that teaching must be flexible according to purpose. As Alexander points out, the structure of the review is not very coherent, and this resulted from the struggle that went on among the authors (Alexander 1997:ch. 10).

29. There is, of course, a long-running dispute about whether 'ought' can be logically derived from 'is'. We have discussed this whole issue in more detail elsewhere: see Foster et al. (2000).

Conclusion

All the chapters of this book have been concerned with what relationships are possible and desirable between educational research, on the one hand, and policymaking or practice, on the other. As I noted in the Introduction, this has been a perennial issue of discussion, and in my view it is unlikely that it will ever be put to rest. This is because, in an important sense, the problem is intractable. What I mean by this is that expectations on both sides of the divide between research and practice will always tend to exceed what is possible. Policymakers and practitioners are always likely to expect that research should provide them with more than it can. Similarly, many researchers will often want their work to have a direct and specific impact on policymaking or practice, even though this can happen only rarely and never without a contribution from other factors. Moreover, when it does occur, it is unlikely to have the consequences they desire, or perhaps even those they anticipate. Excessive expectations are generated, I suggest, by the existence of what was referred to in Chapter 3 as multiple 'worlds', and the tensions that exist amongst these.

One response to my arguments in this book might be to infer that I am denying that research can make any practical contribution. This is not true. My point is simply that, generally speaking, the contribution will be small, often indeterminate, and frequently difficult to trace.[1] And an important implication is that efforts to subject research to 'transparent accountability' can be no more successful, and perhaps even less so, than applying this form of assessment to teaching or other professional occupations. Furthermore, *attempting* to do this will have damaging consequences for the quality of educational research.

It may also be concluded from what I have said in this book that I do not believe that there are any ways in which the practical use of research can be improved. Again, this does not follow from what I have written. There are useful improvements that could be made, though they are modest in both scope and likely effect. Identifying these has not been my prime concern here, though the previous chapter does point to one area where I believe that improvements could be made: in the preparation and presentation of research findings via reviews. Instead, the main task of my book has been to clarify and think through the issues underlying the relationship between educational research and practice. Much previous discussion of this issue, perhaps as a result of pressure from recurrent crises in that relationship, has tended to assume that we already have a good understanding of what is involved, so that the only task is to find 'the solution'. And, indeed, that is also what drives current attempts to reform educational research in England and Wales. I have tried to show in previous chapters that this assumption is an error. Considerable thought is required about the different forms that research can and ought to take, and also about the nature of policymaking and practice and the sorts of social organisation in which they are embedded. Moreover, this must be done with an exploratory attitude, rather than being governed by normative conceptions of how research *needs to be* if it is to be useful, or of how practitioners *ought* to relate to it.

The engineering and strong enlightenment models, which I discussed in earlier chapters, each tends to assume a single mode of use, and one which implies determinacy; in the sense that research findings are regarded as logically implying practical recommendations about goals and/or means. In my view this is a fallacy. Empirical research findings alone cannot tell us what is right or wrong about a situation, who is to blame, or what should be done. Such value conclusions can only be drawn once we bring in value premises, and there is usually scope for reasonable disagreement about the selection and prioritising of these (see Foster et al. 2000). Thus, even if such premises are actually built into the orientation of a piece of research, and the researcher draws value conclusions, these will always be open to challenge on the grounds that they do not follow directly from the factual data. Moreover, in my view, researchers do not have any distinctive authority in the spheres of practical evaluation and prescription, in the way that they do in relation to factual knowledge claims.[2]

One important implication of denying that research findings carry intrinsic practical evaluations or implications is that we must recognise that they can be used in diverse ways, and it may be worth outlining these here. Let me begin with the most obvious and straightforward use that practitioners can make of research findings. Here, research supplies them with information that they did not previously have. Sometimes this will be a matter of practitioners having felt unable to act because they were aware of a gap in their knowledge; with research filling that gap, thereby allowing action to be taken. More commonly, perhaps, practitioners will find it necessary to act despite gaps in their knowledge. Even so, they may subsequently be able to use research to correct the assumptions they have made, and such correction could lead them to change their behaviour in the future, though it need not do so. Nevertheless, we should note the likely limits to this role of research in relation to practice: where research findings seem incompatible with parts of their perspective that they regard as secure, practitioners are less likely to take account of them. In this they may be right or wrong; but it is important to underline that this is a matter of *practical* not simply intellectual judgement; and one on which researchers cannot adjudicate with any great authority.

From this first use of research findings we can move to a closely related one, which may be very common; though many researchers undervalue or positively reject it. Here, research findings are interpreted as confirming existing beliefs and validating existing practice. One reason why this function is undervalued is probably that it shows no obvious sign of the 'impact' of research, since practice remains the same. Indeed, practitioners themselves sometimes deride this contribution, citing it as evidence that 'research tells us nothing we did not already know'. Both arguments are mistaken, however. The value of research is not restricted to cases where it modifies practice. To accept such a restriction is to commit oneself to what might be called modernist idolatry of change. This forgets that change is not always for the better, and that stability has intrinsic benefits. Equally important to underline is that confirmation of what is already believed can be valuable, where it increases the confidence we can reasonably have in those beliefs. Confirmation is worthless only in the case of beliefs that are regarded by virtually everyone as already very secure in their validity.[3]

Another use of their work that is often disparaged by researchers is where their findings are cited in public debates by policymakers or other practitioners in support of positions that have already been reached on other grounds. There is a tendency to assume that this necessarily involves a misuse of research. Of course, it *may* do so, in the sense that the findings are misinterpreted or distorted in order to suit the purposes of legitimation.[4] There are, indeed, likely to be pressures in this direction. However, the line between legitimate interpretation and misinterpretation is not clear-cut; there is usually a broad band within which there is room for disagreement. Moreover, what researchers judge to be misinterpretation, and how they respond to it, may be shaped by their attitude towards the cause in which the research findings are being used. What I want to underline, though, is that there is nothing wrong in principle with the legitimatory use of research findings. The idea that using research findings in support of a position is only justifiable where the findings have themselves led to adoption of that position is one that simply does not take account of the complexities of practical belief formation; in effect, it implies that policy should be based entirely on research findings. So, the only legitimate complaint that researchers can have in this context, it seems to me, is that factual research findings have been seriously misrepresented; not, for example, that these have been used in a way that is contrary to what the researchers themselves took to be the appropriate practical conclusions. As already noted, researchers have some authority, albeit not infallible, over the *meaning* of research findings, but not over judgements about their *significance*; furthermore, the distinction between meaning and significance is itself not clear-cut.

A fourth way in which research may be used is the one that is central to the engineering model. Here, research findings are employed in the production of some technology or procedure which practitioners can employ in their work, the most obvious example in education being psychological tests. Advocates of the enlightenment model often reject this kind of use as impossible or dehumanising. And there are probably good reasons why it is relatively rare in the field of education and in relation to social life generally (see Chapters 1 and 4). I also agree that there is a danger of such technologies and procedures being treated not just as black boxes, so that areas of practice become routinised, but as self-validating. Nevertheless, it is unwise to deny the possibility of this kind of use, or to suggest that it is *necessarily* undesirable. Routinisation of some parts of any form of practice is essential if others are to be opened up to reflection and deliberation. The idea of a fully reflexive form of practice, in which nothing is taken for granted, is another modernist myth. Thus, it seems to me that psychological tests can be of value as a supplement to practitioner judgement. That they sometimes lead, unjustifiably, to a downgrading of the value of such judgement is equally true, but simply indicates the need for caution. What can be usefully routinised or technologised is not always easy to judge, and this can change over time. However, rejecting research-based technologies or procedures is no more sensible than treating them as a *replacement* for practitioner judgement.

The sharpest contrast to this 'engineering' use of research is where research causes practitioners to pause in their work and stimulates them completely to rethink their perspective. This is the kind of impact that many researchers committed to the strong enlightenment model see as the proper role for research in relation to both policymaking and practice. They may believe that research can provide a new comprehensive perspective which will transform practice for the better (we might call this the Marx scenario). Alternatively, they may believe that a continual unsettling of practitioner perspectives is of value in itself (we might call this the Socrates scenario).[5] For reasons already stated (see Chapter 2), I do not believe that research can ever supply a replacement perspective for practice. However, I recognise that it can, very occasionally, throw serious doubt on key elements of practitioners' perspectives and force them substantially to revise both their point of view and their practice. It is important to remember, however, that not all challenges to current perspectives are of value; and no form of challenge is of value at all times. Moreover, once again, what is and is not of value here is a matter of *practical* not just of intellectual judgement.[6]

In this conclusion, I have outlined the diverse ways in which research can influence practice. Two general points can be made about these. First, they are all real possibilities, and in particular contexts they may all be of value. Secondly, and even more important, they can all be damaging, at least as judged from *some* perspective. Most discussion of the role of research in relation to policymaking and practice seems to be governed by the idea that the findings of research carry practical implications which can be 'applied', and that the effects of this will always be beneficial; or, at least, that this will be true in the case of research of the right kind and/or where practitioners adopt the correct attitude towards it. It would be reassuring if the relationship between research and other kinds of practice were so simple and safe. Much of this book has been concerned with demonstrating that it is not.

Notes

1. This is simply to reiterate the judgements of several writers in the field, over a considerable period: see, for example, Cohen and Garet (1975), Weiss (1977, 1979 and 1980), Rule (1978), Lindblom and Cohen (1979), Scott and Shore (1979:appendix), Levin (1991), Adams et al. (1991) and Shove (1998).
2. At most, they can only legitimately provide conditional evaluations and pre-scriptions. See the discussion on page 143 above.
3. Failure to understand this, along with the tendency to 'recognise' the validity of contradictory ideas (see Gage 1991), is one reason why practitioners often undervalue research.
4. It is important to emphasise that my use of the term 'legitimation' here refers to the employment of research findings both to defend existing practices *and* to support proposals for change.
5. These two positions are sometimes combined, with the unsettling of per-spectives being seen as likely to lead to the emergence of a radically new form of social life, as in the case of some kinds of postmodernism: see Chapter 4. Alternatively, writers sometimes simply vacillate between Marx and Socrates.
6. The idea that the *function* of research is to challenge dominant perspectives seems to me to be profoundly mistaken: see Hammersley (2001a).

References

Abbott, A. (1992) 'What do cases do? Some notes on activity in sociological analysis', in C. Ragin and H. S. Becker (eds) *What is a Case? Exploring the foundations of social inquiry*, Cambridge, Cambridge University Press.

Abbott, A. (1998) 'The causal devolution', *Sociological Methods and Research*, 27, 2: 148–81.

Ackrill, J. L. (1981) *Aristotle the Philosopher*, Oxford, Oxford University Press.

Adams, R. M., Smelser, N. J. and Treiman, D. J. (1991) 'The national interest in the support of basic research', in D. S. Anderson and B. J. Biddle (eds) *Knowledge for Policy: improving education through research*, London, Falmer Press. (Original report published in 1982.)

Ahmad, W. I. U., Sheldon, T. A. (1991) 'Race and statistics', *Radical Statistics*, 48, 27–33. Reprinted in M. Hammersley (ed.) *Social Research: philosophy, politics, and practice*, London, Sage, 1993.

Alasuutari, P. (1998) *An Invitation to Social Research*, London, Sage.

Alexander, R. J. (1992) *Policy and Practice in Primary Education*, London, Routledge.

Alexander, R. J. (1997) *Policy and Practice in Primary Education*, 2nd edn, London, Routledge.

Alexander, R. J., Rose, J. and Woodhead, C. (1992) *Curriculum Organisation and Classroom Practice in Primary Schools: a discussion paper*, London, Department of Education and Science, HMSO.

Altheide, D. L. and Johnson, J. M. (1994) 'Criteria for assessing interpretive validity in qualitative research', in N. K. Denzin and Y. S. Lincoln (eds) *Handbook of Qualitative Research*, Thousand Oaks, CA, Sage.

Altman, D. G. (1994) 'The scandal of poor medical research', *British Medical Journal*, 6924, 308: 283–4.

Anderson, B. (1990) *Methodological Errors in Medical Research*, Oxford, Blackwell.

Anderson, D. S. and Biddle, B. J. (eds) (1991) *Knowledge for Policy: improving education through research*, London, Falmer Press.

Archer, M. (1996) 'Social integration and system integration: developing the distinction', *Sociology*, 30, 4: 679–99.

Atkinson, P. (1981) *The Clinical Experience*, Farnborough, Gower.

Atkinson, P. (1992) *Understanding Ethnographic Texts*, Newbury Park, Sage.

Atkinson, P. (1995) *Medical Talk and Medical Work*, London, Sage.

Atkinson, P., Coffey, A. and Delamont, S. (1999) 'Ethnography: post, past, and present', *Journal of Contemporary Ethnography*, 28, 5: 460–71.

Bailey, F. G. (1969) *Strategems and Spoils: a social anthropology of politics*, Oxford, Blackwell.

Baker, D. P. (1997) 'Good news, bad news, and international comparisions: comment on Bracey', *Educational Researcher* 26, 3: 16–17.

Baker, J. R. (1978) 'Michael Polanyi's contributions to the cause of freedom in science', *Minerva*, XVI, 3: 382–96.

Ball, S. J. (1994) *Education Reform: a critical and post-structural approach*, Buckingham, Open University Press.

Ball, S. J. (1995) 'Intellectuals or technicians? The urgent role of theory in educational studies', *British Journal of Educational Studies*, XXXXIII, 3: 255–71.

Ball, S. J. (1997) 'Policy sociology and critical social research: a personal review of recent education policy and policy research, *British Educational Research Journal*, 23, 3: 257–74.

Ball, S. J. (2001) ' "You've been NERFed!" Dumbing down the academy: National Education Forum: "a national strategy-consultation paper": a brief and bilious response', *Journal of Education Policy*, 16, 3: 265–8.

Barrow, R. (1984) *Giving Teaching Back to Teachers*, Brighton, Wheatsheaf.

Bassey, M. (1995) *Creating Education through Research*, Newark, Kirklington Moor Press, in association with the British Educational Research Association.

Bassey, M. (2000) 'Reviews of educational research', *Research Intelligence*, 71: 22–9.

Bauman, Z. (1987) *Legislators and Interpreters*, Cambridge, Polity.

Becker, H. S. (1970) *Sociological Work*, Chicago, Aldine.

Becker, H. S. (1973) *Outsiders: studies in the sociology of deviance*, 2nd edn, New York, Free Press.

Becker, H. S. (1992) 'Cases, causes, conjunctures, stories, and imagery', in C. Ragin and H. S. Becker (eds) *What is a Case? Exploring the foundations of social inquiry*, Cambridge, Cambridge University Press.

Becker, H. S. (1998) *Tricks of the Trade*, Chicago, University of Chicago Press.

Becker, H. S., Geer, B., Hughes, E. C. and Strauss, A. (1961) *Boys in White: student culture in medical school*, Chicago, Chicago University Press.

Beiner, R. (1983) *Political Judgement*, London, Methuen.

Beiner, R. (1997) *Philosophy in a Time of Lost Spirit*, Toronto, University of Toronto Press.

Beiser, F. (1987) *The Fate of Reason*, Cambridge, MA, Harvard University Press.

Bennett, N. (1976) *Teaching Styles and Pupil Progress*, London, Open Books.

Bennett, N. (1985) 'Recent research on teaching-learning processes in classroom settings', mimeo.

Bensman, J. and Lilienfeld, R. (1973) *Craft and Consciousness*, New York, Wiley.

Berlin, I. (1979) *The Age of Enlightenment: the eighteenth century philosophers*, Oxford, Oxford University Press.

Berlin, I. (1990) *The Crooked Timber of Humanity*, London, Murray.

Bernal, J. D. (1939) *The Social Function of Science*, London, Routledge and Kegan Paul.

Bernstein, B. (1971) *Class, Codes and Control, volume 1*, London, Routledge and Kegan Paul.

Bird, G (1986) *William James*, London, Routledge and Kegan Paul.

Blumer, H. (1969) *Symbolic Interactionism*, Englewood Cliffs, NJ, Prentice Hall.

Blunkett, D. (2000) 'Influence or irrelevance: can social science improve government?', *Research Intelligence*, 71: 12–21.

Bogard, W. (1990) 'Closing down the social: Baudrillard's challenge to contemporary sociology', *Sociological Theory*, 8, 1: 1–15.

Bowe, R., Ball, S. J., with Gold, A. (1992) *Reforming Education and Changing Schools: case studies in policy sociology*, London, Routledge.

Bracey, G. W. (1996) 'International comparisons and the condition of American education', *Educational Researcher*, 25, 1: 5–11.

Bracey, G. W. (1997) 'Rejoinder: on comparing the incomparable: a response to Baker and Stedman', *Educational Researcher*, 26, 3: 19–26.

Brahams, D. (1991) 'Effectiveness research and health gain', *Lancet*, 338: 1386.

Brenner, N. (1994) 'Foucault's new functionalism', *Theory and Society*, 23: 679–709.

Bryant, C. G. A. (1976) *Sociology in Action*, London, Allen and Unwin.

Bulmer, M. (1982) *The Uses of Social Research*, London, Allen and Unwin.

Burawoy, M., Blum, J. A., George, S., Gille, Z., Gowan, T., Haney, L., Klawiter, M., Lopez, S. H., O Riain, S. and Thayer, M. (2000) *Global Ethnography: forces, connections, and imaginations in a postmodern world*, Berkeley, CA, University of California Press.

Burczak, T. A. (1994) 'The postmodern moments of F. A. Hayek's economics', *Economics and Philosophy*, 10: 31–48.

Burkett, G. and Knafl, K. (1974) 'Judgment and decision making in a medical speciality', *Sociology of Work and Occupations*, 1, 1: 82–109.

Burnham, J. (1945) *The Managerial Revolution or What is Happening in the*

World Now, Harmondsworth, Penguin. (Originally published 1941.)

Carr, D. (1977) 'Husserl's problematic concept of the life-world', in F. A. Elliston and P. McCormick (eds) *Husserl: expositions and appraisals*, Notre Dame, University of Notre Dame Press.

Carr, W. (1987) 'What is an educational practice?', *Journal of the Philosophy of Education*, 21, 2: 163–75.

Carr, W. and Kemmis, S. (1986) *Becoming Critical*, London, Falmer.

Caswill, C. and Shove, E. (2000) 'Introducing interactive social science', *Science and Public Policy*, 27, 3: 154–8.

Chambers, J. H. (1991) 'The difference between the abstract concepts of science and the general concepts of empirical educational research', *Journal of Educational Thought*, 25, 1: 41–9.

Chambers, J. H. (1992) *Empiricist Research on Teaching: a philosophical and practical critique of its scientific pretensions*, Boston, Kluwer.

Charlton, B. (1995) 'Megatrials are subordinate to medical science', *British Medical Journal*, 311: 257.

Charlton, D. G. (1959) *Positivist Thought in France during the Second Empire 1852–1870*, Oxford, Oxford University Press.

Clancy, C. (1996) 'Evidence-based medicine meets cost-effectiveness analysis' (editorial), *Journal of the American Medical Association*, 276, 4: 329–30.

Clarke, A. (1991) 'Social worlds/arenas theory as organisational theory', in D. Maines (ed) *Social Organisation and Social Process*, New York, Aldine de Gruyter.

Clarke, C. (1998) 'Resurrecting research to raise standards', *Social Sciences: News from the ESRC*, 40, October: 2.

Clarke, J. and Newman, J. (1997) *The Managerial State: power, politics and ideology in the remaking of social welfare*, London, Sage.

Clifford, J. and Marcus, G. (eds) (1986) *Writing Culture: the poetics and politics of ethnography*, Berkeley, CA, University of California Press.

Cochrane, A. L. (1972) *Effectiveness and Efficiency*, Nuffield Provincial Hospitals Trust.

Cohen, A. (1974) *Two-Dimensional Man: an essay on the anthropology of power and symbolism in complex society*, London, Routledge and Kegan Paul.

Cohen, A. P. (ed.) (1986) *Symbolising Boundaries: identity and diversity in British cultures*, Manchester, Manchester University Press.

Cohen, D. K. and Garet, M. S. (1975) 'Reforming educational policy with applied social research', *Harvard Educational Review*, 45, 1: 17–43.

Cohen, G. A. (1978) *Karl Marx's Theory of History*, Oxford, Oxford University Press.

Cohen, N. (2000) 'With our money, they hide the truth', *New Statesman*, 20 March: 17–19.

Collins, H. (1975) 'The seven sexes: a study of the sociology of a phenomenon, or the replication of experiments in physics', *Sociology*, 9: 205–24.

Corey, S. (1953) *Action Research to Improve School Practices*, New York, Teachers' College, Columbia University.

Court, C. (1996) 'NHS Handbook criticises evidence-based medicine', *British Medical Journal*, 312: 1439–1440.

Crocker, L. G. (1992) 'The problem of truth and falsehood in the age of enlightenment', in P. Riley (ed.) *Essays on Political Philosophy*, Rochester, NY, University of Rochester Press. (First published in 1953.)

Cronbach, L. (1975) 'Beyond the two disciplines of scientific psychology', *American Psychologist*, 30: 116–27.

Crystal, D. (1987) *The Cambridge Encyclopaedia of Language*, Cambridge, Cambridge University Press.

Culyer, A. J. (1986) *Health Service Ills: the wrong economic medicine (a critique of David Green's Which Doctor)*, Discussion Paper 16, Centre for Health Economics, University of York.

Davis, M. (1998) *Thinking Like an Engineer: studies in the ethics of a profession*, New York, Oxford University Press.

Dearlove, O., Sharples, A., O'Brien, K. and Dunkley, C. (1995) 'Many questions cannot be answered by evidence based medicine', *British Medical Journal*, 311: 257–8.

Degenhardt, M. A. B. (1984) 'Educational research as a source of educational harm', *Culture, Education and Society*, 38, 3: 232–52.

Deighan, M. and Hitch, S. (eds) (1995) *Clinical Effectiveness from Guidelines to Cost-Effective Practice*, Health Services Management Unit, University of Manchester, Earlybrave Publications.

Delamont, S. and Hamilton, D. (1984) 'Revisiting classroom research: a continuing cautionary tale', in S. Delamont (ed.) *Readings on Interaction in the Classroom*, London, Methuen.

Demerath, N. J. and Peterson, R. A. (eds) (1967) *System, Change, and Conflict*, New York, Free Press.

Denzin, N. K. and Lincoln, Y. S. (eds) (1994) *Handbook of Qualitative Research*, Thousand Oaks, CA, Sage.

Department for Education and Employment (DfEE) (1998) *Proposed Action Plan in Response to the Recommendations from the IES Report 'Excellence in Schools'*, London, DfEE.

Department of Education and Science (DES) (1991) *Primary Education: statement by the Secretary of State for Education and Science*, London, DES.

Dews, P. (1986) 'The *Nouvelle Philosophie* and Foucault', in M. Gane (ed.) *Towards a Critique of Foucault*, London, Routledge and Kegan Paul.

Dews, P. (1987) *Logics of Disintegration: post-structuralist thought and the claims of critical theory*, London, Verso.

Douglas, J. D. (1976) *Investigative Social Research*, Beverly Hills, CA, Sage.

Doyle, W. (1977) 'Learning the classroom environment', *Journal of Teacher*

Education, 28: 51–5.

Drolet, P. M. (1994) 'The wild and the sublime: Lyotard's post-modern politics', *Political Studies*, XLII: 259–73.

Dunkin, M. J. and Biddle, B. J. (1974) *The Study of Teaching*, New York, Holt, Rinehart and Winston.

Economic and Social Research Council (ESRC) (2000) Teaching and Learning Research Programme, July 2000 update at http://www.ex.ac.uk/ESRC-TLRO/backgrnd.htm

Edwards, D. (1988) 'Toleration and Mill's liberty of thought and discussion', in S. Mendus (ed.) *Justifying Tolerance: conceptual and historical perspectives*, Cambridge, Cambridge University Press.

Edwards, T. (1996) 'The research base of effective teacher education', *Research Intelligence*, newsletter of the British Educational Research Association, 57, July: 7–12.

Eisenhart, M. (1998) 'On the subject of interpretive reviews', *Review of Educational Research*, 68, 4: 391–9.

Elliott, J. (1991) *Action Research for Educational Change*, Milton Keynes, Open University Press.

Elliott, J. (1996) 'School effectiveness research and its critics: alternative visions of schooling', *Cambridge Journal of Education*, 26, 2: 199–223.

Elliston, F. A. and McCormick, P. (eds) (1977) *Husserl: expositions and appraisals*, Notre Dame, University of Notre Dame Press.

Elster, J. (1982) 'Marxism, functionalism and game theory: the case for methodological individualism', *Theory and Society*, 11: 453–82.

Embree, L. (1988) 'Schutz on science', in L. Embree (ed.) *Worldly Phenomenology*, Washington, DC, Center for Advanced Research in Phenomenology and University Press of America.

Entwistle, V. A., Sheldon, T. A., Sowden, A. and Watt, I. S. (1998) 'Evidence-informed patient choice', *International Journal of Technology Assessment in Health Care*, 14, 2: 212–25.

Evans-Pritchard, E. E. (1951) *Social Anthropology*, London, Routledge and Kegan Paul.

Fallding, H. (1963) 'Functional analysis in sociology', *American Sociological Review*, 28: 5–13.

Farrow, S. (1999) 'Insulted by Blunkett', *The Guardian*, 21 July.

Fay, B. (1975) *Social Theory and Political Practice*, London, Allen and Unwin.

Fay, B. (1987) *Critical Social Science: liberation and its limits*, Cambridge, Polity.

Ferlie, E., Ashburner, L., Fitzgerald, L. and Pettigrew, A. (1996) *The New Public Management in Action*, Oxford, Oxford University Press.

Ferry, L. and Renaut, A. (1990) *French Philosophy of the Sixties: an essay on antihumanism*, Amherst, MA, University of Massachusetts Press.

Ferry, L. and Renaut, A. (eds) (1997) *Why We Are Not Nietzscheans*,

Chicago, University of Chicago Press.

Feussner, J. (1996) 'Evidence-based medicine: new priority for an old paradigm', *Journal of Bone and Mineral Research*, 11, 7: 877–82.

Finch, J. (1986) *Research and Policy: the uses of qualitative methods in social and educational research*, Lewes, Falmer.

Foster, P. (1990) 'Cases not proven: an evaluation of two studies of teacher racism', *British Educational Research Journal*, 16, 4: 335–48.

Foster, P. (1993a) 'Teacher attitudes and Afro-Caribbean achievement', *Oxford Review of Education*, 18, 3: 269–82.

Foster, P. (1993b) 'Some problems in identifying racial/ethnic equality or inequality in schools', *British Journal of Sociology*, 44, 3: 519–35.

Foster, P. (1993c) 'Equal treatment and cultural difference in multi-ethnic schools: a critique of teacher ethnocentrism theory', *International Studies in the Sociology of Education*, 2, 1: 89–103.

Foster, P. (1994) 'The use of "ethnic data" in education', *New Community*, 20, 4: 647–54.

Foster, P. (1999) ' "Never mind the quality, feel the impact": a methodological assessment of teacher research sponsored by the Teacher Training Agency', *British Journal of Educational Studies*, 47, 4: 380–98.

Foster, P., Gomm, R. and Hammersley, M. (1996) *Constructing Educational Inequality: an assessment of research on school processes*, London, Falmer.

Foster, P., Gomm, R. and Hammersley, M. (2000) 'Case studies as spurious evaluations: the example of research on educational inequalities', *British Journal of Educational Studies*, 48, 3: 215–30.

Foucault, M. (1980) *Power/Knowledge: selected interviews and other writings 1972–7*, New York, Pantheon Books.

Foucault, M. and Deleuze, G. (1972) 'Intellectuals and power', translated in M. Foucault, *Language, Counter-Memory, Practice*, edited by D. F. Bouchard, Oxford, Blackwell.

Fowler, P. B. S. (1995) Letter, *Lancet*, 346: 838.

Freese, L (1980) 'The problem of cumulative knowledge', in L. Freese (ed.) *Theoretical Methods in Sociology*, Pittsburgh, PA, University of Pittsburgh Press.

Freidson, E. (1970) *Profession of Medicine: a study of the sociology of applied knowledge*, New York, Dodd, Mead.

Fuller, S. (1999) 'Making the university fit for critical intellectuals: recovering from the ravages of the post-modern condition', *British Educational Research Journal*, 25, 5: 583–96.

Fuller, S. (2000) *The Governance of Science*, Buckingham, Open University Press.

Gage, N. L. (1985) *Hard Gains in the Soft Sciences: the case of pedagogy*, Bloomington, IN, Phi Delta Kappa.

Gage, N. L. (1991) 'The obviousness of social and educational research results', *Educational Researcher*, 20, 1: 10–16.

Gage, N. L. (1994) 'The scientific status of the behavioral sciences: the case of research on teaching', *Teaching and Teacher Education*, 10, 5: 565–77.

Galton, M. (1996) *Crisis in the Primary Classroom*, London, Fulton.

Galton, M., Simon, B. and Croll, P. (1980) *Inside the Primary Classroom*, London, Routledge and Kegan Paul.

Garfinkel, H. (1967a) 'The rational properties of scientific and commonsense activities', in H. Garfinkel, *Studies in Ethnomethodology*, Englewood Cliffs, NJ, Prentice-Hall.

Garfinkel, H. (1967b) *Studies in Ethnomethodology*, Englewood Cliffs, NJ, Prentice-Hall.

Gay, P. (1966) *The Enlightenment: an interpretation*, London, Weidenfeld and Nicolson.

Gewirtz, S. (1998) 'Post-welfarist schooling: a social justice audit', *Education and Social Justice*, 1, 1: 52–64.

Gibbons, M. (2000) 'Mode 2 society and the emergence of context-sensitive science', *Science and Public Policy*, 26, 5: 159–63.

Gibbons, M., Limoges, C., Nowotny, H., Schwartzman, S., Scott, P., and Trow, M. (1994) *The New Production of Knowledge: the dynamics of science and research in contemporary societies*, London, Sage.

Gillborn, D. and Gipps, C. (1996) *Recent Research on the Achievements of Ethnic Minority Pupils*, London, Office for Standards in Education, HMSO.

Gillborn, D. and Gipps, C. (1998) 'Watching the watchers: research, methods, politics and equity. A response to Foster and Hammersley', *British Educational Research Journal*, 24, 5: 629–33.

Gillborn, D. and Mirza, H. S. (2000) *Educational Inequality: mapping race, class and gender and synthesis of research evidence*, London, Office for Standards in Education.

Gipps, C. (1992) *What We Know About Effective Primary School Teaching*, The London File, Papers from the Institute of Education, London, Tufnell Press.

Glass, G. V. (1994) 'Review of Chambers, John H. 1992 empiricist research on teaching', *Journal of Educational Thought*, 28, 1: 127–30.

Glass, G., McGaw, B. and Smith, M. L. (1981) *Meta-Analysis in Social Research*, Beverly Hills, CA, Sage.

Goffman, E. (1959) *The Presentation of Self in Everyday Life*, Garden City, NY, Doubleday.

Goffman, E. (1961) *Asylums*, Harmondsworth, Penguin.

Goffman, E. (1975) *Frame Analysis*, Harmondsworth, Penguin.

Goldstein, H. and Mortimore, P. (1997) 'Misinterpreting Key Stage 1 test scores', at http://www.ioe.ac.uk/publications/ofs-crit.html

Gomm, R., Hammersley, M., and Foster, P. (eds) (2000) *Case Study Method:*

key issues, key texts, London, Sage.

Goodson, I. (1999) 'The educational researcher as public intellectual', *British Educational Research Journal*, 25, 3: 277–97.

Gould, S. J. (1989) *Wonderful Life*, Harmondsworth, Penguin.

Gouldner, A. (1973) *For Sociology*, Harmondsworth, Penguin.

Gouldner, A. W. (1965). 'Explorations in applied social science', in A. W. Gouldner, and S. M. Miller (eds) *Applied Sociology: opportunities and problems*, New York, Free Press.

Gourevitch, V. (ed.) (1997) *Rousseau: the discourses and other early political writings*, Cambridge, Cambridge University Press.

Graaf, J. de V. (1957) *Theoretical Welfare Economics*, Cambridge, Cambridge University Press.

Grahame-Smith, D. (1995) 'Evidence-based medicine: Socratic dissent', *British Medical Journal*, 310: 1126–27.

Grathoff, R. (ed.) (1989) *Philosophers in Exile: the correspondence of Alfred Schutz and Aron Gurwitsch, 1939–1959*, Bloomington, IN, Indiana Press.

Gray, J. (1996) *Berlin*, London, Fontana.

Gray, J., Jesson, D. and Sime, N. (1990) 'Estimating differences in the examination performances of secondary schools in six LGAs: a multilevel approach to school effectiveness', *Oxford Review of Education*, 16, 2: 137–58.

Habermas, J. (1968) *Knowledge and Interest* (English translation, Cambridge, Polity, 1987).

Habermas, J. (1971) *Theory and Practice* (English translation, Cambridge, Polity, 1988).

Hague, D. (1990) 'Establishing research priorities in the social sciences', in P. Deane (ed.) *Frontiers of Economic Research*, London, Macmillan.

Hague, D. (1991) *Beyond Universities: a new republic of the intellect*, Hobart Paper 115, London, Institute of Economic Affairs.

Ham, C., Hunter, C.J. and Robinson, R. (1995) 'Evidence based policymaking', *British Medical Journal*, 310: 71–2.

Hammersley, M. (1979) 'Towards a model of teacher activity', in J. Eggleston (ed.) *Teacher Decision Making in the Classroom*, London, Routledge and Kegan Paul, pp. 181–92.

Hammersley, M. (1985) 'From ethnography to theory', *Sociology*, 19: 244–59.

Hammersley, M. (1987a) 'Ethnography and cumulative development of theory: a discussion of Woods' proposal for "phase two" research', *British Educational Research Journal*, 13, 3: 283–96.

Hammersley, M. (1987b) 'Ethnography for survival? A reply to Woods', *British Educational Research Journal*, 13, 3: 309–17.

Hammersley, M. (1989) 'The problem of the concept: Herbert Blumer on the relationship between concepts and data', *Journal of Contemporary Ethnography*, 18: 133–59.

Hammersley, M. (1992) *What's Wrong with Ethnography?*, London, Routledge.
Hammersley, M. (1993) 'On the teacher as researcher', in M. Hammersley (ed.) *Educational Research: current issues*, London, Paul Chapman.
Hammersley, M. (1995a) *The Politics of Social Research*, London, Sage.
Hammersley, M. (1995b). 'Theory and evidence in qualitative research', *Quality and Quantity*: 29: 55–66.
Hammersley, M. (1996) 'Post mortem or post modern? Some reflections on British sociology of education', *British Journal of Educational Studies*, 44, 1: 395–408.
Hammersley, M. (1997a) 'Educational research and teaching: a response to David Hargreaves' TTA lecture', *British Educational Research Journal*, 23, 2: 141–61.
Hammersley, M. (1997b) Educational inequalities, Block 5, Unit 1, Open University Course EU208 *Exploring Educational Issues*, Milton Keynes, Open University.
Hammersley, M. (1998a) *Reading Ethnographic Research: a critical guide*, London, Longman.
Hammersley, M. (1998b) 'Partisanship and credibility: the case of anti-racist educational research', in P. Connolly and B. Troyna (eds) *Researching 'Race' in Educational Settings*, Buckingham, Open University Press.
Hammersley, M. (1999a) 'Not bricolage but boatbuilding: exploring two metaphors for thinking about ethnography', *Journal of Contemporary Ethnography*, 28, 5: 574–85.
Hammersley, M. (1999b) 'Sociology, what's it for? A critique of the grand conception', *Sociological Research Online*, 4, 3, September. http://www.socresonline.org.uk/socresonline/4/3/hammersley.html
Hammersley, M. (2000a) 'The sky is never blue for modernisers: the threat posed by David Blunkett's offer of "partnership" to social science', *Research Intelligence*, 72: 12–13.
Hammersley, M. (2000b) *Taking Sides in Social Research: essays on partisanship and bias*, London, Routledge.
Hammersley, M. (2000c) 'The relevance of qualitative research', *Oxford Review of Education*, 26, 3–4: 393–405.
Hammersley, M. (2000d) 'Review of Ann Oakley *Experiments in Knowing*', *Sociological Review*, 48, 3: 483–5.
Hammersley, M. (2001a) 'Critical or uncritical: is that the question?', unpublished paper available from the author.
Hammersley, M. (2001b) 'On "systematic" review of research literatures', *British Educational Research Journal*, 27, 5: 543–54.
Hammersley, M. and Atkinson, P. (1995) *Ethnography: Principles in Practice*, London, Routledge.
Hammersley, M. and Scarth, J. (1993) 'Beware of wise men bearing gifts:

a case study in the misuse of educational research', in R. Gomm and P. Woods (eds) *Educational Research in Action*, London, Paul Chapman.

Hampson, N. (1968) *The Enlightenment*, Harmondsworth, Penguin.

Hargreaves, A. (1982) 'Resistance and relative autonomy theories: problems of distortion and incoherence in recent Marxist analyses of education', *British Journal of Sociology of Education*, 3, 2: 107–26.

Hargreaves, D. H. (1972) *Interpersonal Relations and Education*, London, Routledge and Kegan Paul.

Hargreaves, D. H. (1978) 'Whatever happened to symbolic interactionism?', in L. Barton and R. Meighan (eds) *Sociological Interpretations of Schooling and Classrooms*, Driffield, Nafferton Books.

Hargreaves, D. H. (1979) 'A phenomenological approach to classroom decision-making', in J. Eggleston (ed.) *Teacher Decision Making in the Classroom*, London, Routledge and Kegan Paul.

Hargreaves, D. H. (1981) 'Schooling for delinquency', in L. Barton and S. Walker (eds) *Schools, Teachers and Teaching*, Lewes, Falmer Press.

Hargreaves, D. H. (1994) *The Mosaic of Learning: schools and teachers for the next century*, London, Demos.

Hargreaves, D. H. (1996) *Teaching as a Research-Based Profession: possibilities and prospects*, Teacher Training Agency Annual Lecture, London, Teacher Training Agency.

Hargreaves, D. H. (1997) 'In defence of research for evidence-based teaching: a rejoinder to Martyn Hammersley', *British Educational Research Journal*, 23, 3: 405–19.

Hargreaves, D. H. (1999a) 'Revitalising educational research: lessons from the past and proposals for the future'. *Cambridge Journal of Education*, 29, 2: 239–49.

Hargreaves, D. H. (1999b) 'The knowledge-creating school', *British Journal of Educational Studies*, 47: 122–44.

Hargreaves, D. H. (1999c) 'Helping practitioners explore their school's culture', in J. Prosser (ed.) *School Culture*, London, Paul Chapman.

Hargreaves, D. H., Hester, S. and Mellor, F. (1975) *Deviance in Classrooms*, London, Routledge and Kegan Paul.

Harvey, L. (1990) *Critical Social Research*, London, Unwin Hyman.

Hayek, F. A. (1952) *The Counter-Revolution of Science: studies in the abuse of reason*, Glencoe, Free Press.

Hayek, F. A. (1978) *New Studies in Philosophy, Politics, Economics, and the History of Ideas*, London, Routledge and Kegan Paul.

Heidegger, M. (1977) 'Only a god can save us now: an interview with Martin Heidegger', *Graduate Faculty Philosophy Journal*, 6, 1: 5–27. (Originally published in German in *Der Spiegel*, Spring, 1976.)

Herbert, A. (1889) *The Sacrifice of Education to Examinations*, London, Macmillan.

Hickox, M. S. H. (1982) 'The Marxist sociology of education: a critique',

British Journal of Sociology, 3, 2: 107–26.

Hillage, J., Pearson, R., Anderson, A. and Tamkin, P. (1998) *Excellence in Research on Schools*, London, Department for Education and Employment.

Hindess, B. (1987) *Freedom, Equality and the Market*, London, Tavistock.

Hirsch, E. D. (1967) *Validity in Interpretation*, New Haven, CT, Yale University Press.

Hirst, P. H. (1983) 'Educational theory', in P. H. Hirst (ed.) *Educational Theory and its Foundation Disciplines*, London, Routledge and Kegan Paul.

Hirst, P. H. (1990) 'The theory-practice relationship in teacher training', in M. B. Booth, V. J. Furlong and M. Wilkin (eds) *Partnership in Initial Teacher Training*, London, Cassell.

Hodgkinson, H. L. (1957) Action research: a critique, *Journal of Educational Sociology*, 31, 4: 137–53.

Hodgkinson, P. (2000) 'Who wants to be a social engineer? A commentary on David Blunkett's speech to the ESRC', *Sociological Research Online*, 5, 1 at http://www.socresonline.org.uk/5/1/hodgkinson.html

Hodkinson, P. (2001) 'Response to the National Strategy Consultation Paper, for the National Educational Research Forum', *Research Intelligence*, 74, February.

Hodkinson, P. and Garratt, D. (2000) 'Living with diversity in the educational research community: a response to technically rational attacks on qualitative educational and sociological research', unpublished revised version of a paper given at the British Educational Research Association Annual Conference, University of Sussex, September 1999.

Horkheimer, M. and Adorno, T. (1944) *Dialectic of Enlightenment*, London, Allen Lane (1973 edn).

Horowitz, I. L. (1961) *Radicalism and the Revolt against Reason: the social theories of Georges Sorel*, London, Routledge and Kegan Paul.

Hudson, W. D. (ed.) (1969) *The Is/Ought Question*, London, Macmillan.

Hughes, H. S. (1959) *Consciousness and Society: the reorientation of European thought 1890–1930*, London, MacGibbon and Kee.

Hustler, D., Cassidy, A. and Cuff, E. C. (eds) (1986) *Action Research in Classrooms*, London, Allen and Unwin.

Jackson, P. (1968) *Life in Classrooms*, New York, Holt, Rinehart and Winston.

Jadad, A. R. (1996) 'Are you playing evidence-based medicine games with our daughter?', *British Medical Journal*, 347: 247.

Jamous, H. and Pelloile, B. (1970) 'Professions or self-perpetuating system: changes in the French university-hospital system', in J. A. Jackson (ed.) *Professions and Professionalisation*, Cambridge, Cambridge University Press.

Janowitz, M. (1972) *Sociological Models and Social Policy*, Morristown, NJ, General Learning Systems.

Jay, M. (1973) *The Dialectical Imagination: a history of the Frankfurt School and the Institute of Social Research 1923–1950*, Berkeley, CA, University of California Press.

Jenett, B. (1988) 'Medical ethics and economics in clinical decision-making', in G. Mooney and A. McGuire (eds) *Medical Ethics and Economics in Health Care*, Oxford, Oxford University Press.

Jennings, J. (1997) 'Of treason, blindness and silence: the dilemmas of the intellectual in modern France', in J. Jennings and A. Kemp-Welch (eds) *Intellectuals in Politics*, London, Routledge.

Jones, G. and Sagar, S. (1995) 'No guidance is provided for situations for which evidence is lacking', *British Medical Journal*, 311: 258.

Judt, T. (1992) *Past Imperfect: French intellectuals, 1944–56*, Berkeley, CA, University of California Press.

Kristeva, J. (1977) 'A new type of intellectual: the dissident', translated in J. Kristeva (ed.) *The Kristeva Reader*, Oxford, Blackwell.

Kuhn, K. (1940) 'The phenomenological concept of "horizon"', in M. Farber (ed.) *Philosophical Essays in Memory of Edmund Husserl*, Cambridge, MA, Harvard University Press.

Kuhn, T. S. (1970) *The Structure of Scientific Revolutions*, Chicago, University of Chicago Press.

Lacey, C. and Lamont, W. (1976). *Partnership with Schools: an experiment in teacher education*, Occasional Paper 5, University of Sussex Education Area.

The Lancet (1995) Editorial, 346: 785.

Landgrebe, L. (1940) 'The world as a phenomenological problem', *Philosophy and Phenomenological Research*, 1: 38–58.

Larmore, C. (1987) *Patterns of Moral Complexity*, Cambridge, Cambridge University Press.

Larmore, C. (1996) *The Morals of Modernity*, Cambridge, Cambridge University Press.

Lassman, P. and Velody, I. (eds) (1989) *Max Weber's 'Science as a Vocation'*, London, Unwin Hyman.

Lather, P. (1991) *Getting Smart: feminist research and pedagogy with/in the postmodern*, New York, Routledge.

Lather, P. (1999) 'To be of use: the work of reviewing', *Review of Educational Research*, 69, 1: 2–7.

Latour, B. (1987) *Science in Action*, Milton Keynes, Open University Press.

Levin, H. M. (1991) 'Why isn't educational research more useful?', in D. S. Anderson and B. J. Biddle (eds) *Knowledge for Policy*, London, Falmer. (Reprinted from *Prospects*, 8, 2: 157–66, 1978.)

Lewin, K. (1948) *Resolving Social Conflicts*, New York, Harper and Row.

Lilla, M. (ed.) (1994) *New French Thought: political philosophy*, Princeton,

NJ, Princeton University Press.

Lincoln, Y. and Guba, E. (1985) *Naturalistic Inquiry*, Beverly Hills, CA, Sage.

Lindblom, C. and Cohen, D. (1979) *Usable Knowledge: social science and social problem solving*, New Haven, CT, Yale University Press.

Little, I. M. D. (1950) *A Critique of Welfare Economics*, Oxford, Oxford University Press.

Livingston, G. (1999) 'Beyond watching over established ways: a review as recasting the literature, recasting the lived', *Review of Educational Research*, 69, 1: 9–19.

Lobkowicz, N. (1967) *Theory and Practice*, Notre Dame, Notre Dame University Press.

Lobkowicz, N. (1977) 'On the history of theory and praxis', in T. Ball (ed.) *Political Theory and Praxis: new perspectives*, Minneapolis, MN, University of Minnesota Press.

Lockwood, D. (1964) 'Social integration and system integration', in G. K. Zollschan and W. Hirsch (eds) *Explorations in Social Change*, London, Routledge and Kegan Paul.

Lofland, J. (1972) *Analysing Social Settings*, Belmont, CA, Wadsworth.

Lomax, P. (1999) 'Working together for educative community through research (Presidential Address)', *British Educational Research Journal*, 25, 1: 5–21.

Lomax, P. (2000) 'The value of pluralism in educational research', paper given at a conference on Diversity or Control in Educational Research, City University, January.

Long, N. (1958) 'The local community as an ecology of games'. *American Journal of Sociology*, 50: 251–61.

Luckmann, B. (1970) 'The small life-worlds of modern man', *Social Research*, 37, 4: 580–96. (Reprinted in T. Luckmann (ed.) *Phenomenology and Sociology*, Harmondsworth, Penguin, 1978.)

Lukes, S. (1985) *Marxism and Morality*, Oxford, Oxford University Press.

Lynch, M. (1988) 'Alfred Schutz and the sociology of science', in L. Embree (ed.) *Worldly Phenomenology: the continuing influence of Alfred Schutz on North American Human Science*, Washington, DC, Center for Advanced Research in Phenomenology and University Press of America.

Lynch, M. (1993) *Scientific Practice and Ordinary Action: ethnomethodology and social studies of science*, Cambridge, Cambridge University Press.

MacDonald, B. (1974). 'Evaluation and the control of education', in B. MacDonald and R. Walker (eds.) *SAFARI I: Innovation, Evaluation, Research and the Problem of Control*. Norwich: Centre for Applied Research in Education, University of East Anglia. (Also in D. Tawney (ed.) *Curriculum Evaluation Today*, London, Macmillan, 1976.)

McGucken, W. (1978) 'On freedom and planning in science: the Society for Freedom in Science 1940–6', *Minerva*, XVI, 1: 42–72.

McIntyre, D. (1997a) 'The profession of educational research', *British Educational Research Journal*, 23, 2: 127–40.

McIntyre, D. (1997b) 'President's proposal for a new BERA journal', *Research Intelligence*, 60: 5–6.

McIntyre, D., Hagger, H. and Wilkin, M. (eds) (1993) *Mentoring perspectives on school-based teacher education*, London, Kogan Page.

Macintyre, S. (1977) *Single and Pregnant*, London, Croom Helm.

McKinstry, L (1997) 'Sending out research parties: on educational researchers who look for everything except how to improve education', *Spectator*, 20 September: 24–5.

Maines, D. R. (ed.) (1991) *Social Organization and Social Process: essays in honor of Anselm Strauss*, New York, Aldine de Gruyter.

Manuel, F. (1962) *The Prophets of Paris*, Cambridge, MA, Harvard University Press.

Mao Zedong (1972) *Quotations from Mao TseTung*, Peking, Foreign Languages Press.

March, J. G. (ed.) (1988) *Decisions and Organisations*, Oxford, Blackwell.

Marris, P. and Rein, M. (1967) *Dilemmas of Social Reform*, 2nd edn, London, Routledge and Kegan Paul.

Marrow, A. J. (1969) *The Practical Theorist: the life and work of Kurt Lewin*, New York, Teachers College Press.

Matza, D. (1963) *Delinquency and Drift*, Englewood Cliffs, NJ, Prentice-Hall.

Matza, D. (1969) *Becoming Deviant*, Englewood Cliffs, NJ, Prentice-Hall.

Mayne, J. and Zapico-Goni, E. (eds) (1997) *Monitoring Performance in the Public Sector*, New Brunswick, Transaction Books.

Meacham, S. J. (1998) 'Threads of a new language: a response to Eisenhart's "On the subject of interpretive review"', *Review of Educational Research*, 68, 4: 401–7.

Meehl, P. (1957) 'When shall we use our heads instead of the formula?', *Journal of Counselling Psychology*, 4, 4: 268–73.

Mendus, S. (ed.) (1988) *Justifying Tolerance: conceptual and historical perspectives*, Cambridge, Cambridge University Press.

Merleau-Ponty, M. (1973) *Adventures of the Dialectic*, Evanston, IL, Northwestern University Press.

Merquior, J. G. (1985) *Foucault*, London, Fontana.

Merton, R. K. (1957) 'The bureaucratic personality', in *Social Theory and Social Structure*, New York, Free Press.

Merton, R. K. (1973a) 'The normative structure of science', in R. K. Merton, *The Sociology of Science: theoretical and empirical investigations*, Chicago, University of Chicago Press.

Merton, R. K. (1973b) *The Sociology of Science: theoretical and empirical investigations*, Chicago: University of Chicago Press.

Mies, M. (1991) 'Women's research or feminist research? The debate surrounding feminist science and methodology', in M. M. Fonow and J. A. Cook (eds) *Beyond Methodology*, Bloomington, IN, Indiana University Press.

Mortimore, P. and Goldstein, H. (1996) *The Teaching of Reading in 45 Inner London Primary Schools: a critical examination of OFSTED research*, London, Institute of Education.

National Educational Research Forum (NERF) (2000) *A National Strategy Consultation Paper*, Nottingham, NERF.

Nietzsche, F. (1874) 'On the uses and disadvantages of history for life', in F. Nietzsche, *Untimely Meditations*, Cambridge, Cambridge University Press (1983 edn).

Nisbet, J. and Broadfoot, P. (1980) *The Impact of Research on Policy and Practice in Education*, Aberdeen, Aberdeen University Press.

Nixon, J. (ed.) (1981) *A Teacher's Guide to Action Research*, London, Grant McIntyre.

Noblit, G. W. and Hare, R. D. (1988) *Meta-Ethnography: synthesising qualitative data studies*, Newbury Park, CA, Sage.

Norman, G. R. (1995) Letter, *The Lancet*, 346: 839.

Norris, N. (1995) 'Contracts, control and evaluation', *Journal of Education Policy*, 10, 3: 271–85.

Nove, A. (1969) *The Soviet Economy*, 3rd edn, London, Allen and Unwin.

O'Connor, D. J. (1957) *An Introduction to the Philosophy of Education*, London, Routledge and Kegan Paul.

Oakeshott, M. (1962) *Rationalism in Politics*, London, Methuen.

Oakley, A. (2000) *Experiments in Knowing: gender and method in the social sciences*, Cambridge, Polity Press.

Olson, J. (1992) *Understanding Teaching*, Milton Keynes, Open University Press.

Pettigrew, M. (1994) 'Coming to terms with research: the contract business', in D. Halpin and B. Troyna (eds) *Researching Education Policy*, London, Falmer.

Peursen, C. van (1977) 'The horizon', in V. A. Elliston and P. McCormick (eds) *Husserl: expositions and appraisals*, Notre Dame, University of Notre Dame Press.

Pocock, J. G. A. (1975) *The Machiavellian Moment*, Princeton, NJ, Princeton University Press.

Polanyi, M. (1940) *The Contempt of Freedom: the Russian experiment and after*, London, Watts.

Polanyi, M. (1946) *Science, Faith and Society*, London, Oxford University Press. (Second edition, Chicago, University of Chicago Press, 1964.)

Polanyi, M. (1959) *Personal Knowledge*, Manchester, Manchester University Press.

Polanyi, M. (1951) *The Logic of Liberty: reflections and rejoinders*, Chicago,

University of Chicago Press.

Polanyi, M. (1962) 'The republic of science: its political and economic theory', *Minerva*, 1, 1: 54–73.

Polanyi, M. (1964) *Science, Faith and Society*, 2nd edn, Chicago, University of Chicago Press.

Pollitt, C. (1990) *Managerialism and the Public Services*, Oxford, Blackwell.

Popper, K. R. (1959) *The Logic of Scientific Discovery*, London, Hutchinson. (First published in German in 1935.)

Popper, K. R. (1963) *Conjectures and Refutations*, London, Routledge and Kegan Paul.

Poster, M. (1974) 'Sartre's concept of the intellectual: a Foucauldian critique', in N. F. Cantor and N. King (eds) *Notebooks in Cultural Analysis: an annual review*, vol. 1, Durham, NC, Duke University Press.

Power, M. (1997) *The Audit Society: rituals of verification*, Oxford, Oxford University Press.

Price, D. de Solla (1963) *Little Science, Big Science*, New York, Columbia University Press.

Pring, R. (2000) *Philosophy of Educational Research*, London, Continuum.

Prosch, H. (1986) *Michael Polanyi: a critical exposition*, Albany, NY, State University of New York Press.

Putnam, H. (1993) 'The "corroboration" of theories', in T. Honderich and M. Burnyeat (eds) *Philosophy as It Is*, Harmondsworth, Penguin. (This paper was originally published in P. A. Schilpp (ed.) *The Philosophy of Karl Popper*, La Salle, IL, Open Court, 1974.)

Pyke, N. (1996) 'Black sociologist attacks race "doom and gloom" ', *Times Educational Supplement*, 13 September: 12.

Quinton, A. (1980) *Bacon*, Oxford, Oxford University Press.

Ransom, S. (ed.) (1998) *Inside the Learning Society*, London, Cassell.

Rapoport, R. (1970) 'Three dilemmas in action research', *Human Relations*, 23, 6: 499–513.

Ravetz, J. R. (1971) *Scientific Knowledge and its Social Problems*, Oxford, Oxford University Press.

Readings, B. (1991) Introduction, in J.-F. Lyotard, *Political Writings*, Minneapolis, MN, University of Minnesota Press.

Rescher, N. (1984) *The Limits of Science*, Berkeley, CA, University of California Press.

Reynolds, D. (1998) 'Teacher effectiveness', Lecture delivered at the Teacher Training Agency Corporate Plan Launch 1998–2001, May 1998.

Reynolds, D. and Farrell, D. (1996) *Worlds Apart? A review of international surveys of educational achievement involving England*, London, Office for Standards in Education, HMSO.

Ringer, F. (1969) *The Decline of the German Mandarins*, Cambridge, MA, Harvard University Press.

Roberts, C., Lewis, P., Crosby, D., Dunn, R., and Grundy, P. (1996) 'Prove it', *Health Service Journal*, 106, 5493, 7 March: 32–3.

Robinson, P. (1997) *Literacy, numeracy and economic performance*, London, Centre for Economic Performance, London School of Economics.

Rothschild, Lord (1971). 'The organisation and management of government R and D', in *A Framework for Government Research and Development*, Cmnd 4184, London, HMSO.

Rothschild, Lord (1982). *An Enquiry into the Social Science Research Council*, London, HMSO.

Rudduck, J. and McIntyre, D. (eds) (1998) *Challenges for Educational Research*, London, Paul Chapman.

Rule, J. B. (1978) *Insight and Social Betterment: a preface to applied social science*, New York, Oxford University Press.

Ryle, G. (1949) *The Concept of Mind*, London, Hutchinson.

Sackett, D. L. (1996) *The Doctor's (Ethical and Economic) Dilemma*, Office of Health Economics Annual Lecture, London, Office of Health Economics.

Sackett, D. L., Haynes, R. B. and Tugwell, P. (1985) *Clinical Epidemiology: a basic science for clinical medicine*, Boston, Little, Brown.

Sammons, P. and Reynolds, D. (1997) 'A partisan evaluation: John Elliott on school effectiveness', *Cambridge Journal of Education*, 27, 1: 123–36.

Sanders, W. B. (1974) *The Sociologist as Detective*, 2nd edn, New York: Praeger.

Sartre, J.-P. (1949) *What is Literature?* New York, Philosophical Library.

Scarth, J. and Hammersley, M. (1986a) 'Some problems in assessing closedness of tasks', in M. Hammersley (ed.) *Case Studies in Classroom Research*, Milton Keynes, Open University Press.

Scarth, J. and Hammersley, M. (1986b) 'Questioning ORACLE's analysis of teachers' questions', *Educational Research*, 28, 3: 174–84.

Schmidt, J. (ed.) (1996) *What is Enlightenment? Eighteenth century questions and twentieth century questions*, Berkeley, CA, University of California Press.

Schön, D. (1983) *The Reflective Practitioner*, London, Temple Smith.

Schön, D. (1987) *Educating the Reflective Practitioner*, San Francisco, Jossey-Bass.

Schütz, A. (1962) 'The problem of rationality in the social world', in *Collected Papers vol. 1*, The Hague, Martinus Nijhoff.

Schütz, A. (1967) *The Phenomenology of the Social World*, Evanston, IL, Northwestern University Press.

Schütz, A. (1970) *Reflections on the Problem of Relevance*, New Haven, CT, Yale University Press.

Schütz, A. and Luckmann, T. (1974) *The Structures of the Life-World*, London, Heinemann.

Schwab, J. J. (1969) 'The practical: a language for curriculum', *School Review*, 78: 1–24.

Schwandt, T. (1996) 'Farewell to criteriology', *Qualitative Inquiry*, 2, 1: 58–72.

Schwandt, T. (1998) 'The interpretive review of educational matters: is there any other kind?', *Review of Educational Research*, 68, 4: 409–12.

Scott, R. A. and Shore, A. R. (1979) *Why Sociology Does Not Apply: a study of the use of sociology in public policy*, New York, Elsevier.

Shahar, E. (1997) 'A Popperian view of "evidence-based medicine" ', *Journal of Evaluation in Clinical Practice*, 3, 2: 109–16.

Shotland, R. L. and Mark, M. M. (eds) (1985) *Social Science and Social Policy*, Beverly Hills, CA, Sage.

Shotter, J. and Gergen, K. J. (eds) (1989) *Texts of Identity*, London, Sage.

Shove, E. (ed.) (1998) *Researchers, Users, and Window Frames*, Lancaster, Lancaster University.

Shove, E. and Rip, A. (2000) 'Users and unicorns: a discussion of mythical beasts in interactive science', *Science and Public Policy*, 27, 3: 175–182.

Shuchman, M. (1996) 'Evidence-based medicine debated', *The Lancet*, 347: 1396.

Simon, H. (1955) 'A behavioral model of rational choice', *Quarterly Journal of Economics*, 69: 99–118.

Simon, W. M. (1963) *European Positivism in the Nineteenth Century*, Ithaca, NY, Cornell University Press.

Simons, H. (1987). *Getting to Know Schools in a Democracy*, London, Falmer.

Slee, R. and Weiner, G. (eds) (1998) *School Effectiveness for Whom? Challenges to the school effectiveness and school improvement movements*, London, Falmer.

Smith, B. H. and Taylor, R. J. (1996) 'Medicine: a healing or a dying art?', *British Journal of General Practice*, 46: 249–51.

Smith, G. (2000) 'Research and inspection: HMI and OFSTED, 1981–1996 - a commentary', *Oxford Review of Education*, 26, 3–4: 333–52.

Smith, J. K. (1993) *After the Demise of Empiricism: the problem of judging social and educational inquiry*, Norwood, NJ, Ablex.

Smyth, J. and Hattam, R. (2000) 'Intellectual as hustler: researching against the grain of the market', *British Educational Research Journal*, 26, 2: 157–75.

Sperber, D. and Wilson, D. (1986) *Relevance*, Oxford, Blackwell.

Spradley, J. P. (1979) *The Ethnographic Interview*, New York, Holt, Rinehart and Winston.

Stedman, L.C. (1997a) 'International achievement differences: an assessment of a new perspective', *Educational Researcher*, 26, 3: 4–15.

Stedman, L.C. (1997b) 'Response: deep achievement problems: the case for reform still stands', *Educational Researcher*, 26, 3: 27–9.

Stehr, N. (1978). 'The ethos of science revisited: social and cognitive norms', in R. Gaston (ed.) *Sociology of Science*, San Francisco: Jossey-Bass.

Stenhouse, L. (1975) *An Introduction to Curriculum Research and Development*, London, Heinemann.

Strauss, A. L. (1978) *Negotiations: variation, contexts, process, and social order*, San Francisco, Jossey-Bass.

Strauss, A. L. (1993) *Continual Permutations of Action*, New York, Aldine de Gruyter.

Ströker, E. (1987) *Husserl's Transcendental Phenomenology* (English translation, Stanford, CA, Stanford University Press, 1993).

Strong, P. (1984) 'Viewpoint: the academic encirclement of medicine?' *Sociology of Health and Illness*, 6, 3: 341–58.

Tanenbaum, S. (1993) 'What physicians know', *New England Journal of Medicine*, 329: 1268–71.

Taylor, K. (ed.) (1975) *Henri Saint-Simon*, London, Croom Helm.

Taylor, M. J. (1981) *Caught Between: a review of research into the education of pupils of West Indian origin*, Windsor, National Foundation for Educational Research–Nelson.

Taylor, M. J. (1986) *Chinese Pupils in Britain: a review of research into the education of pupils of Chinese origin*, Windsor, National Foundation for Educational Research–Nelson.

Taylor, M. J. (1988) *Worlds Apart? A review of research into the education of pupils of Cypriot, Italian, Ukrainian, and Vietnamese origin, Liverpool Blacks and Gypsies*, Windsor, National Foundation for Educational Research–Nelson.

Taylor, M. J. and Hegarty, S. (1985) *The Best of Both Worlds? A review of research into the education of pupils of South Asian origin*, Windsor, National Foundation for Educational Research–Nelson.

Taylor, W. (1973) 'Knowledge and research', in W. Taylor (ed.) *Research Perspectives in Education*, London, Routledge and Kegan Paul.

Teacher Training Agency (TTA) (1996) *Teaching as a Research-based Profession*, London, Teacher Training Agency/Central Office of Information.

Thomas, G. (1998) 'The myth of rational research', *British Educational Research Journal*, 24, 2: 141–61.

Thornton, H. M. (1992) 'Breast cancer trials: a patient's viewpoint', *The Lancet*, 339: 44–5.

Tiles, J. (1989) *John Dewey*, London, Routledge and Kegan Paul.

Tomlinson, S. (1983) *Ethnic Minorities in British Schools: a review of the literature 1960–82*, London, Heinemann.

Tooley, J. (1999) 'The Popperian approach to raising standards in educational research', in J. Swann and J. Pratt (eds) *Improving Education: realist approaches to method and research*, London, Cassell.

Tooley, J., with Darby, D. (1998) *Educational Research: a critique*, London, OFSTED.

Trinder, L., with Reynolds, S. (eds) (2000) *Evidence-based Practice: a critical appraisal*, Oxford, Blackwell Science.

Troman, G. (1996) 'No entry signs: educational change and some problems encountered in negotiating entry to educational settings', *British Educational Research Journal*, 22, 2: 71–88.

Turner, S. P. (1990) 'Forms of patronage', in S. Cozzens and T. F. Gieryn (eds) *Theories of Science in Society*, Bloomington, IN, Indiana University Press.

Usher, R. (2000) 'Deconstructive happening, ethical moment', in H. Simons and R. Usher (eds) *Situated Ethics in Educational Research*, London, Routledge/Falmer.

Venturi, F. (1971) *Utopia and Reform in the Enlightenment*, Cambridge, Cambridge University Press.

Wallach, J. (1992) 'Contemporary Aristotelianism', *Political Theory*, 20, 4: 613–41.

Watson, G. (1973) 'Were the intellectuals duped? The 1930s revisited', *Encounter*, XLI, 6, December: 20–30.

Watson, P. (1996) 'Knowing the score', *Health Service Journal*, 106, 5494, 14 March: 28–31.

Weightman, J. (1993) 'Fatal attraction: review of T. Judt *Past Imperfect*', *New York Review of Books*, 11 February: 9–12.

Weinberg, A. (1978) 'The obligations of citizenship in the republic of science', *Minerva* XVI, 1: 1–3.

Weiss, C. (ed.) (1977) *Using Social Research in Public Policy Making*, Lexington, MA, D. C. Heath.

Weiss, C. (1979) 'The many meanings of research utilisation', *Public Administration Review*, 39: 426–31.

Weiss, C., with Bucuvalas, M. (1980) *Social Science Research and Decision Making*, New York, Columbia University Press.

Wenham, P. (1994) 'A Study of the Impact of the DES pamphlet "Curriculum Organisation and Classroom Practice in Primary Schools: a discussion paper" ', Milton Keynes, unpublished M.Phil dissertation, Open University.

Wheeler, S. (1966) 'The structure of formally organized socialization settings', in O. G. Brim and S. Wheeler, *Socialization after Childhood: two essays*, New York, Wiley.

Whyte, W. F. (1955) *Street Corner Society*, 2nd edn, Chicago, University of Chicago Press.

Wiles, K. (1953) 'Can we sharpen up the concept of action research?', *Educational Leadership*, 10: 408–10.

Wilkie, T. (1991) *British Science and Politics since 1945*, Oxford, Blackwell.

Winch, P. (1958) *The Idea of a Social Science and its Relationship to Philosophy*, London, Routledge and Kegan Paul.

Wood, A. (1991) 'Marx against morality', in P. Singer (ed.) *A Companion to Ethics*, Oxford, Blackwell.

Woodhead, C. (1998) 'Academia gone to seed', *New Statesman*, 20 March: 51–2.

Woods, P. (1985) 'Ethnography and theory construction in educational research', in R. G. Burgess (ed.) *Field Methods in the Study of Education*, Lewes, Falmer.

Woods, P. (1987) 'Ethnography at the crossroads: a reply to Hammersley', *British Educational Research Journal*, 13: 297–307.

Woods, P. (1996) *Researching the Art of Teaching: ethnography for use*, London, Routledge.

Woods, P. , Jeffrey, B., Troman, G. and Boyle, M. (1997) *Restructuring Schools, Reconstructing Teachers: Responding to change in the primary school*, Buckingham, Open University Press.

Woods, P. and Wenham, P. (1995) Politics and pedagogy: a case study in appropriation, *Journal of Education Policy*, 10, 2: 119–41.

Woolgar, S. (1988) *Science: the very idea*, London, Routledge.

Woolgar, S. (2000) 'The social basis of interactive social science', *Science and Public Policy*, 27, 3: 165–73.

Wragg, E. C. (1976) 'The Lancaster Study: its implications for teacher training', *British Journal of Teacher Education*, 2, 3: 281–90.

Ziman, J. (1978) 'Solidarity within the republic of science', *Minerva*, XVI, 1: 4–19.

Index